Critical Religious Education in Practice

Critical Religious Education in Practice serves as an accessible handbook to help teachers put Critical Religious Education (CRE) into practice. The book offers straightforward guidance, unpicking some of the key difficulties that teachers encounter when implementing this high-profile pedagogical approach.

In-depth explanations of CRE pedagogy, accompanied by detailed lesson plans and activities, will give teachers the confidence they need to inspire debate in the classroom, tackling issues as controversial as the authority of the Qur'an and the relationship between science and religion. The lesson plans and schemes of work exemplify CRE in practice and are aimed at empowering teachers to implement CRE pedagogy across their curriculum. Additional chapters cover essential issues such as differentiation, assessment, the importance of subject knowledge and tips for tackling tricky topics. The accompanying resources, including PowerPoint presentations and worksheets, are available via the book's companion website.

Key to developing a positive classroom culture and promoting constructive attitudes towards Religious Education, this text is essential reading for all practising and future teachers of Religious Education in secondary schools.

Christina Easton is undertaking a Philosophy PhD at the London School of Economics, UK. She has eight years of experience teaching Religious Education, including as a Head of Department.

Angela Goodman is undertaking a PhD focusing on Critical Religious Education. She contributes to Initial Teacher Training in Religious Education at King's College London, UK, and has taught Religious Education at secondary level for seven years.

Andrew Wright is Professor of Religious and Theological Education at the Institute of Education, University College London, UK.

Angela Wright directs the Secondary Religious Education PGCE at King's College London, UK. She has worked in Initial Teacher Training for over twenty years.

Critical Religious Education in Practice

A Teacher's Guide for the Secondary Classroom

**Christina Easton,
Angela Goodman,
Andrew Wright and
Angela Wright**

LONDON AND NEW YORK

First published 2019
by Routledge
2 Park Square, Milton Park, Abingdon, Oxon OX14 4RN

and by Routledge
52 Vanderbilt Avenue, New York, NY 10017

Routledge is an imprint of the Taylor & Francis Group, an informa business

British Library Cataloguing in Publication Data
A catalogue record for this book is available from the British Library

Library of Congress Cataloging in Publication Data
Names: Easton, Christina, author.
Title: Critical religious education in practice: a teacher's guide for the secondary
classroom / Christina Easton, Angela Goodman, Andrew Wright and Angela Wright.
Description: Abingdon, Oxon ; New York, NY : Routledge, 2019. I Includes
bibliographical references.
Identifiers: LCCN 2017053099I ISBN 9781138123212 (hbk) I ISBN 9781138123229
(pbk) I ISBN 9781315648989 (ebk)
Subjects: LCSH: Religious education—Great Britain. I Religion—Study and
teaching (Secondary)—Great Britain. I Critical pedagogy—Great Britain.
Classification: LCC LC410.G7 E36 2018 I DDC 372.84—dc23
LC record available at https://lccn.loc.gov/2017053099

ISBN: 978-1-138-12321-2 (hbk)
ISBN: 978-1-138-12322-9 (pbk)
ISBN: 978-1-315-64898-9 (ebk)

Typeset in Helvetica
by Swales & Willis Ltd, Exeter, Devon, UK

Visit the companion website: www.routledge.com/cw/easton

Printed and bound in Great Britain by
TJ International Ltd, Padstow, Cornwall

Contents

Preface

The manuscript for this book was completed before the publication of the Final Report of the Commission on RE. Nevertheless, we have been able to acknowledge it in minor updates. It is, as yet, unclear what impact the report will have on the future of our subject. Its recommendations are wide-ranging, and we are delighted to see its focus on Religion and Worldviews, as reflected in the call for a re-naming of RE.

Our subject is, as the Commission reports, in a dangerous position with low uptake in schools and on associated courses at universities. The RE community is lobbying strongly, as evidenced by the response of those teachers and teacher educators at the recent 20:20 Conference in Crewe, but we need the government to listen to us about the vital importance of our subject and to act.

In order for us to see the positive changes that we are hoping for, it is imperative that we learn from the mistakes of the past. For many years our subject has been heavily influenced by philosophies and associated pedagogies which deny that we can explore (and in some cases even talk about!) the truth about ultimate reality. This has led to our subject being viewed as entirely subjective which, in turn, has allowed it to be devalued. However, the focus on knowledge in the Commission's report, in the new GCSE and A Level specifications and at recent national RE conferences implies a shift towards realism. This is to be welcomed but also raises questions about the preparedness of the RE community to enact the new vision for RE in a consistent way. We need to commit ourselves to the unique subject matter of 'Religion and Worldviews' and aim at producing high calibre philosophical and theological study, rather than reducing our subject to social science. We hope that this book may serve as an effective tool in ensuring this.

As the only approach to RE which has explicitly forwarded a non-confessional realist approach over the last two decades, CRE is well positioned to act as a model for the outworking of the new emerging vision for RE. In light of the Commission's report we are confident that this book can play a role in promoting a positive way forward for our subject, enabling teachers to enact the recommendations, in relation to pedagogy, in an effective and comprehensive way.

How to use this book

This book is all about empowering you to improve your teaching and your students' learning. Critical Religious Education (CRE) provides an innovative and powerful understanding of the nature and purpose of learning in our subject. Our hope is that you will be inspired and empowered through engaging with the ideas and seeing some of these brought to life in the schemes of work and resources we provide. These include handouts, assessment frameworks and PowerPoint (PWP) presentations with explanatory notes. All resources are made available for download on the book's companion website: www.routledge.com/cw/easton

The organisation of the book is systematic but can still be dipped into. We recommend that you read Chapters 1 and 2 before you look at any exemplification. When looking at the exemplification we suggest you begin with the Year 7 scheme of work in Chapter 3 – this is a great way to get your head around the philosophy of critical realism and the implications of this for CRE. Although the other chapters of exemplification can be read in any order, we would suggest that you read them in the order given, as they do build on one another. In a similar way the chapters which relate to practical concerns can also be read in any order but also have some cross-referencing between them. So, in short, we have ordered the chapters in a way which we think makes most sense!

Some considerations before you begin

We do not know your particular circumstances, what your school is like, the nature and needs of the students you are teaching, or the time you are allocated, so we have not sought to be prescriptive in the length of lessons, or indeed their number. We realise that in some contexts there may be a need to split what we have presented as single lessons across a couple of lessons, and this is entirely reasonable. It will be up to you to adapt the ideas embedded in the lessons and the resources we have provided to work in your school and in your situation. This is particularly true for the purposes of differentiation. Do not be put off by the need to make changes; you will need enthusiasm and commitment, but it will be worth it. Please be aware that the idea is *not* to give you stand-alone schemes of work to use but rather that we are inducting you into a pedagogical approach that we believe could revolutionise your teaching and your students' learning overall.

Overview

In Chapter 1 we provide an introduction to critical realism as the philosophical basis for this enterprise and to Critical Religious Education (CRE) as its pedagogical application.

In Chapter 2 we seek to explore the most obvious characteristic of CRE in the classroom – it deals with controversy head on. This has been taken as an objection to its use, and as it may stop teachers in their tracks, we feel that it is really important to explore this and offer some justification for it before providing any specific exemplification.

Exemplification: schemes of work

In Chapter 3 we include a Year 7 scheme of work that provides an introduction to CRE for the students. This was piloted in over 20 schools and shared with many more. It has been very well received. The purpose of this scheme of work is to explore with the students the nature and processes of CRE – what it is, what it is hoping to achieve and how it is intrinsically relevant to them.

In Chapter 4 we provide a Year 8 scheme of work on Islam. This chapter works as exemplification of how to use a CRE pedagogy to ensure that the teaching of world religions is characterised by depth and authenticity. We seek to show the importance of exploring core beliefs as well as the internal diversity of faiths, and to show how all of these variations are necessarily only made sense of through the lens of each individual student, through their own world-view. We seek to highlight the critical issues and the critical questions and to show the importance of exploring these in the classroom.

In Chapter 5 we provide a Year 9 scheme of work on science and religion. We begin by arguing that for any philosophical learning to be effective, students must first be equipped with the necessary language and concepts. It is worth very little to do such investigations superficially. To this end, time is taken at the beginning of the chapter to explore the philosophical tools which can be used and to ensure teachers are clear about what these look like and how they can be utilised. These are then exemplified through the example of a scheme of work on science and religion – a popular topic through which we hope to show the significant difference that a CRE approach can make.

In Chapter 6 we provide another Year 9 scheme of work, this time on ethics. In a similar way to the philosophy chapter, time is taken at the start of the chapter to explain the nature of and processes involved in any rigorous ethical investigation. Again, concepts and language are explained before these are then applied to a scheme of work that focuses on empowering students to understand what is involved in moral decision making and the importance of consistency with regard to this.

In Chapter 7 we consider the new GCSE specifications and explore the opportunities they afford us as teachers to embed CRE and bring about outcomes of rigorous learning. The purpose of this chapter is to exemplify the longer term planning processes needed to facilitate learning from exam specifications, in an attempt to show how CRE can impact the way the content is organised and tackled.

And so into practice

Chapters 8 to 10 explore fundamental concerns which run alongside any planning. These are assessment, differentiation and subject knowledge.

In Chapter 8 we explore the current context with regard to assessment and recognise this as a great opportunity to develop something really innovative, something which is embedded in gaining insight into what students really know and understand. We use the tenets of critical realism as the basis for our assessment criteria and provide exemplification of what this could look like.

In Chapter 9 we explore the nature of differentiation in a CRE classroom and show it to be centrally about knowledge of your students and a relationship of trust. It does not rehearse lots of techniques but argues that effective differentiation is fundamentally linked to assessment and is all about dialogue, sharing ideas and developing the type of learning environment in which students are secure to voice beliefs and opinions and to listen to and respect those of others.

Chapter 10 reiterates the importance of really secure subject knowledge, without which CRE is not possible.

Acknowledgements

This book is the result of a collaborative exercise that has taken place over many years. During this time, we have had the privilege of working with lots of fantastic colleagues, many of whom have contributed their ideas to this book.

The Forum of Religious and Spiritual Education (FORASE), from which this project was born, started out as a large group with many involved. Although the book and related resources are primarily the work of the authors, many people were involved in the formative stages of this endeavour.

Most notably, we would like to thank Tom Hibberd and Dave Aldridge, who were involved from the outset of this venture and who contributed their ideas on the planning process of CRE as well as their resources. Dave Aldridge contributed significantly to the Year 7 scheme of work. Tom Hibberd was involved in both the Year 7 and the Year 8 schemes of work, and his work with the group ended only relatively recently in the process after his relocation to Devon.

We would also like to give very special thanks to Tony Wenman, who convened FORASE for its first eight years. Not only did he take care of the administrative side of our meetings, but he also pushed us to think further about our assumptions, and particularly about the implications for primary age children. Don't worry, Tony, we'll get that book on CRE in the primary sector out eventually!

We would also like to thank Elina Wright, Will Griffith and Ciro Genovese (amongst others) who were involved in the early planning stages of the book. Thanks also to Wahida Begum, Ayse Demirel Ucan and Zameer Hussain who we consulted over the Islam scheme of work and to Jaymie Pauvaday, consulted over Buddhist ethics.

In providing the resources for this book, we have often drawn on shared collective practice, and so it is not possible to thank every person who has contributed. We apologise sincerely to those who we may miss out. We would like to thank colleagues previously at St Saviour's & St Olave's School, especially Mary Montgomery who has contributed some significant resources and Tim Sanders, Faith Kirby and Martha Prescott who have trialled many of the resources and contributed some PowerPoint slides. We would also like to thank the staff at Surbiton High School, who were open-minded and enthusiastic in their trialling of some schemes of work and resources. Stuart Bachelor and Fiona Etherington both contributed specific ideas and resources to the Year 9 Science and Religion scheme of work. Many schools were involved in the piloting of the Year 7 scheme of work, but we would particularly like to thank Dave Smith, then at Archbishop Tenison's Church of England School in Lambeth, and James Melligan, then at Guildford County School, who both gave useful feedback on ways to access the resources for students whatever their prior attainment.

Writing this book has been a long process, and it has not always been easy. We have been supported by our families and friends through anxieties, stresses and disagreements, and for this we are truly grateful: for Christina, Stuart and Lily Easton, Paul and Valerie Davis; for Angela G., Kim and Izzy Goodman, Vivien and John Salisbury and Juliet and Kevin Goodman; for Andy, Elina, Juliana and Mariana; and for Angela W., Paul, Alfie and Yazmin. But our biggest thanks must go to each other. We work in very different ways and so it has not always been an easy process. We have supported each other through difficult times as well as enjoyed joyous occasions including marriages, babies and first puppies (and hawks). We might have written the book quicker if we hadn't sometimes opened the wine before the end of our meetings, but we'd have had a lot less fun.

Critical Religious Education

An introduction

Once there were two pigs in a sty. They had everything that a pig would want, shelter, food, water and a huge puddle of mud. One night there was a terrible thunderstorm. Hail came crashing down on the ground, thunder roared and lightning flashed in the distance. As the storm grew closer, a bolt of lightning struck the sty and part of the fence around it fell to the ground leaving a big hole behind it. When the first pig awoke he took one glance at the outside world and just snorted. The second pig, however, peered through the gap and his mouth fell open, his ears pricked up, his tail straightened and his snout wrinkled. "Wow," he said. He stepped out into the big wide world. "Come on," he said to the other pig, but the other pig just snorted again so the pig went by himself. On his travels he saw a family weeping over the body of a young child. This upset him greatly. Further up the path he saw a father and his son playing together, smiling brightly. This made him extremely happy. As he journeyed even further up the path he saw a fox being beaten up by a badger. This made him feel really angry. The poor pig was confused by his emotions. He went on, his ears drooping and snout dragging along on the ground. At the top of a very large hill he stopped to rest under an apple tree. In that tree there was an owl. The pig asked the owl, "What is the meaning of life? I am confused. Why are we here?" The owl replied, "I cannot tell you. You can either return home and be a contented pig, or stay and be a discontented philosopher."

Teachers tend to take it for granted that students understand what their subject is about, and why it is important to study it. This is not always the case in religious education. It is important that students begin to develop an understanding of the nature and value of religious education and that students own this understanding for themselves; it is not enough for the teacher simply to tell them. A flourishing religious education classroom is one in which the students themselves openly debate the nature and value of religious education.

Critical Religious Education (CRE) is grounded in the belief that controversial issues should be discussed openly in the classroom. This is a challenging task, and many teachers are concerned that they lack the confidence to facilitate this effectively and that it may be disruptive. However difficult this may be, we suggest that students can only become religiously literate if they are empowered to tackle controversial issues head-on.

The idea that students should explore the possibility that religious education is irrelevant is a very scary prospect for any teacher. However, it is an uncomfortable fact that many students will bring that attitude with them into the classroom. If it is left unaddressed it is likely to fester throughout Years 7–11. By tackling the issue head-on from the beginning, and encouraging the debate to flourish, there is a far greater chance that students will develop positive attitudes. This book is intended to introduce you to ways of enabling your students to perceive the intrinsic value of the subject.

Critical realism: the philosophy

Critical realism provides the philosophical framework for CRE. It adopts three basic principles: ontological realism, epistemic relativity and judgmental rationality:

(1) **Ontological realism** argues that there is a reality which exists, and that it exists independently of human perception. Thus, if God exists, then whether human beings are aware of this fact or not has no impact whatsoever on the reality of God.

(2) **Epistemic relativity** accepts the contingency of our knowledge of the world. On the one hand, we have no absolute certain knowledge of the actual ontological order of things; contra religious and secular fundamentalists. On the other hand, our knowledge is not completely arbitrary; contra radical constructivists and anti-realists. We have knowledge of the world, though such knowledge is always subject to revision and never complete; thus, despite the fact that science has much still to learn, we are still able to walk on the moon and perform heart surgery.

(3) **Judgmental rationality** argues that the relationship between ontology and epistemology is necessarily a critical one. Our knowledge of the world is not based on absolute proof or arbitrary construction, but rather on informed judgment. This means that the basic paradigm of our relationship to the world is one of 'faith seeking understanding'. This is so both for secularists and religious believers.

CRE: the pedagogy

Religious education is concerned with developing the beliefs, values, worldviews and spiritualities of students. However, this process cannot be reduced to the level of mere self-expression since we are relational creatures, whose identities are bound up with the way we relate to ourselves, to other human beings, to the natural world and to the presence or absence of God – or some other transcendent reality – in our lives. This means that our personal development is bound up with the way we experience the world, and the crucial question as to whether such experience is in harmony with the actual order of things. At the same time, religious and secular traditions cannot be reduced to the level of mere lifestyle options. Such traditions make claims about ultimate reality and about the appropriate way of living life in harmony with it. The common factor here is the ontological (and existential) question of our relation to the way things actually are. In CRE, students are encouraged to articulate their own understanding of ontological reality, with an awareness that their views are limited by epistemic relativity. They are then introduced to a range of alternative accounts of reality. They do so from within the horizon of their own given world-view. Consequently, they explore the relationship between their own worldview and the worldview of the religious or secular tradition they are studying.

In CRE, the fact that a plurality of worldviews is taught means that there can be no common agreement assumed between the worldview of the student and the topic studied. CRE deals with contested worldviews and hence inevitably operates with tensions both between different religious and secular horizons of meaning, and the horizons of meaning of the students. However, this does not mean that this necessitates a fundamental gulf between them. What unites them is a common desire to understand reality and to live in harmony with it. Such exploration does not require adherence to the religion being studied, since to teach or learn about something is not necessarily to advocate it.

This focus for learning will require students to reflect on the variation between different worldviews. Indeed, students *need* to experience such variation *in order to* learn. Deep understanding is only possible by considering how and why something is similar or different to something else. These are the fundamental assertions of the Variation Theory of Learning, which began with the work of Ference Marton, and which underpins CRE in practice. By carefully considering other worldviews, students will come to see their own tradition in a new light.

The tension between ontology and epistemology – between ultimate reality and the various accounts we offer of ultimate reality – forms the driving force of CRE. It is not acceptable for a teacher to attempt to impose a particular world-view on students, nor is it sufficient for students to merely express an unjustified personal preference for one belief system or another. Instead, by cultivating a deep understanding of students' horizons of meaning and the horizons of various religious and secular traditions, religious education should aim to empower students to make informed judgments about the ultimate nature of reality and the implications of this for the way in which they choose to live their lives.

CRE: pedagogy into practice

A religiously literate person is one able to think, feel and act wisely in relation to ultimate questions about the nature of reality (truth) and the meaning of life (truthful living).

Learning is *not* just about

- inserting facts into empty minds
- enabling students to express their thoughts and feelings

Learning *is* about

- bringing students into a richer and more discerning relationship with the world

Knowledge is a developing two-way relationship between

- the horizon of meaning of each student
- the – normally disputed and controversial – horizon of meaning of the topic being studied

Knowledge is personal - it has to do with students'

- reason and comprehension
- feelings and emotions
- actions and behavior
- judgments and commitments

CRE: curriculum planning

Stage 1: expression

- students come to class with an understanding of the topic, however limited
- they are given the opportunity to express their initial preliminary understanding

Stage 1 enables students to express the various experiences, perspectives and attitudes towards the topic that they are bringing with them into the classroom. Self-expression is not the main aim of CRE, but rather an important means to a greater end.

Stage 2: variation

- students are introduced to new ways of understanding the topic
- because most topics are controversial, they are introduced to more than one perspective on it

Teachers often avoid introducing new perspectives to students because they worry about indoctrinating them. This means that they are often left to rely on their own experiences and their horizons are not expanded. If students are offered more than one perspective on a topic, the issue of indoctrination becomes redundant.
    In selecting a variety of new perspectives, teachers should

- take account of the previous experiences of students and seek to add to them
- seek to identify variations that are relevant and important
- avoid too many variations within a single lesson

Stage 3: exploration

- there will be tensions between students' preliminary understanding and these new perspectives
- exploring these tensions will develop their religious literacy

Our understanding of the world is limited. There is much that we do not know. Though we put our faith in particular understandings of the world, it is important that we remain open to new ways of making sense of life. There is a tendency to think that a learning sequence must end in the resolution of a controversial issue. CRE contends that leaving an issue unresolved can be a vital aspect of learning. Students will develop their religious literacy by struggling to answer unresolved questions. What matters is that they engage in the process, rather than arrive at a commonly shared view.

Critical thinking is non-negotiable

The stress on epistemic relativity focuses on students' learning. It should be part of the teacher's thinking in so far as they have a responsibility for expanding the horizons of students by introducing them to disputed variations. The teacher should be committed to enabling students to develop into discontented philosophers. Fundamentalism (in terms of only presenting one view) and relativism (in terms of avoiding grappling with the possibility of an ultimate truth) are not an option for the teacher when planning and implementing lessons. However, they can of course be addressed as specific truth claims, in and of themselves, within the classroom.

CHAPTER 2

Critical Religious Education

Handling controversy in the classroom

Teaching religious education (RE) can sometimes feel a bit like leading a large, unruly crowd across a minefield. At every moment, there is a risk of an 'explosion'; someone might say 'the wrong thing' and cause offence and upset. You might think that adopting a critical pedagogy in your RE teaching makes it an even riskier business; drawing attention to disagreements between (and within) religions, and asking students to critically reflect on these disagreements is a bit like asking children to approach and examine dangerous mines!

In this chapter we show that, contrary to this, CRE *alleviates* rather than exacerbates classroom conflict. We look at the issues that all RE teachers face in virtue of teaching about controversial issues, and suggest that CRE by its very nature provides principles and strategies that respond to these difficulties. In particular, we explain the implications of a CRE pedagogy for developing a positive classroom culture and how this promotes a specific understanding of respect and tolerance.

A good government of a country plagued with mines will not ignore them. It will educate people to know what mines look like, how to negotiate them and make them safe. By making students sensitive to existing disagreements and skilled at negotiating these, CRE produces religiously literate students prepared for life in a pluralist society. As such, teaching CRE helps meet the Government's requirement to teach 'British values'. Adopting a critical pedagogy also makes it easier to justify RE's place on the curriculum to parents who are concerned about their child participating in RE.

Introduction to RE and controversial issues

The prospect of encouraging students to debate matters as controversial as the authority of the Qur'an or the ethical status of homosexuality might fill some teachers with fear. Thoughts abound of discussions getting out of control, arguments breaking out, statements being taken out of context and reported to parents . . . These fears might be enough to persuade a teacher to stick to learning about *how* Muslims show their beliefs about the Qur'an in practice and *what* the Bible says about homosexuality.

We encourage you not to retreat to perceived 'safer' territory. The worries mentioned above come with the territory of teaching RE. Most teachers will encounter issues like these at some point in their career, regardless of their pedagogical approach. However, some may view CRE as particularly dangerous, because CRE explicitly encourages students to engage critically with truth-claims. Ofsted reports that there is apprehension over critical learning in RE; teachers have "uncertainties about the relationships between fostering respect for pupils' beliefs and encouraging open, critical, investigative learning in RE" (Ofsted, 2010).

This apprehension about raising controversial issues might put some teachers off adopting a CRE approach. Research has suggested that often teachers will deliberately avoid contentious issues in order to 'keep the peace'. For example, teachers at an integrated school in Northern Ireland deliberately avoided discussing religious and cultural issues about which Protestants and Catholics disagree, citing fear of "lots of rows" and "confrontation" (Donnelly, 2004, p.11). Oulton et al. (2004, p.504) found that some teachers feel unable to present any views as wrong, with only one in three teachers saying that they would try to affect their students' views on racism. Similarly, a number of social studies teachers interviewed as part of a US study intentionally avoided discussion of controversial issues in their lessons. This was justified by reasons of "safety, fairness or personal discomfort" (Hess and McAvoy, 2015, p.174).

These research findings suggest that teachers need to be supported and enabled so that they feel more confident in tackling the issues that may arise in response to controversy. The philosophy underpinning CRE naturally gives us principles to guide our responses to these issues, such as a specific understanding of what respect for others requires. The classroom culture that CRE creates and sustains is one where conflict can be managed and seen as productive.

Creating the right classroom culture

The key to managing discussion of controversial topics is to have the right classroom culture set up from the beginning. The environment needs to be one of **trust** (that your viewpoint will be shown respect and that you will not be made to feel stupid), **active engagement** (with the views of others), and **tolerance** (as discussed in the 'CRE, tolerance and respect' section below).

You may wish to start the year with a new class by mind-mapping what might go wrong in the RE classroom (e.g. offence, upset, argument) and then constructing a set of rules to guide discussion around controversial issues.

Successful discussion of controversial issues is unavoidably tied up with good behaviour management, and so it is important that expectations for behaviour are high. This poses a particular challenge for RE teachers, who want to encourage active discussion at the same time as maintaining tight control. You might experiment with strategies for managing discussion such as only allowing students to speak when they are holding a ball (which they then throw back to you or on to the next person). In the Year 7 scheme of work, students practise 'RE boxing' in their first formal RE debate. Here students are awarded points if their arguments successfully respond to previous arguments. This helps to teach the skills of academic debate, including the discipline of *engaging* with other people rather than simply shouting louder than them! Alternatively, you can give out Duplo bricks that everyone has one of and must 'play' as an argument and connect with the previous one, so as to encourage students to link their arguments with those that precede them.

The suggested Year 7 scheme of work provides ample opportunities for practising the type of respectful behaviour that will be all the more important when the topics become more emotive. Since the focus of that scheme of work is not on a particular religion, students should not feel that they are being 'got at' from the start, and time should be spent at this early stage modelling respectful language and 'how to disagree well'.

Tips:

- *Make rules for the classroom explicit.*
- *Consider having the rules permanently on display.*
- *Rigidly stick to the rules you have set to guide discussion.*

CRE, tolerance and respect

Given the importance of 'tolerance' and 'respect' in creating the best environment for good learning in RE, it is worth spending some time thinking about what should be meant by these terms and how best to promote tolerance and respect.

Students will often have been told by their parents and teachers about the importance of 'respecting everyone', but the chances are that this has not been accompanied by reflection on what this means. Indeed, research has suggested that students can be quite confused about what the requirement to respect asks of them. Some students think that respect entails that they do not question the truth of other people's views. For example, one student responded to the Qur'an sorting exercise (see Chapter 4) by saying "It is really mean to say it might not be [the direct word of God]. It is really rude if you don't treat it respectfully" (Davis, 2012, p.32). On this student's view, to say that somebody is wrong is to disrespect them. You might have heard something similar voiced by your students. We can refer to this understanding as the **'respecting-as-agreeing' view**.

Yet in our pluralist society, there exist a variety of conflicting viewpoints. Reflecting on this fact gives us reason to challenge the respecting-as-agreeing view. If respecting everyone requires that you agree with everyone, then (since in some cases opinions conflict) this would mean agreeing with *contradictory* opinions – which cannot be done with sincerity. The only way to make sense of this view would be to see beliefs as *metaphorical* rather than as making significant truth claims about the way things actually are in the world. This allows for beliefs to be held true without them coming into conflict with other beliefs. This thought process is reflected in some of the theoretical literature on this topic. For example, Andrew Davis (2010, p.190) argues that it is impossible to hold an **exclusivist** approach to religion (believing that your view is true and others false) and yet show respect to those who hold conflicting beliefs. Davis suggests that this is not a problem, since we should take a metaphorical interpretation of what initially seem to be exclusivist beliefs such as 'Jesus is the Son of God'.

The trouble with this 'solution' is that it distorts the way that beliefs are in fact held by many religious people. Davis says that "All Christians know that Jesus is not *literally* the Son of God" (2010, p.198), but this simply is not true. To refer to exclusive approaches as "primitive" (2010, p.198) is patronising to believers. It represents an 'ivory tower' approach to religion that does not tally with the lives of the majority of religious adherents. Many religious believers do hold their beliefs as **propositional** beliefs. That is, they are beliefs about the way things actually are in the world. In light of this fact, for students to achieve an *authentic* understanding of *lived* religious belief, there is a need to challenge the respecting-as-agreeing view. Indeed, concern for respect gives a reason itself to challenge the respecting-as-agreeing view, since it does not seem very respectful to distort the way that religious believers see their beliefs so that they fit comfortably with conflicting religious beliefs. If teachers want to encourage a deeper respect that goes beyond what can be achieved when students are engaging only on a superficial, empathetic level, they will need to encourage their students to engage with viewpoints as (significantly) true, i.e. as sometimes making claims about the way things truly are. Someone engaging with a religious worldview as making propositional claims "will be demonstrating deep respect: even more so if they extend the courtesy of engaging with the possibility that an alternative worldview might actually be true" (Wright, 2007, p.112).

Instead of respecting-as-agreeing, CRE encourages students to adopt an alternative understanding of respect. This focuses on respecting the *person*, as a person, rather than respecting *each one of the person's beliefs*. A variety of non-religious and religious arguments support the view that simply in virtue of their status as a human being, the person with whom we disagree has dignity and rationality that makes them worthy of respect. Persons are marked out by their acting on the basis of reasons, and so perhaps the appropriate way to respect the person whose view you oppose is to *engage with their reasons*. How have they reached this conflicting viewpoint? What reasons are there for why they stand where they stand? True respect for a person should therefore motivate an interest in, and engagement with, their reasons.

What does this preferred understanding of respect look like in classroom practice? Essentially, it involves being *interested* in other people's reasons, *listening* to these being expressed, and engaging in a way that is *polite* and does not make the person feel stupid. This can be summarised as 'taking each other seriously'. We would encourage you to teach students to be able to say that they disagree (if they do) and that they think that a viewpoint is wrong, but to be able to do so politely and non-dismissively. One way to do this is to model language that targets *beliefs* rather than people. Encourage your students to say 'I think what Jenny said is wrong because . . . ' rather than 'Jenny is wrong because . . . ' Encourage speech that pinpoints where there is the disagreement, e.g. 'I can see where you are coming from, but I still find it hard to understand how that view explains evil in the world because . . . '.

This is not to say that students will not get offended, for it is a fact of human nature that we do not like being told that we are wrong! But if students engage in discussion in the spirit of a *mutual pursuit of truth*, with a focus on evaluating a belief (or belief-set) rather than with the purpose of showing that *this person* is wrong, then criticism is likely to be better received.

Once we understand 'respect' as a basic requirement for politeness and as an acknowledgement of human dignity, rather than as a requirement to agree, it becomes easier to understand what is meant by 'tolerance'. Tolerating beliefs certainly does not mean 'accepting that they are true', since this would involve having to accept contradictory beliefs. We should also avoid interpreting tolerance as 'agreeing to disagree', as this implies that we do not need to engage with the person with whom we disagree, and instead we can pretend that the disagreement does not exist. Rather, tolerance is best interpreted as **allowing other people to hold their beliefs**, as part of your respect for them as a person, **whilst being willing to voice reasons for why you think that they are wrong**.

Since this understanding of tolerance requires critical engagement with opposing viewpoints, it will also encourage students to be *discerning* in what they believe and in what they tolerate. CRE does not advocate a blanket tolerance of *all* viewpoints; not all opinions are good opinions. If a viewpoint is harmful and cannot stand up to critical scrutiny, then this might suggest to us that the actions that follow from this viewpoint should not be tolerated. These are tricky issues, and there is no easy formula for the boundaries of tolerance. But these are exactly the sorts of issues that need thinking about in a democratic society marked by difference and often disagreement. It is therefore important that our students, as the citizens of the future, think about how best to deal with such issues.

The groundwork of CRE, explored in the Year 7 scheme of work, should naturally lead students to this view of tolerance and away from unreflective, blanket tolerance. Students are exposed to a variety of conflicting truth claims and learn that there are not conclusive, universally accepted arguments in favour of their own point of view. They should, therefore, come to possess some level of *humility* about their beliefs and be less likely to be dogmatic when faced with opposing views. The hope is that students will gradually develop a level of intellectual maturity such that they are able to stand unresolved tensions and live peacefully in spite of them, but who are at the same time impelled to engage in discussion and further investigation in order to attempt to resolve the tensions. Recognition of **epistemic relativity**, alongside the fact that there is wide disagreement in society on some important issues, should lead students to develop the virtue of **epistemic humility** (being humble about their beliefs, and recognising the possibility that they could be wrong). Epistemic humility is part of what motivates us to think that the viewpoints of others are worthy of open and serious discussion, and so is a prerequisite for good classroom debate.

CRE therefore offers an understanding of tolerance and respect that is deep and authentic, rather than surface-level and involving belief-distortion. Respect for persons is affirmed, and built up, through the process of discourse and discussion.

Tips:

- *Use the terms 'respect' and 'tolerance' as part of your everyday RE classroom language.*
- *Explicitly discuss what these terms mean. Consider re-visiting the Year 7 Tolerance lesson later in the RE curriculum, perhaps in relation to a topic you are currently studying.*
- *Challenge students who state viewpoints aggressively, e.g. 'How could you have phrased that more respectfully?', 'Don't raise your voice; improve your argument!'*
- *Model respectful speech and language in your own questioning, e.g. 'Why might someone disagree with Prina's view?'*
- *If necessary, help less able students, especially those representing minority positions, by contributing arguments (as part of your role as devil's advocate).*

CRE and its contribution to social cohesion

If we take a critical approach to RE, which does not hide disagreements between religions and openly asks students to voice disagreement in the classroom, surely this will further increase discord in our multi-religious society? The above discussion on tolerance and respect should already have gone some way to respond to this question. However, it is important that this objection is properly addressed, since the contribution of RE to the 'social cohesion agenda' is often seen as an important justification for RE's place on the curriculum. Woodward (2012, p.132) explains that "the community cohesion agenda values diversity and accepts all regardless of race, belief, gender, disability, sexual orientation or age". RE is seen as an important way of pushing forward this agenda. Indeed, Watson even points to the poor provision of RE in the schools which the 7/7 tube bombers attended as a reminder of the importance of good RE (Watson, 2012, p.19).

The CRE approach may initially seem in conflict with the social cohesion agenda because it openly acknowledges the fact of "religious particularity" (Wright, 2007, p.90) (that is, the fact that religions make at least some exclusive truth claims). The social cohesion agenda's aim is to be *inclusive* whereas the approach set out in this book does not hide the fact that religions are often *exclusive*. The CRE approach does not have as its aim to promote social cohesion. However, we do believe that the approach better contributes to social cohesion than alternative approaches that may ignore or downplay difference. In this section, we offer a number of reasons as to why.

First, the CRE approach is likely to result in a longer-lasting, more genuine tolerance. This is because it requires more than merely surface respect and does not 'brush over' distinctive truth claims made by religions. Since it is an inevitable feature of life in a multi-faith society that we come into contact with people with conflicting beliefs, an ability to cope with such disagreement is best developed in the safe and structured environment of the classroom.

Second, being on a journey together in search of the right answers can act as a uniting force between those who disagree. The very passion with which we can have a heated disagreement shows our shared concern for truth. With those with whom we disagree, we share uncertainty about the ultimate nature of reality, awareness that we can only make judgements based on the limited amount we know, and a concern to get the answer right so that we can live truthfully. These commonalities go at least some way to providing a basis for solidarity and respect.

Third, by questioning the approach to tolerance and respect that asks that we accept all views, CRE undermines the plausibility of a potentially dangerous relativism. Relativism leads people to think that they do not need to provide reasons for beliefs and that it is always wrong to question the beliefs of others. Some evidence of this has been found in classroom research, where some students used references to 'respect' as an end-point or default answer so as to avoid having to give reasons (Davis, 2012, p.32). This is of particular concern where beliefs are harmful (for example, the belief that some races are superior to others, or that God commands indiscriminate, large-scale violence as part of lesser jihad). We need to be able to challenge harmful beliefs if we are to have a peaceful, flourishing society. CRE equips students with the tools to do this.

CRE therefore contributes to a cohesive society better than a policy of accepting all beliefs. By examining truth claims, students are better able to understand the complexity of controversial issues and are forced to embrace the need to find ways to live together peacefully despite disagreement.

Tips:

- *Acknowledge both agreements and disagreements between and within religions.*
- *Use group terms to describe the group's project; 'together we explored why regular prayer might be worthwhile', 'today we're trying to work out what we should think about . . . '.*
- *Emphasise that the aim is not agreement – take disagreement as a given!*

CRE and 'British values'

Since 2012, the Teachers' Standards have required that teachers enact good professional conduct by "showing tolerance of and respect for the rights of others" and by "not undermining fundamental British values, including democracy, the rule of law, individual liberty and mutual respect, and tolerance of those with different faiths and beliefs" (Department for Education, 2011). This was followed by the 2014 announcement that all schools "have a duty to 'actively promote'" these values. Schools must demonstrate that they have "a clear strategy for embedding these values and show how their work with pupils has been effective in doing so" and this will form part of the school inspection process (Department for Education, 2014).

The Government has stated several motives for the policy, including "to ensure young people leave school prepared for life in modern Britain", to "tighten up the standards on pupil welfare to improve safeguarding, and the standards on spiritual, moral, social and cultural development of pupils to strengthen the barriers to extremism", and to ensure that children become "valuable and fully rounded members of society who treat others with respect and tolerance, regardless of background" (Department for Education, 2014). However, the policy is clearly also motivated by the need to respond to violent extremism. Its first appearance (in the 2012 Teachers' Standards) came alongside mention of the *Prevent* strategy, which focuses on addressing the ideological causes of extremism.[1]

In light of the Government's stated purposes and the background of the policy in the fight against extremism, it is unhelpful to interpret the policy as being primarily about promoting *British* values or a sense of nationality. Rather, the policy is better viewed as a response to the difficulty of how to cope with pluralism in a way that is consistent with the ideals of tolerance and freedom, and yet robust enough to cope with harmful beliefs and ways of life. We can also see the policy as part of a more general motivation to stabilise the state by cultivating in the next generation of citizens a desire to comply with, support, but also critically engage with, political institutions. How might a CRE approach help achieve these goals?

First, as discussed above, CRE encourages tolerance, understood so that being tolerant does not mean accepting all views and can mean *intolerance of extremism*. We must assume that this is what the Government wants and thus that we should be teaching *intolerance* of certain beliefs and practices (such as racism and terrorism). By teaching students how to engage critically with views that they oppose, students are equipped with the tools to tackle extremist views and dismiss them as unworthy of tolerance.

Second, discussions in CRE lessons help develop skills and virtues that are conducive to the flourishing of society. Students gain practice at how to conduct themselves in a dispute over truth, in a civilised way that does not pose a danger to others. As part of the learning process, virtues are cultivated that are desirable in our citizens; **attentiveness** (to the beliefs of others), **depth** of understanding of similarity and difference, **discernment** (for example, people who aim to be consistent in their beliefs and who avoid quick, rash judgements) and **responsibility** (people who act on the basis of their beliefs). Moreover, encountering different beliefs as *potentially true* helps cultivate **epistemic humility**, the realisation that one might be wrong even about one's most deeply held beliefs. Encouraging students to think about *reasons* behind beliefs also helps students develop epistemic humility, for there is always the potential for revising beliefs when new reasons come to light. Importantly, people with these virtues are the sorts of people who can be reasoned with, which is a desirable trait of citizens if society is to be a safe place.

Third, CRE encourages a level of critical questioning which allows that even the most basic values and assumptions are up for debate. It is one of the responsibilities of the RE teacher not to indoctrinate, even about assumptions that underlie discussion (such as the need to respect everyone). Critical questioning must extend to the 'British values' themselves, and students must be free to question and debate what these values are and how they should be interpreted.

Adopting this approach is important if the Government policy is to be able to meet two obvious objections. The first objection raises concern that the values are controversial, liberal values. Arguably, teaching these values is to indoctrinate children into liberalism – a clear example of liberal hypocrisy! The second objection worries that the imposition of *any* values (however uncontroversial) on children is problematic, for it means that when they become full citizens they are unable to give free, rational and informed consent to the state's authority, with the consequence that state authority and laws are illegitimate (see Brighouse, 1998, p.723). Both these objections lose their force if children are allowed to exercise their growing rationality by questioning the values themselves, by being involved in the process of shaping what these values are and their implications for how we should behave. The values are then not to be seen as illegitimately 'imposed from above', but mutually agreed upon and shaped. To avoid such concerns, students need to be given opportunities to critically reflect on the values and what they mean. CRE gives students the tools to do so with intelligence and rigour.

Tips:

- *Make use of the language of the 'British values' policy.*
- *Openly discuss what these values mean, acknowledging and allowing discussion of their controversial nature.*

Withdrawal from the subject

Parents can withdraw their children from RE without giving a reason. This right is most commonly exercised by parents who do not want their child exposed to other faiths and/or to have their religious beliefs questioned, or because they are from a no-faith background and disagree with the subject forming any part of their child's curriculum. In terms of the aims of the 'British values' policy and the need for a society of citizens that can get on despite its differences, these are usually the students we *most want* in the RE classroom. So, anything that you can do to persuade parents to keep their children in RE is helpful. A CRE approach may make it easier for you to explain and justify the subject's place to such parents. In our experience, the motivations for withdrawal usually result from a misunderstanding of the nature and content of the subject. The following strategies might help:

- Make clear to secular parents the non-confessional pedagogy adopted in your lessons and (if relevant) how RE has changed since when they were at school.
- Invite parents in for you to take them through schemes of work.
- Emphasise that the principles underlying RE, and the importance and place of different values, are not imposed, they are themselves up for discussion.
- Point out that the students are always encouraged to make their *own* critical judgements having first looked at relevant information and engaged in discussion.

In our experience, this last point (students making independent critical judgements) is what some parents of faith find particularly objectionable. If this is the case, then you could try to convince parents of the value of critical reflection even from within a faith perspective:

● Most people, if they think through what indoctrination means and its implications for later life, will not want their children to be indoctrinated. This is something all the major religious traditions claim to want to avoid. For example, the Qur'an indicates that people are to come to Islam through free choice; "Let there be no compulsion in religion" (2:256). The Jewish and Christian traditions have a long history of critical examination of truth claims (think of, for example, the discussions of the Talmudic scholars or the Medieval scholastics). "The essence of indoctrination is that it always eliminates choice" (Copley, 2005, p.263), and to have a choice, one has to have access to more than one viewpoint.

● Children are more likely to hold onto their beliefs in the long term if they have considered the reasons for and against them and independently arrived at their conclusions. In our multicultural society, it is almost impossible to avoid encountering those with opposing beliefs, and increasingly, coming face-to-face with secular criticism. If someone has never had to defend their beliefs, and has not rehearsed arguments in favour of both sides, they may be more likely to lose their beliefs since they do not truly understand the grounds for holding their beliefs. (This is a version of John Stuart Mill's 'dead dogma' argument; Mill quoted Cicero's famous dictum that "He who knows only his own side of the case knows little of that" (Mill, 2006, p.44).) For this reason, Thiessen (1992, p.82) argues in relation to Christian nurture in faith schools that it should "foster honest and serious grappling with doubt, questions and objections to Christian convictions".

● People are more likely to *act* on their beliefs if they have been discussed in the manner suggested above, for a 'dead dogma' becomes "deprived of its vital effect on the character and conduct: the dogma becoming mere profession, inefficacious for good" (Mill, 2006, p.61). For example, if we've just been engaged in discussions about the value of recycling for the environment, we are more likely to be moved to recycle next time we visit the bin. Presumably if parents believe that they are in the possession of the truth, they will want their children to *live their lives truthfully* in accordance with that truth. They should therefore support discussion as a means for 'bringing home' the importance of beliefs as well as its implications for action.

● Most religious and non-religious worldviews accept a view of personhood as being marked by the capacity for rationality and autonomy (although the interpretation of and emphasis on these concepts varies). Following from this, most people are willing to accept that it is good to exercise these capacities and is in some sense a loss when these capacities are not being exercised. Therefore, it is right that students should be encouraged to question their beliefs and this should not be viewed as dangerous. Mill puts forward a similar point, arguing that holding beliefs without good reasons (for example, adhering to a belief solely because this is what your parents believe) means you are not exercising your human faculties; "to conform to custom, merely as custom, does not educate or develop in him any of the qualities which are the distinctive endowment of a human being" (Mill, 2006, p.67).

Conclusion

Guiding controversial discussions in RE is something of an art, but it is something that teachers become better at through experience. We acknowledge that in some classrooms, particularly those with large numbers of faith students, critically reflecting on truth claims raises difficult issues. But CRE can be done, and be done well, in such settings. Watch other teachers. Set rules for discussion. Reflect when you are planning your lessons on your particular set of students and their sensitivities. If necessary, inform students in advance of topics that they will find difficult. With good planning and behaviour management, a healthy dose of sensitivity, as well as the streak of bravery required to tackle controversy head-on, teachers can teach CRE without problems, and its benefits will extend beyond the classroom to society as a whole.

Note

1 Extremism is defined in Prevent as "vocal or active opposition to fundamental British values, including democracy, the rule of law, individual liberty and mutual respect and tolerance of different faiths and beliefs" (HM Government, 2011, p.107). The implementation of Prevent continues to be highly controversial, particularly since the Counter-Terrorism and Security Act 2015 made it a *statutory* duty for public sector organisations to prevent people from getting drawn into terrorism. Schools are required to identify potential signs of extremism and refer these students to 'Channel', the Government's de-radicalisation programme. Some suggest that this has had the effect of stifling freedom of expression in the classroom (Bowcott and Adams, 2016). This is supported by anecdotal reports by teachers that they have noticed that their Muslim students are more afraid to speak out, and are less involved in classroom discussion (e.g. Faure-Walker, 2016). This does seem an almost inevitable consequence of teachers being required to be 'on the lookout' for certain speech and behaviours, and will add additional challenges to creating the environment of trust and open debate discussed in the section 'Creating the right classroom culture'.

References

Bowcott, O. and Adams, R. (2016). Human rights group condemns Prevent anti-radicalisation strategy. *The Guardian*. 13/07/2016. Available online at: https://www.theguardian.com/politics/2016/jul/13/human-rights-group-condemns-prevent-anti-radicalisation-strategy (accessed 28/04/17).

Brighouse, H. (1998). Civic Education and Liberal Legitimacy. *Ethics* 108, no.4, 719–745.

Copley, T. (2005). Young People, Biblical Narrative and "Theologizing": A UK Perspective. *Religious Education* 100, no. 3: 254–265.

Davis, A. (2010). Defending Religious Pluralism for Religious Education. *Ethics and Education* 5, no. 3: 189–202.

Davis, C. (2012). *Countering the postmodern turn: Re-engaging students with truth in the classroom*. Unpublished Master's Thesis. Sheffield Hallam University, UK.

Department for Education (2011). Teachers' Standards: Guidance for school leaders, school staff and governing bodies. Available online at: https://www.gov.uk/government/uploads/system/uploads/attachment_data/file/301107/Teachers__Standards.pdf (accessed 13/06/16).

Department for Education (2014). News. Available online at: https://www.gov.uk/government/news/guidance-on-promoting-british-values-in-schools-published (accessed 16/05/16).

Donnelly, C. (2004). What price harmony? Teachers' methods of delivering an ethos of tolerance and respect for diversity in an integrated school in Northern Ireland. *Educational Research* 46, no.1, 3–16.

Faure-Walker, R. (2016). How the Prevent Counter-Terrorism Strategies Create a Muslim Outgroup and Might Increase the Threat of Terrorism. Presentation on 11/07/16 to the Third ISA Forum on Sociology. Abstract accessed online at: https://isaconf.confex.com/isaconf/forum2016/webprogram/Paper77998.html (accessed 28/04/17).

Hess, D. E. and McAvoy, P. (2015). *The Political Classroom: Evidence and Ethics in Democratic Education*. New York: Routledge.

HM Government (2011). *Prevent Strategy*. Available online at: https://www.gov.uk/government/uploads/system/uploads/attachment_data/file/97976/prevent-strategy-review.pdf (accessed 17/05/16).

Mill, J. S. (2006). *On Liberty*. London: Penguin.

Ofsted (2010). *Transforming Religious Education*. Available online at: http://dera.ioe.ac.uk/1121/1/Transforming%20religious%20education.pdf (accessed 06/01/18).

Oulton, C., Day, V., Dillon, J. and Grace, M. (2004). Controversial Issues: Teachers' Attitudes and Practices in the context of Citizenship Education. *Oxford Review of Education* 30, no. 4: 489–507.

Thiessen, E. J. (1992). Christian Nurture, Indoctrination and Liberal Education. In *The Contours of Christian Education*, eds. J. Astley and D. Day, 67–83. Essex: McCrimmons.

Watson, B. (2012). Why Religious Education Matters. In *Debates in Religious Education*, ed. L. Philip Barnes, 13–21. Oxon: Routledge.

Woodward, R. (2012). Community Cohesion. In *Debates in Religious Education*, ed. L. Philip Barnes, 132–145. Oxon: Routledge.

Wright, A. (2007). *Critical Religious Education, Multiculturalism and the Pursuit of Truth*. Cardiff: University of Wales Press.

CHAPTER 3

Critical Religious Education

An introductory scheme of work (Year 7)

In 2008 Andrew Wright formed FORASE – The Forum on Religious and Spiritual Education – at King's College London (KCL). This was in response to a call by other notable academics for there to be more concrete examples of the pedagogy of Critical Religious Education (CRE) in practice. FORASE was initially a seminar group incorporating a number of religious education (RE) teachers working in and around London, who came together to discuss issues surrounding RE pedagogy. The need became apparent for a smaller group, dedicated to creating a publication which would model CRE in practice, and thus the writing group was formed. The introductory scheme of work outlined in this chapter was the first project that the writing group undertook. Once completed, the scheme of work was trialled in the schools of two of the authors and was subsequently piloted in a number of schools associated with KCL. The pilot process confirmed the viability of the project, with a very positive response to the materials from all the RE departments involved. A number of schools embedded the introductory scheme of work into the curriculum.

The aim of the scheme of work is to provide an introduction to CRE, and for this to become the foundation for embedding CRE across the curriculum. It achieves this in two ways. First, the scheme of work implicitly introduces both students and teachers to the framework of critical realism. Rather than using the language of 'ontological realism', 'epistemic relativity' and 'judgemental rationality', which may be inappropriate for Year 7 students, the scheme of work is designed to explore these concepts by embedding them in curriculum content and focusing the students' learning on unpacking them. This is perhaps most clear in lessons 3–5 which ask the questions: 'What is real?' (ontological realism); 'Can we know what is real?' (epistemic relativity); and 'How do we know what is real?' (judgemental rationality). Second, the scheme of work exemplifies how to explore **ultimate questions**. It introduces students to the processes and tools necessary for approaching RE critically. This involves developing an understanding of different worldviews and how these impact the way in which we live, of the criteria which may be used for making judgements about truth claims and how to debate and evaluate. The scheme of work is an effective introduction to a critical realist pedagogy and provides an excellent way to begin your students' secondary religious education.

Ultimate questions: Important questions about reality which do not have a certain answer and thus are still debated. The major world religions and secular traditions give different answers to many of these questions.

This chapter gives an overview of the scheme of work, followed by a closer look at each of the individual lessons. For each lesson we provide a rationale for the learning, clear learning objectives and a set of key activities, with an explanation of how these should be enacted. In addition, there is a list of resources for each lesson and images of key resources. All resources can be accessed on the accompanying website. It is intended that this chapter will support teachers in delivering CRE to their students. Ideally teachers should use the entire scheme of work as it stands, but it is possible that particular lessons or even individual resources could be used by teachers within other complementary units of study.

Lessons, resources and teacher guidance

Each lesson has simply expressed learning objectives and the process of the lesson is described. The activities have been planned to fit into an hour-long lesson. You will need to adapt the activities to fit into your particular school's timings. The teacher guidance provides you with some suggestions, both for ways to adapt lessons to suit different contexts and practical ways to deliver the activities outlined. The actual PowerPoints and worksheets are available on the companion website.

Specific differentiation will always be personal to the individual students you have in your classes.[1] The nature of the tasks is very much driven and formed by the responses that the students bring to them. One of the significant challenges of teaching the scheme of work will be the responsiveness you will need as a teacher to ensure that all the students' voices are heard and their contributions are valued. The learning is likely to be very fluid as the students enjoy the opportunity to grapple with their own emerging understanding of those existential questions which puzzle us all and the plethora of answers available!

A note on introducing worldviews

The worldviews are an essential tool in enabling children to intelligently and respectfully engage with and critique the views of others. Your worldview embodies what you believe and how you live. Through this scheme of work students will recognise that they hold differing views from each other. What worldviews enable students to understand is that these beliefs are **coherent** based on each worldview's initial premise on the nature of truth.

Dividing worldviews into three categories – Theism, Secularism and Postmodernism – is clearly an oversimplification. However, it must be remembered that their role is to provide a heuristic tool – a formulation serving as a guide in the solving of a problem. As with many stereotypes they are not perfect but if they can begin to enable students to understand broadly different ways in which people believe truth can be known, as well as the difference between absolute and relative truth and their implications, then this is clearly a significant step forward.

Postmodernism

Postmodernism is the most challenging issue to teach yet arguably the most essential. The understanding of postmodernism here is based entirely on a **commitment to subjective truth**. Nothing has objective truth. Truth is constructed by individuals and exists only subjectively. Therefore all beliefs and values must be understood as being equally 'valid', on the basis that they have no objective meaning. However, postmodernism should not be confused with the understanding of moral relativism that appears in A Level textbooks – that positions of right and wrong are culturally based. It also must not be confused with liberal theist views – liberal theists may accept that they are less certain about their beliefs but they do not believe that all truth is subjective.

It is also worth noting that the critical realist, whilst committed to a single reality and therefore opposed to postmodernism, would argue that we should *of course* study postmodernism. Due to our epistemic relativity, we must always come to learning with a degree of humility when interrogating the views of others; this cannot and should not preclude the consideration of views whose compatibility seem improbable or indeed impossible! We trust our judgemental rationality to lead us to a more discerning view of the world and to an active understanding of the beliefs to which we are committed. Not to critically evaluate postmodernism would betray a lack of courage in our convictions.[2]

Theism

The theistic worldview is fairly self-explanatory. It is imperative that you do not let students get away with saying that theists don't find truth in science. You might also point out that historical evidence also plays a part; for example, the historical records of the lives of Jesus, Muhammad, etc. As one of the two worldviews that argue absolute truth exists independently of humanity, it may be helpful to point out that this does not necessarily mean that theists are all certain of their beliefs, just that they think that there is more evidence to believe in God than to not.

Secularism

The secular worldview is also self-explanatory. When delivering it, make sure that students recognise that truth does not only come from natural science but also human sciences, social and political sciences, history, discussion, etc.

A fourth way – agnosticism

This is a belief to which someone can be committed, but it must be made clear to your students that such a potentially ambivalent position does not change the nature of reality – either God exists or God does not exist. Many theists and secular thinkers would argue that it is worth working out which side you feel has better evidence.

Through such engagement we hope to begin a process by which students are empowered to engage with the complexity and controversy of different ontological positions. Once established, even at a basic level, the worldviews become a transferable tool which can be applied to other topics. For example, when studying the life of Jesus, an atheist will be able to criticise a Christian response by linking his views to his understanding of the nature of truth; for example, he could argue that there is a lack of empirical evidence for Jesus' miracles. He would understand that a Christian may believe these stories, based on a belief in the authority of scripture, but would be able to intelligently explain why he feels that this is misplaced. He could argue that the Bible is more likely to have been written by humans than be divinely inspired. It also establishes a link between beliefs about truth and connected beliefs/actions which can act as a model when greater specialisation and diversity is required, such as in the distinction between liberal and fundamentalist Christians, Islamists and moderate Muslims, etc.

If you are working in a faith school, your students are more likely to share the same worldview (though do not take this for granted!). You will need to introduce the others as alternatives and encourage your students to empathetically and intelligently speculate about the reasons someone may hold a different worldview.

An overview of the introductory scheme of work

Sequence	Lesson title	Learning objectives
1	Introducing the ultimate questions	To identify your own answers to the ultimate questions To have begun to reflect on how others answer the ultimate questions
2	Exploring the nature of ultimate questions	To understand what an ultimate question is To recognise how ultimate questions interlink To respond to one of three ultimate questions
Baseline assessment		To respond to the question 'Does God exist?'
3	How do we know what is REAL?	To recognise different accounts of what is real To begin to make judgements about what is real and what is not
4	How do we KNOW what is real?	To understand ways in which philosophers and theologians have cast doubt on even our most basic beliefs about what is real To apply and explore the four accounts of what is real introduced last lesson To reflect on how much you really know about the world

Sequence	Lesson title	Learning objectives
5	How do WE know what is real?	To identify some of the ways we make judgements between conflicting truth claims To make a judgement about whether we are faced with 'utter ignorance' in 'theologic' disputes
6	Introducing different worldviews	To understand three different worldviews To apply the language of the worldviews in order to interpret and diagnose the worldview of a peer To identify your own worldview and respond to the worldviews of others
7	Applying worldviews	To consolidate your understanding of the three worldviews studied To understand that these worldviews can impact how we live
8	Evaluating worldviews	To describe and attempt to explain why you hold your worldview To critically respond to the worldviews of others
9	The need for tolerance	To understand that conflicting truth claims can be difficult to negotiate To recognise that there are different views about what tolerance is, and what these views are To make your own critical judgement about which view of tolerance is best
10–12	Assessment and feedback	To demonstrate your learning on the topic To receive feedback on your progress To self-assess your response to the topic

Lesson 1: introducing the ultimate questions

Key activities:

- Ultimate Questions Questionnaire
- Comparison with partner
- Independent task – try it on the parents!

Resources:

- PowerPoint
- Ultimate Questions Questionnaire

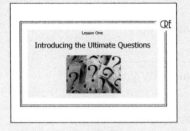

Learning objectives

1. To identify your own answers to the ultimate questions
2. To have begun to reflect on how others answer the ultimate questions

The aim of Lesson 1 is to introduce students to the scope of the subject. However, as this scheme of work is intended to introduce CRE to students at secondary level, the first lesson is fairly minimal in terms of activities and resources in order to allow for the general set-up which may occur at the beginning of the school year. It may be that books are given out, mark schemes stuck in, games played to learn names, etc. before moving on to the suggested activities.

The key task for this lesson is the Ultimate Questions Questionnaire. Students should be given the questionnaire and asked to complete it on their own, without discussing it with anyone else. How much time is given for this activity can be decided by the individual teacher as is appropriate in their context, but we would suggest a minimum of 15 minutes in order that students can give adequate answers. The questionnaire serves to begin the process of students' critical engagement with questions of ultimate truth. As well as being a tool for the students, it is also a tool for the teacher, who can deduce much about individual students' worldviews from their responses. The extent to which students have already thought critically about questions of this nature may also be clear from their responses.

Once students have completed the questionnaire, they should be given time to share and compare their answers with a partner. It is hoped that students will have answered at least some of the questions differently to their partners. Thus they should begin to encounter variation as a result of this task and will hopefully recognise that there is more than one possible answer to each of the questions posed. Teachers may wish to further this with some whole-class feedback if time allows.

Students can then take home a blank copy of the questionnaire to complete with a member of their family. This should encourage some critical discussion in the home and may also encourage the students to consider where their beliefs come from. These questionnaires are drawn upon in later lessons, as will become apparent.

Lesson 2: exploring the nature of ultimate questions

Learning objectives

1. To understand what an ultimate question is
2. To recognise how ultimate questions interlink
3. To respond to one of three ultimate questions

The aim of Lesson 2 is to help students better understand what ultimate questions are and how they interlink. Broadly speaking, ultimate questions tend to fall under one (or more) of three important areas/questions for RE: personal identity (Who am I?), ethical implications (How should I live?) and metaphysical explorations (What is real?).

To start, students are encouraged to generate ultimate questions by writing (on sticky notes) examples of questions which are important to them. As a stimulus you could show the PowerPoint slide with key words such as 'good', 'evil', 'the world'. (You could also direct them back to last lesson's questionnaire.) Use of student questions serves to illustrate the range of questions which might be studied, whilst highlighting to students that ultimate questions are ones that they can generate themselves.

The second stage of the lesson involves categorising the questions. Draw a chart on the whiteboard with the three key questions (Who am I?, How should I live?, What is real?). As a class, add their questions to the relevant columns. Arranging the questions can be difficult in that many of them overlap. For example, the question, 'Did God make me?' would relate to both 'Who am I?' and 'What is real?'. You could thus separate the question by writing 'Was I created by God?' under 'Who am I?', and 'Does God exist?' under 'What is real?'. You could also discuss how the answers may have implications for the way we live. This example serves to illustrate that many ultimate questions are interrelated and that the beliefs we hold impact our actions and attitudes to others. It is also worth having a 'dump' column for questions that are not ultimate.

Who am I?	How should I live?	What is real?	Dump
Do I have a soul?	What is the purpose of life?	Does God exist?	Who will win the League?
What makes me, me?	Is there a code to live by?	Is there life after death?	

Following this task, students discuss with a partner which of the three main questions ('Who am I?', 'How should I live?', and 'What is real?') they consider to be the most important and why. They can then answer their chosen question in writing, demonstrating their new understanding of the scope that the question poses.

Baseline assessment

The baseline assessment is suggested at this stage in the scheme of work for a number of reasons. The assessment of an extended piece of writing from each student at the beginning of the scheme (indeed at the beginning of their secondary school career) should help teachers to understand the general strengths their students bring with them to the classroom and any particular learning needs they may have. In addition, the assessment serves to inform teachers of the quality and depth of the knowledge and understanding that their students already have in relation to the content being studied. Related to this, it also serves as a practical tool for teachers in beginning to assess their students' academic virtues (see Chapter 8 on assessment). This is important for monitoring their progress, as the baseline assessment will be able to be compared with their final assessment. Furthermore, all of this information will empower teachers to pitch discussion appropriately throughout the scheme of work, in light of the differing qualitative responses of the students.

The question 'Does God exist?' has been chosen for its open-ended nature. All students should be able to engage with the question on some level yet undoubtedly some students will give a more developed response to the question than others. As this is a baseline assessment, there are no expectations as to the knowledge and understanding the students should already have. For this reason, amongst others, we suggest that the assessment is marked with comments only (see teachers' marking guidance on the website). The purpose of the assessment is to find out what the students bring with them to the classroom and this should be made clear to the students. It should also be made clear that you are interested in seeing how well they express themselves and how well they can identify and consider viewpoints which are different to their own.

How you choose to enact the baseline assessment will be dependent on the context in which you teach. If you have relatively short lessons and are able to dedicate an entire lesson to this task, it could serve as an opportunity to introduce students to the assessment framework. Following the completion of the baseline assessment, you may also have time for students to have a discussion about what they have written. If, on the other hand, you have longer lessons, you may have time to perform the baseline assessment as a task at the end of Lesson 2 or at the beginning of Lesson 3. What is important, regardless of context, is that students are given adequate time to think about and respond to the question.

ACTIVITIES

Resources

- Baseline assessment guidance for students
- Baseline teachers' marking guidance

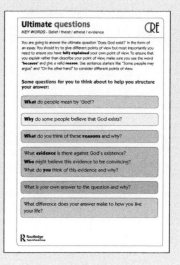

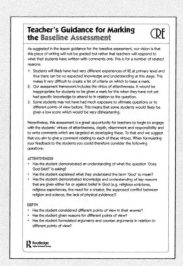

Baseline assessment: continued

We suggest a minimum of 20 minutes for this. We also suggest that this is done in the classroom and not as a homework task as it is important that it is the students' own work. Finally, we suggest that, however you arrange this task, you do not ask the students to discuss the question in advance of the written task as this will detract from your ability to assess what each student has brought with them to the classroom.

Lesson 3: how do we know what is REAL?

Learning objectives

1. To recognise different accounts of what is real
2. To begin to make judgements about what is real and what is not

The aim of Lesson 3 is to introduce students to the idea that RE consists of the study of what is actually real, or of what 'reality' is. Students are intended to *begin to* offer an account of reality, and in particular to identify examples of what is real or not real and whether some things are more real than others.

The lesson is largely structured around a card sort resource which includes various objects and concepts which may or may not be considered to be 'real'. In the first activity – card sort 1 – students are asked to work in pairs or groups to divide the cards into three piles – 'Real', 'Not real' and 'Not sure'. Following this a class discussion can ensue, especially drawing out reasons why students are 'not sure' whether things are real or not. Next, the same cards are used again for a second activity – card sort 2 – in which the students are placed into four groups, and each group is given a different account of reality – physical objects are real, human ideas are real, eternal principles are real, what is most valuable is real. These accounts do not necessarily conflict but are intended to point students alternatively to the role of the senses in determining what is real, the possibility of a social reality, the requirement that what is real be permanent or independent of human beings, the possibility that ideas are more real than objects, and the possibility of a transcendent metaphysical reality. It may be wise to order the students in appropriate groups given that these categories arguably increase in conceptual difficulty. For the second card sort activity, the students have to find examples in the cards which they think match their group definition of 'reality'. For example, 'squirrels' would come under 'physical objects' and 'Homer Simpson' under 'human ideas', whereas 'justice' could arguably come under either 'human ideas', 'eternal principles' or 'most valuable'. Groups will then feedback, justifying their categorisations, and this may lead to another class discussion.

As a plenary, students can discuss the questions on the PowerPoint. For homework, students can write a response to the question 'What is real?'. Alternatively, they can create an illustrated mind-map to show different ways of interpreting 'What is real?'. The handout offers a template, but students may choose to make a bigger version, suitable for display.

Key activities:

- Card sort 1 – what is real?
- Class discussion
- Card sort 2 – types of reality
- Reflection and response

Resources:

- PowerPoint
- 'What is real?' card sort
- Definitions of 'What is real?'
- 'What is real?' homework template

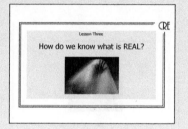

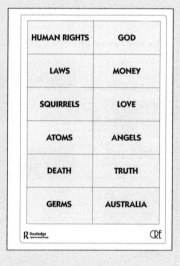

HUMAN RIGHTS	GOD
LAWS	MONEY
SQUIRRELS	LOVE
ATOMS	ANGELS
DEATH	TRUTH
GERMS	AUSTRALIA

Lesson 4: how do we KNOW what is real?

Key activities:

- Discussion surrounding 'The Blind Men and the Elephant'
- Questions relating to Plato's Cave
- Chart – how might I be mistaken?

Resources:

- PowerPoint including videos
- Blind Men poem handout
- 'How do we know what is real?' chart

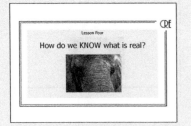

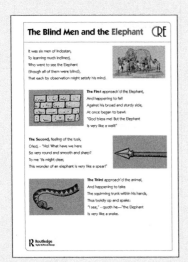

Learning objectives

1. To understand ways in which philosophers and theologians have cast doubt on even our most basic beliefs about what is real
2. To apply and explore the four accounts of what is real introduced last lesson
3. To reflect on how much you really know about the world

The aim of Lesson 4 is for students to recognise the tension between our accounts of reality (epistemology) and the way that reality actually is (ontology). This is accomplished by drawing on the definitions of reality from the previous lesson and exploring them in light of two famous allegories – 'The Blind Men and the Elephant' and Plato's Cave.

The lesson begins with exploration of the fable of 'The Blind Men and the Elephant' (minus the moral at the end as it is returned to in the following lesson) in order to introduce the idea that we may be to some extent 'blind' about reality. Students can watch it on YouTube or read it from a hard copy and can consider questions such as 'What do you think the elephant might represent?' and 'How are we like the blind men?'

Following this discussion, students move on to watching a video summarising Plato's Allegory of the Cave. They discuss how to understand its meaning using the questions on the PowerPoint.

After class discussion, students can complete the chart, drawing on the previous lesson in order to give an explanation and examples of each account of reality. For each category of the 'real', they can suggest ways that they could be mistaken or deceived about what they take to be real. Perhaps our senses or other people who we trust deceive us...

Finally, you can relate the chart back to the 'The Blind Men and the Elephant' and Plato's Cave. In what ways are the two stories linked? How do both stories lead us to question what we really KNOW?

A homework or extension task could be to respond to Plato's ideas about what is real. Do you agree that only eternal principles are real? Why / why not?

Lesson 5: how do WE know what is real?

ACTIVITIES

Learning objectives

1. To identify some of the ways we make judgements between conflicting truth claims
2. To make a judgement about whether we are faced with 'utter ignorance' in 'theologic' disputes

The aim of Lesson 5 is to introduce the concept of judgemental rationality and to consider how we might make judgements about what is real or true. The whodunit story 'Who ate Freddy's chocolate?' enables students to consider how we go about making judgements between different truth claims. Judgemental rationality, a cornerstone of critical realism, is not unproblematic. How can we weigh up different truth claims? What criteria are available? This story enables students to consider the importance of evidence, experience and testimony.

Read the story 'Who ate Freddy's chocolate?' as a class. Students should then be given time to discuss and respond to the questions on the sheet in pairs or groups. This is followed by a whole-class discussion, where all groups should be encouraged to feedback their ideas. If students suggest for the third question that Freddy should just leave the matter, this might lead to discussion of whether or not it is important to seek the truth.

The bulk of the discussion should be devoted to the last question. You can use the whiteboard to highlight evidence, experience and testimony as examples of sources that help us make judgements between truth claims. You will also need to use the explanations in the PowerPoint to consider the importance of credibility and coherence when coming to conclusions. Thinking about how a judge makes use of all of these tools when making her judgement in a court case may aid understanding here. To demonstrate their understanding, students can create a mind-map or short piece of writing entitled 'How can we make decisions about what is real or true?'

Finally, students can now pull the last three lessons together by returning to the fable of 'The Blind Men and the Elephant' and making a judgement about whether they agree with the moral of the story as offered in the poem by John Godfrey Saxe. The vocabulary here is tricky and may need 'translating' for some students. Spend time on it together, before getting the students to respond individually to the question: Do you agree with his moral of the story? Encourage them to draw on their learning over the last three lessons: What do we mean by 'real'? How do we *know* what is real? How do we make those judgements?

Key activities:

- Discussing 'Who ate Freddy's chocolate?'
- Discussing criteria for making judgements
- Judgement on the moral of 'The Blind Men and the Elephant'

Resources:

- PowerPoint
- Freddy's chocolate worksheet
- Moral of the Blind Men poem worksheet

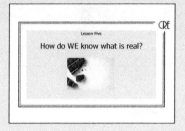

ACTIVITIES

Key activities:

- Comparison of answers to ultimate questions
- Introduction to worldviews
- Diagnosis of peers' worldview
- Explanation of own worldview

Resources:

- PowerPoint
- Questionnaire from Lesson 1
- Three worldviews handout

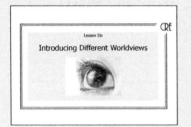

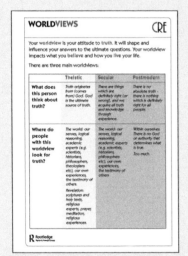

Lesson 6: introducing different worldviews

Learning objectives

1. To understand three different worldviews
2. To apply the language of the worldviews in order to interpret and diagnose the worldview of a peer
3. To identify your own worldview and respond to the worldviews of others

The aim of Lesson 6 is to introduce students to three common worldviews and help them to identify which they hold themselves. The worldviews are an essential tool in enabling children to intelligently and respectfully engage with and critique the views of others. One's worldview impacts what one believes and how one lives. Students have already begun to explore the fact that people hold different beliefs. Introducing worldviews enables students to understand that different beliefs are based on different views of truth which stem from different worldviews. This can help them to realise that a variety of answers to the same question can at least be coherent.

To start, students compare the answers that they gave to the questionnaire in Lesson 1 to those of a partner. Where did they agree? Where did they disagree? You can then introduce the idea of a worldview. One fun way to do this is by showing an optical illusion such as the famous old woman / young woman. Students will disagree about what the picture is of; they see the world differently.

The teacher should then introduce the three different worldviews: theistic, secular and postmodern. This can be done through the handout or PowerPoint. What is important is that students understand how the worldviews differ regarding the nature of truth and how it can be accessed. Clearly the worldviews are simplified for Year 7, but they enable students to understand broadly different ways in which people believe truth can be known, as well as the difference between absolute and relative truth and their implications.

Once the teacher has explained the worldviews, students move on to diagnosing the worldview of a partner by considering the answers that they gave in their questionnaire. Partners should feedback to each other and can then discuss the question: How do the different worldviews help explain why their answers are either similar or different? Finally, students can reflect on their own worldview and begin to explain where it might come from, either vocally or in writing.

Lesson 7: applying worldviews

Learning objectives

1. To consolidate your understanding of the three worldviews studied
2. To understand that these worldviews can impact how we live

The aim of Lesson 7 is for students to learn that our worldview should affect the way we live. The lesson begins by consolidating the students' understanding of the three worldviews presented in the previous lesson. This can take the form of a test, a think-pair-share activity or any other activity that the teacher sees fit. It is important that the students recap this information as without it they will not be able to complete the tasks in the remainder of the lesson.

Students should then be put into groups of three and be allocated a role – Theo the theist, Sophia the secular thinker or Pete the postmodernist. They should then consider which of the statements on the worldview statements worksheet their character would agree with and should work in their groups to complete the tick box activity. This can be fed back as a whole-class discussion to ensure accuracy and understanding.

Students can then work in the same groups and potentially even maintain the same 'roles' for the dialogue writing / role-play activity. Here they are asked to consider a scenario and how one's worldview might affect the choices that one makes. Students should be encouraged to draw on the evidence on the sheet in their script writing and it should be clear to the class which character each student is playing from their dialogue and actions when the role plays are performed. The performances can be used for the plenary of the lesson and there can be some peer evaluation of how effectively the worldviews were put across in the drama.

A good homework task for this lesson is to ask the students to explain how their worldview impacts their own life.

ACTIVITIES

Key activities:

- Recap worldviews
- Group work – worldview statements
- Role plays

Resources:

- PowerPoint
- Worldview statements worksheet
- Scenario for role-play task

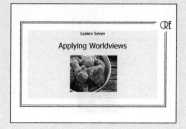

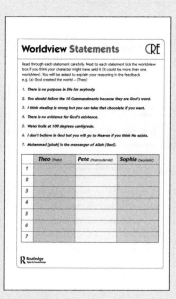

Lesson 8: evaluating worldviews

Key activities:

- Forming groups – composing arguments for each worldview
- Worldview dialogue ordering
- RE boxing
- Reflection

Resources:

- PowerPoint
- Sugar paper/large sheets of paper
- Worldview dialogue large

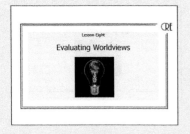

Learning objectives

1. To describe and attempt to explain why you hold your worldview
2. To critically respond to the worldviews of others

The aim of Lesson 8 is for students to begin to evaluate the differing worldviews.

To start, recap from the last lesson using the questions on the PowerPoint. Students should then be asked to move to a physical position in the class to represent their emerging worldview commitments. A possible practical problem may be that the majority of your students self-identify as the same worldview. If, for example, you have 20+ theists, 7 secularists and 2 postmodernists, you may wish to ask some students to join the other groups (this is potentially a good challenge for gifted and talented students). Students then work in their groups to come up with arguments for their worldview. They should be aiming to get at least five different points written down on their sugar paper. Remind them to think back to the criteria identified by 'Who ate Freddy's chocolate?' What evidence/experience/credible testimonies do they have?

Once this task is complete, students should break into smaller groups of three or four and be given the worldview dialogue to arrange in the correct order (N.B. you will need to have cut this up beforehand). This activity helps students to understand what good debate/evaluation looks like and the need to respond with relevant counter-arguments. It may also give them extra points to add to their arguments for their worldview. Following this each group should discuss how Pete would respond and this should be fed back in order to give the postmodernists some extra ideas.

Students should then move back into the three big groups and add any last-minute arguments to their sugar paper. RE boxing can then commence (see rules in PowerPoint). One group makes a point for their worldview and another group then has to respond directly to that point and so on. If your class is particularly competitive this can be scored so that points are awarded when a good point/counter-argument is raised. This finishes at your discretion.

Finally, each student should write a few sentences about which arguments from the debate they thought were the strongest and why. This could lead into a homework task evaluating the worldviews.

Lesson 9: the need for tolerance

Learning objectives

1. To understand that conflicting truth claims can be difficult to negotiate
2. To recognise that there are different views about what tolerance is, and what these views are
3. To make your own critical judgement about which view of tolerance is best

The aim of Lesson 9 is to encourage students to follow through the implications of the previous lessons and look at how they should react to different opinions put forward by their peers in the classroom. It is hoped that students will realise that if there is an answer out there (ontological realism), even though we might not be certain what the correct answer is (epistemic relativity), it is right to enter into critical debate about which viewpoint is the correct one (using judgemental rationality). Tolerance is not about accepting that all views are equally true and thus avoiding critical discussion but rather is about ensuring that discussions are conducted in a respectful manner.

The lesson begins with students arranging a pyramid of definitions of tolerance. This is designed to promote some initial ideas on how 'tolerance' might be understood. Once this has been fed back in pairs and some peer assessment of their arrangement has taken place, there will then be some whole-class discussion as to what the best definition of tolerance is. The teacher should ask questions to guide critical evaluation of their definitions.

Following this, the students will be introduced to two particular definitions of tolerance (as on the handout) and will be asked to discuss which definition makes the most sense when applied to a number of scenarios. It is hoped that students will work out that 1) is the best definition of tolerance. Importantly, they should realise that tolerance is not about 2).

Finally students can discuss in pairs what the implications of this definition of tolerance are going forward with their RE lessons.

As a homework, students can complete the writing frame asking them to justify, with examples, what they think is the best definition of tolerance.

Key activities:

- Pyramid 6
- Tolerance scenarios – deciding between definitions

Resources:

- PowerPoint
- 'What is tolerance?' pyramid handout
- 'What is tolerance?' scenario worksheet
- 'What definition of tolerance is best?' homework worksheet

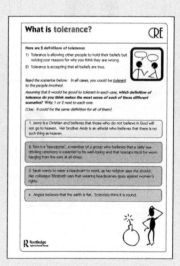

ACTIVITIES

Key activities:

- Recapping learning
- Developing and performing a debate (potential for self/peer assessment)
- Constructing an essay/dialogue to demonstrate understanding
- Completing self-assessment

Resources:

- PowerPoint
- 'Does God exist?' assessment guidance for students
- 'Does God exist?' mark sheet
- Some arguments for and against the existence of God handout

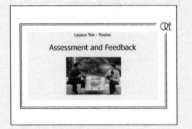

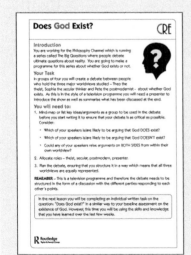

Lessons 10–12: assessment and feedback

Learning objectives

1. To demonstrate your learning on the topic
2. To receive feedback on your progress
3. To self-assess your response to the topic

Lessons 10–12 involve preparing for and then completing an assessment of student learning across the scheme of work. The assessment aims to draw together the concepts studied throughout the scheme of work in a way which enables teachers to assess the students' learning. However, the scheme of work is unusual in that it provides an introduction to the nature of CRE, giving a conceptual foundation rather than focusing on a specific religion or philosophical/ethical topic. This created a challenge when deciding on an appropriate question for the end of topic assessment. The question 'Does God exist?' was chosen as it relates to the learning objectives throughout and allows the students to see a qualitative difference between their baseline assessment and their enriched 'end of topic' assessment. This will be evidenced in particular through the accurate use of the technical terminology of worldviews and the exploration of the nature of reality. However, it must be acknowledged that the question 'Does God exist?' has only been looked at briefly before these lessons and not in the same kind of depth as one would expect if it were to be the sole focus of the learning. Therefore, there is a need to revisit and unpack the varying arguments for and against God's existence which were raised in Lesson 8 and to ensure that students understand the links between the question and other aspects of their learning (e.g. the idea that it is not only physical objects which are real) before students answer the question in written form. In order for these things to be possible, activities have been suggested prior to the written assessment to ensure that the students are appropriately prepared. We thus envision three separate lessons for the completion of the assessment, although there are variations which can be applied should this be problematic.

In the first lesson, the teacher should return to the learning from Lesson 8 and provide students with a copy of the conversation between Theo, Sophia and Pete which they had to order correctly in that lesson. In groups of four, they should extract and summarise the theist and secular arguments for or against the existence of God as well as reflecting on what the postmodern responses were to those arguments. These can then be shared as a class for consolidation purposes along with any other arguments that students raised in Lesson 8 as part of the

RE boxing exercise. Following this, in the same groups, students are asked to create a television debate with one student representing each of the three worldviews studied and a further student to act as 'presenter'. These debates are to be performed in the second lesson and can be peer marked, teacher assessed or simply used as preparation, as the teacher sees fit.

Teachers should use their knowledge of their students to organise them into appropriate groups to achieve the best possible results. Students do not have to represent the worldviews they hold, although teachers can ensure that this is the case should they deem it appropriate.

Students will be given sheets to guide their planning for the debate. These will link them back to key aspects of the scheme of work, as well as providing them with some additional arguments and evidence to use. The support sheets will also suggest a structure for the debate, although more able students may wish to deviate from this.

The task enables students to share and develop ideas in a group setting before individually responding to the question in written form in the third lesson. Through watching other performances of the group debates in the second lesson, the students will all be exposed to a number of different responses to draw on in their written pieces.

The written task should be completed in the third lesson and the time given for this will depend on individual school contexts. The support sheet may also be useful for structuring their written answer. Students can respond to the question in the form of an essay or in the form of a dialogue, as directed by their teacher. For some students, writing the piece as a dialogue may help to develop their evaluative skills. Should the teacher wish to complete the assessment in one or two lessons rather than three, the group task can be side-lined and students can individually write the dialogue as if it were a television debate. The exact form this takes can be chosen by the teacher dependent on the learning styles and competencies of students in their classes. What is important is that students engage with the question and seek to respond to it in a critical way, in light of what they have studied.

The CRE virtues assessment framework is used to formulate a subject specific mark scheme around the virtues of attentiveness, depth, discernment and responsibility. You should provide comments and marks as appropriate for the first three virtues and give your students an opportunity to self-assess how well they have exercised the virtue of responsibility. Ideally, allow lesson time for the students to share and discuss their self-assessments with each other if they want to.

Notes

1 See Chapter 9 for guidance on differentiation.
2 For further discussion of the relationship between critical realism and postmodernism, and the impact of postmodernism on religious education, see Wright (2004).

Reference

Wright, A. (2004). *Religion, Education and Post-modernity*. London: RoutledgeFalmer.

Critical Religious Education and world religions

An exemplar scheme of work for teaching Islam (Year 8)

As CRE is concerned with truth claims about reality, it is often considered more palatable when applied to schemes of work concerning philosophical issues than those addressing world religions. Indeed, in our liberal, multicultural society, the idea of questioning and analysing the truth claims of a particular religious tradition is somewhat taboo. Nevertheless, if CRE is about creating religiously literate individuals who can grapple with the nature of reality, then the truth claims made by religious traditions must be understood and evaluated similarly to all other claims to truth.

Since the work of Ninian Smart in the 1960s (see, for example, Smart, 1968) teaching and learning about 'world religions' has been central to most religious education (RE) programs. Historically, 'world religions' has tended to mean the 'big six' – Judaism, Christianity, Islam, Hinduism, Buddhism and Sikhism – but in recent years it has become increasingly popular to include other influential traditions – both theistic and secular – in RE curriculums. CRE seeks to draw students into discussion of reality and thus any truth claim could legitimately be considered and discussed in a CRE classroom. Nevertheless, given that the specific content of the RE curriculum is religion and given the prevalence of specific religious traditions in most RE curricula, demonstrating how to plan a scheme of work on a world religion within CRE is particularly important. We thus intend to give some guidelines for the planning of such a scheme of work in general, followed by a model scheme of work on Islam.

Key elements to consider in your planning

Teachers who have attempted to apply the theory of CRE to their practice have been faced with the choice of systematic verses of thematic schemes of work with regards to religious claims. Early attempts often settled on the thematic route, choosing a particular ultimate question which would be answered from a variety of perspectives over a scheme of work or, indeed, within a single lesson. However, whilst this may be more appropriate for content of a philosophical nature, over time it became apparent that approaching CRE in this way meant that students did not develop sufficient theological depth to answer such questions in a truly critically manner. This was at least partially because they never gained an authentic understanding of religious traditions as a whole. For example, one could not possibly analyse the truth claims surrounding the virgin conception without an understanding of Christian beliefs about the Trinity, Jesus as the Son of God, God's omnipotence and immanence etc. The same is true of other religious truth claims and thus an authentic representation of religious beliefs has to take place in the CRE classroom before questions of truth can be considered critically. Thus, whilst there is no hard and fast rule and how you arrange your schemes of work will largely depend on the context in which you teach, with regards to world religions, we believe a systematic approach is preferable. Students need to understand the central beliefs of a religious tradition before they can make sense of particular practices or ethical conclusions. Thus, we suggest that a scheme of work on a world religion should ideally follow a particular order;

BELIEFS → **PRACTICES** → **ETHICAL ISSUES**

We also suggest that there are three key elements which the teacher needs to consider at the outset of the planning process:

Authenticity – What is the most important content to facilitate an authentic understanding of that religious tradition?

Coherence – What needs to be included in order to facilitate an understanding of the internal consistency and coherence of the religious tradition? N.B. Ordering the material as described above (Beliefs – Practices – Ethical Issues) also helps with this.

Variation – Where is there variation within the tradition? What are the most significant variations from other traditions? What variations should you include?

The first two of the three 'key elements' of planning a scheme of work on a world religion are relatively uncontroversial. All good RE should be marked by authenticity, ensuring that religious traditions are presented in a way which is true to the beliefs and practices of their various adherents. Thus, the first element, ensuring that you have the correct content to make the learning **authentic**, should be a priority within any pedagogical frame.

The second element, **coherence**, is also something one would expect in most schemes of work, regardless of pedagogy. It is necessary under most frameworks to at least be able to explain how fundamental beliefs relate to associated practices and ethical standpoints. Within a CRE framework, there may be more critical discussion about exactly which practices and ethical standpoints are most coherent with the fundamental beliefs about reality held in the tradition being studied, than one may expect in other schemes of work. Understanding how beliefs, practice and ethical standpoints fit together is a key part of the critical process as, if someone rejects a fundamental belief, they are unlikely to accept practices etc. which proceed from it. However, generally speaking, a focus on content and coherence is not exclusive to a CRE approach.

However, the third key element to a CRE scheme of work, **variation**, is a much less common feature and is thus more controversial. Many liberal forms of RE seek to emphasise similarities between and within religious traditions and often side-line differences, claiming that an understanding of common beliefs and values is more conducive to nurturing tolerance than an understanding of conflicting claims. CRE, on the other hand, whilst not ignoring similarities, also places emphasis on discussion of difference. It actively recognises where truth claims about ontological reality conflict with one another and highlights this as a key aspect in developing religious literacy. As with all other forms of liberal RE, the importance of respect and tolerance between students with differing standpoints is upheld within a CRE framework, but this is not considered to be at odds with recognising where differences exist or, ultimately making judgements between the differing standpoints under consideration. The premise of epistemic relativity ensures this – as we cannot claim the infallibility of our own knowledge, we have to be humble when discussing differences between our beliefs and those held by others. Thus, we should be able to discuss differences without this undermining respect or tolerance.

The Variation Theory of Learning (VTL) (see, for example, Marton, 2015), associated with CRE (see Hella and Wright, 2009), suggests that effective learning only occurs when variation is present. Asking students to discern between variations gives a focus and purpose to their study – they are able to make more informed and, in turn, more critical judgements about reality. Furthermore, by introducing variation, we not only bring criticality to the scheme of work but, as suggested by VTL, we actually help students to understand the content they are studying better in and of itself. For example, a student has a far more nuanced understanding of the concept of Tawhid when they understand how it differs from the trinity or polytheistic conceptions of God. Hence, planning world religions schemes of work in this way is just as applicable in a single faith context as a multi-faith one. Furthermore, acknowledging these differences makes the learning experience more authentic and allows students to engage with questions about reality on a deeper level.

Critical questions – your essential tool for effective planning

In order to incorporate variation into your scheme of work, you need to identify **critical questions** to be posed. We suggest that in a CRE scheme of work on a world religion there will be three layers of critical questioning. These will surround;

1. Questions relating to truth claims which are fundamental to the religion itself i.e. Is there one God?
2. Questions relating to different truth claims posited within a religion i.e. Is there a 'Hidden Imam'?
3. Questions relating to different truth claims posited between religions i.e. Was Jesus the Son of God?

Within any world religion, there are numerous claims to truth and thus it is important when planning to prioritise the critical questions which will be the most fruitful for the students' learning. Therefore, once you have selected the appropriate content for the scheme of work and ordered it effectively to promote coherence, you will then have to decide on specific questions to pose. This is a challenging aspect of CRE and you will need to build your confidence in making these choices. You may find the list of criteria below helpful to apply when constructing critical questions. This list is by no means exhaustive, but will hopefully serve as a useful staring point.

1. Critical questions are best posed where variation or conflict is **obvious**. If you are aware that there are significantly different perspectives held on a particular issue then asking a question about this may be most fruitful.

2. Critical questions should also arise from the **specific material** being studied. All too often, those trying to apply CRE will hunt for critical questions to tack on to content in order to try and make it 'critical'. However, if this doesn't organically lend itself to the material being studied, it is a pointless exercise and doesn't actually aid learning. It may in fact result in the lesson(s) leading off on a tangent which is not the most effective use of already limited lesson time. Furthermore, it is necessary for students to fully understand the reasons behind any judgements being made; thus, critical questions need to directly relate to the specific material being covered in depth, in order for the students to be able to respond critically and intelligently to them.

3. Critical questions may be more fruitful if there is **breadth** and **depth** of variation which you are aware of in response to them (and which is presented at an appropriate level for your students).
   Many historic GCSE syllabuses and other RE resources pose evaluative questions to which there is essentially a 'yes' or 'no' answer such as 'Should people pray?' Whilst this is a critical question which may well be worthwhile asking, the range of responses one may give to it are relatively narrow – essentially theists will say yes as He answers prayer and atheists will say no as God doesn't exist. If you are limited on time and can thus only ask a small number of critical questions, it may be better to ask a question which inspires a wider range of responses such as 'Should giving to the poor be obligatory?' Whilst again, the answer is essentially 'yes' or 'no', there is much more variation in the responses people will give. Muslims will say yes due to the pillar of Zakah but Christians may be split on the issue – some would say yes we should pay tithes, others no it should be voluntary as an act of love to God. Similarly, atheists may be split – some humanists may say yes as all people are equally valuable whereas others will say no due to a belief in freedom of choice. This could even then relate to certain political positions. This question allows for a richer dialogue as a result of the breadth and depth of variation involved which leads to the need for greater discernment and, in turn, a better quality of response than a question with a minimal range of answers.

The critical questions you pose will also be dependent on the stage of education which the students are at. As suggested above, clearly some subject matter is inappropriate until a certain age is reached and thus some questions may not be prioritised in the earlier years. Similarly, whilst certain questions may have a breadth and depth of variation if accessed at a certain level, some variations may be too conceptually demanding at an earlier stage. If we take the question discussed earlier – 'Should we pray?' – as an example, this may in fact be a very rich question, should you be able to incorporate concepts such as deism or pre-determinism but this is unlikely to be appropriate for your Year 8 students.

Which variations?

After you have selected your critical questions and decided on where they should be posed in the scheme of work, your final job is to select the most appropriate variations in answer to them. Your professional judgement as a teacher will again be required here. As one criteria for selecting critical questions is that conflict should be obvious, it is clearly prudent to select the conflicting variations as your starting point. If the subject matter you are covering relates to the Muslim view that God cannot be depicted for example then it may be more prudent to juxtapose a Hindu view than a Jewish one if you are limited by time. Whilst Muslim and Jewish views on this may be different, the differences are not as pronounced as they are between Muslims and Hindus (and have been both historically and in recent times).

Similarly, it may be more prudent to incorporate a variation which is a commonly held belief, rather than a minority view, if you have to choose based on time or other constraints. Furthermore, the make-up of the area in which your school is located, the school itself or even your individual class may provide some guidance as to what variations it is wise to include. Your students will arrive at the learning process with their own emergent beliefs and assumptions about the subject matter being studied and thus it is likely that variation will exist in the classroom organically. You will therefore need to consider the variations that are most likely to appear in your context, ensure that these will be covered in sufficient depth and then, where appropriate, select other variations which you think will be most fruitful to the learning process.

Ultimately what variation is introduced (aside from that which happens organically as a result of student beliefs) should be based on your professional judgement, using your subject knowledge to make informed and justified decisions.

In summary, the context which you are in, the students you are teaching, and the amount of time you have to cover a tradition, will play a large part in deciding which critical questions to pose and which variations to include. If you consider carefully the issues and criteria as discussed above, you will choose questions and introduce variation which will challenge and extend your students and develop their understanding of the reality in which we exist.

The importance of religious texts

Within a CRE framework it is vital that students are given opportunities to engage with religious texts such as Holy Scripture and documentation from religious organisations. Religious texts are viewed as **authoritative** by many religious believers and, as such, are the basis for the beliefs that they hold about reality. Therefore, engagement with these sources is fundamental to an **authentic** understanding of world religions. For CRE this engagement is particularly important as it is impossible to make truly **critical judgements** about the claims to truth which religious believers and traditions make, without recourse to the sources from which they stem. The exercise of judgemental rationality includes being able to use **evidence and examples** in support of the claims to truth which one makes. As sources of authority, religious texts are often a primary source of evidence for people's beliefs, including the judgements that they make about practical and ethical issues. Hence, if students are not given opportunities to study religious texts, the conclusions they come to about religious claims will be severely limited. For example, it would be entirely inappropriate to engage in critical discussion about whether Muslim (or, indeed all) women should wear headscarves without considering the guidance given on the issue in the Qur'an and Hadith.

In addition, the **interpretation** of religious texts is often a reason for contention within religious traditions. Thus, the study of these texts is also of the utmost importance for understanding these disputes and attempting to overcome them. Students need to engage with the texts first-hand so that they can critically discuss the various interpretations. This is necessary if they are to make informed, critical judgements over areas of controversy. Again, for example, it would be outrageous to suggest that a critical judgement can be made on whether gay couples should be allowed in marry in a church without consulting the relevant passages in the Bible. When studying issues such as this, about which there is a wealth of relevant material, it is important to achieve appropriate breadth and depth in relation to the religious texts under scrutiny. This will require a level of **systematic study** (accepting that the extent of this will have to be suitable for the age of the students and the lesson time available). Simply selecting one or two verses to consider is vacuous as it ignores extensive academic wrangling over inter-related passages. It is thus important to consider which combination of passages it is necessary to explore in order to reach an informed judgement.

Finally, it is important to ensure that students are given ample opportunity to engage with religious texts in order to challenge prevalent and potentially misplaced views about them. As discussed above, many religious believers view religious texts as authoritative but their **truth-value** has been called into question by scientific and historical discoveries as well as popular philosophies which suggest that religious claims are subjective or even meaningless (see further discussion on this in Chapters 5 and 6). These developments may explain the decline in the use of scripture in the classroom. Nevertheless, critical realism, with its acknowledgement of the possibility of transcendence and its emphasis on epistemic relativity, allows for the conversation about the authority of these sources to be reignited. Engaging with different interpretations of these texts is one of the best ways to ensure that judgements about their truth-value are suitably informed. Indeed, the student who wishes to disregard religious scriptures needs to justify rejecting their authority as much as the religious believer needs to justify upholding it.

Why Islam?

We have chosen to focus on Islam for a sample scheme of work under "world religions" for a number of reasons. Firstly, and probably most importantly, the global context at the time of writing means that Islam is in the forefront of popular consciousness. Due to political tensions over the last couple of decades, Islamic belief and practice has become increasingly controversial. RE teachers are often hesitant to tackle truth claims as it is, and truth claims about Islam seem to carry an even higher risk. Furthermore, the public perception of the Islamic tradition has been tainted by inaccurate media reporting. This has highlighted both extreme fundamentalist versions of the tradition as well as Westernised, liberal accounts. Attention is rarely paid to the majority middle ground, or to the reasons behind differing beliefs and practices within the tradition. As a result, the average student may have a warped picture of what Muslims believe, from which no credible evaluation of truth can take place. A CRE scheme of work on Islam would seek to address some of these issues, to present young people with an authentic representation of Islamic beliefs and practices and to ensure that it was from this springboard that truth claims prominent in the tradition were discussed.

Secondly, as the practice of Islam is increasingly common in Britain, it seemed like a credible choice. Related to this, we have a large number of colleagues and associates who are Islamic believers/practitioners (from differing sects) with whom we can validate the authenticity of our work.

Finally, the Islamic tradition lends itself to critical discussion having originated as a result of differing truth claims (Muhammad (PBUH) challenged the religious beliefs and practices of the time from the outset), having been divided due to differing truth claims immediately after Muhammad's death (disagreements over leadership lead to the Sunni/Shi'a split which accounts for many of the differences in the practice of Islam today) and, crucially, claiming itself to correct the false teaching of its believed predecessors (Judaism and Christianity). These obvious frictions are exactly the sort of disputes about truth which CRE attempts to allow students to discuss and evaluate intelligently.

What should be included?

It has to be acknowledged from the outset that the Islamic tradition is vast and thus it would be untenable to expect students to have a thorough comprehension of all aspects of it by the end of a single scheme of work. However, the material we have selected aims:

1. To present the beliefs and practices which we consider to be fundamental to the tradition authentically.
2. To highlight areas of disagreement regarding truth which we believe would be most fruitful to explore.

The consensus among scholars (both within and outside the tradition) is that all Muslims hold six fundamental beliefs:

1. That there is one God (Allah) who is above all.
2. That God has revealed himself to the world through the work of prophets, the final of which was Muhammad.
3. That the Qur'an is the word of Allah, revealed to the Prophet Muhammad.
4. That there is a Day of Judgement.
5. That angels exist and are active in the world.
6. That Allah has predestined everything.

These beliefs differ in complexity. The final belief (predestination), for example, is arguably more complex to teach and discuss than the first one (monotheism).

Thus, it may not be appropriate for all of these to be considered independently at this stage. Rather, it may be most appropriate to categorise these into three overarching areas (as many educational resources do): Tawhid (the oneness and otherness of God), Risalah (Allah's work in the world through the prophets), and Akhirah (belief in the afterlife). It would not make sense to create a scheme of work on Islam which ignores the concept of Tawhid as all other beliefs and practices in Islam follow on from the belief in the authority of this one God. Similarly, it would make little sense to present Islam without Risalah as it is only through the work of the prophets (Muhammad especially) that the truth about God is known (from which beliefs and practices are formed). Finally, belief in Akhirah is so fundamental to the tradition that all of the practices within Islam occur in preparation for this e.g. through acknowledgement of the angels during Salah, Sunni Muslims are reminded of the day of judgement at least five times per day. Akhirah is a belief which underlies much of what Muslims do and is thus important to include.

A credible scheme of work on Islam would also need to include:

1. An overview of the life of the Prophet Muhammad, especially focusing on context. The context in which Islam originated highlights and makes sense of the emphasis on the key teachings of Muhammad.
2. The Qur'an and the Hadith: This needs to be 'standalone' even if the six key beliefs are amalgamated (as discussed above) because discussion of truth claims necessitates discussion of authority and the way in which Muslims are aware of the truth about, and will of, God is through these sources. In addition, the Islamic claim that the Qur'an was given to correct the mistakes in the Bible/Torah (and a comparison between particular texts) brings about obvious variation for critical discussion.
3. The five pillars – Shahadah, Salah, Zakah, Sawm, and Hajj: – These are the fundamental practices of Islam through which a Muslim demonstrates his/her beliefs. These are acknowledged and accepted by all Muslims, irrespective of sect.
4. Groups within Islam – Sunni, Shi'a, Sufi: It is inauthentic to present only one aspect of the Islamic tradition, even if it is the majority (e.g. Sunni Islam). As a result of acknowledging the authority of differing people/texts, much of the other beliefs and practices associated with Islam differ between these groups, and this must be acknowledged if/when any of them are discussed. This also gives organic variation for discussion of truth.

In addition, we also agreed that there were areas which should be covered, not because of their inherent importance within the Islamic tradition, but because of their relevance and importance in our society today. These include:

1. The role/dress etc. of women
2. Shari'ah law
3. Jihad

These are the issues which we feel have caused significant controversy in relation to the Islamic tradition of late and thus it seems natural for them to be discussed and analysed as ethical issues (in relation to truth) within this scheme of work. This cannot happen, however, without the prior material being covered, as students could not understand the position from which Muslims approach these issues without that basis.

An overview of the Islam scheme of work

Sequence	Lesson title	Learning objectives
1	Muhammad: his life and context	To know about the life of Muhammad To understand the context in which Muhammad lived and delivered his message To begin reflecting on the truth claims made about God
2	The Qur'an and Hadith	To understand the importance of the Qur'an and Hadith to Muslims To critically reflect on these as sources of authority
3	The six key beliefs of Islam	To know the six key beliefs of Islam and to specifically understand the concepts of Tawhid / Risalah / Akhirah To critically reflect on whether it is wrong to depict God
4	Shahadah	To understand the meaning of the Shahadah To understand the importance of the Shahadah To reflect on submission in our own lives
5	Salah	To understand the practices of Salah and Wudu To critically compare these to other religious traditions
6	Zakah	To understand the Islamic practice of Zakah To critically reflect on whether giving should be compulsory
7	Sawm	To understand the Islamic practice of Sawm To critically compare it to other religious traditions
8	Hajj	To understand the Islamic practice of Hajj and how it reflects beliefs
9	Hajj and equality	To critically discuss whether the Hajj demonstrates equality

(continued)

Sequence	Lesson title	Learning objectives
10	Muhammad: religious, political and military leader	To critically reflect on Muhammad's role as a political and military leader To analyse the last sermon of Muhammad
11	The Sunni and Shi'a split	To identify differing groups within Islam To compare and critically discuss beliefs and practices within Islam To recognise the impact of history and context on these groups
12	Shari'ah law	To identify areas of the world where Islam is practised today To consider the legal systems in some majority Muslim countries To critically reflect on the concept of Shari'ah law and critically discuss whether Shari'ah law should be allowed in Britain
13	Western perspectives on Islam	To reflect on your own responses to Islam To consider reasons behind general Western perspectives on Islam
14	Hijab	To understand Islamic beliefs about gender and equality To analyse Islamic teachings relating to hijab To critically reflect on how Islamic women should dress and how this relates to our context
15	Jihad	To understand the concepts of Greater and Lesser Jihad
16	Jihad debate	To critically assess whether the Lesser Jihad might justify acts of violence today
17 and 18	Assessment and feedback	To demonstrate your learning on the topic To receive feedback on your progress To self-assess your response to the topic

Lesson 1: Muhammad: his life and context

Learning objectives

1. To know about the life of Muhammad (PBUH)
2. To understand the context in which Muhammad lived and delivered his message
3. To begin reflecting on the truth claims made about God

The aim of lesson one is to introduce students to the study of Islam and to help them understand the context in which it originated. Students thus begin the lesson by either writing down or discussing what they already know about Islam and what questions they would like answered over the course of the scheme of work.

Following this, students should create a timeline of Muhammad's life in their books whilst watching the video of how Islam began. They should try to record as many of the dates and events referred to as possible. After the video, the teacher can take feedback from the students and create a shared timeline on the board using all the information that they have managed to record. The PowerPoint includes a link to a completed timeline which can be used for additional information if desired.

Once the timelines are complete, students should reflect on the context in which Muhammad preached his message by discussing the questions on the PowerPoint in pairs or as a class. There is a link to a second animated video in the notes of the PowerPoint which can be used to stimulate this discussion if time allows. After this discussion, students should take part in a hot-seating activity with the aim of consolidating significant features of the historical context that Muhammad lived in. Students are put into groups and given a written account from one of several 'characters' (a Jew, a Christian, a Polytheist, a young girl and a rich merchant). Each group should contain one student confident to play the character in the hot seat. Students should read through the information in their groups and discuss what their character is likely to have thought of Muhammad and his message. The characters then take it in turns to introduce themselves to the class. After each introduction, the rest of the class can be given 30 seconds to each write down one question that they have for that character (there are prompts on the PowerPoint). A selection of these questions can be posed to the character before the next one takes the hot seat. This serves as a plenary for the lesson from which the teacher can assess understanding.

ACTIVITIES

Key activities:

- Initial reflections
- Timeline of Muhammad's life
- Hot-seating activity

Resources:

- Meccan characters worksheet
- PowerPoint including videos

ACTIVITIES

Key activities:

- Listing holy books and associated discussion
- Qur'an information sheet
- Diamond 9
- Storytelling activity (Hadith)
- Human continuum

Resources:

- Qur'an worksheet
- PowerPoint
- Diamond 9 worksheet

Lesson 2: the Qu'ran and Hadith

> ### Learning objectives
>
> 1. To understand the importance of the Qur'an and Hadith to Muslims
> 2. To critically reflect on these as sources of authority

The aim of Lesson 2 is to introduce students to the Qur'an and Hadith and to begin reflecting on these as sources of authority for Muslims. An understanding of the Qur'an and Hadith is important for both religious and ethical application in the religion and will thus continue to develop as the scheme of work progresses.

As a starter, students are asked to write down examples of holy books which they are already aware of. This introduces variation from the start of the lesson. Students can discuss whether, in order for one to be entirely true, another must be fallible. To stimulate this discussion, a text from the Qur'an could be displayed in which there is clear variation from another holy book e.g. the text from surah 4 on the PowerPoint. Students are then introduced to an Islamic understanding of the Qur'an via the Qur'an information sheet and should answer the comprehension questions.

Following this, students complete a diamond 9 activity in which they are given different statements about the Qur'an to order in terms of importance. In the first instance, students should order these according to what they think a Muslim perspective may be. This can be discussed as a class before moving on to students rearranging the diamonds according to their own perspectives. This activity introduces further variation and encourages critical discussion around the nature of the Qur'an.

In the next activity, a student is selected to come to the front and tell a story (this can be entirely improvised or their version of a story that they already know). Whilst the student is telling the story, all other students are attempting to write it down word for word. Once the storyteller has finished, students can compare their accounts. The teacher will use this to draw out the fallibility of the Hadith, in comparison to the Qur'an, and the fact that this has led to differences within the Islamic tradition.

To finish, the statement 'the Qur'an is infallible' will be displayed on the board. Students should create a human continuum with regards to their own position on this statement, with strongly agree at one end of the room and strongly disagree at the other. They can be called upon to explain their current position as the teacher sees fit.

Lesson 3: the six key beliefs of Islam

Learning objectives

1. To know the six key beliefs of Islam and to specifically understand the concepts of Tawhid / Risalah / Akhirah
2. To critically reflect on whether it is wrong to depict God

The aim of Lesson 3 is to introduce students to the six key beliefs of Islam. As discussed in the rationale above, these will be presented to students in three groups – Tawhid, Risalah and Akhirah. Understanding these beliefs is fundamental to understanding religious practices and ethical guidance within Islam.

As a starter, students are played a song entitled 'Al Khaaliq' by Yusuf Islam. Students are to listen to the song and write down what they think the key beliefs of Islam may be. Students should then be presented with the six key beliefs of Islam via PowerPoint with an explanation of how these can be said to fit into three groups.

Students should complete a think-pair-share on the question 'What does it mean to say there is only one God?' Following this, students should be introduced to the concepts of Tawhid and Shirk, via the PowerPoint. To further their understanding, using variation, students should read the Islamic scriptures relating to the Trinity and discuss their meaning. Students should then be presented with the five sources and asked to discuss how a Muslim would respond to: the use of icons in Orthodox Christianity; the concept of the Christian Trinity; Hindu worship using *murtis*; a teenager with celebrity heartthrob pictures; the 99 names of Allah.

Students could be asked to name as many prophets from the Old Testament or Jewish scriptures as they can – this could be a competition. Students should then be introduced to the concept of Risalah and Muhammad as 'Seal of the Prophets' via the PWP.

Students will then participate in a creative thinking exercise in pairs. They should be given key words relating to Muslim beliefs about the afterlife (e.g. heaven, hell, angels, genies, day of judgement, God, devil) and asked to piece together what Muslims believe based on these words alone. The teacher can then take a few examples and elaborate on the actual beliefs.

Finally, a triangle can be displayed on the board linking these key beliefs. Students are asked to come to the board and annotate how the beliefs are related.

ACTIVITIES

Key activities:

- Listening to a song
- Introduction of beliefs
- Analysing scripture
- Exploring possible challenges to Tawhid
- Prophet competition
- Creative and speculative thinking around beliefs
- Relationship between six key beliefs explored

Resources:

- PowerPoint
- Sources relating to the Nature of God

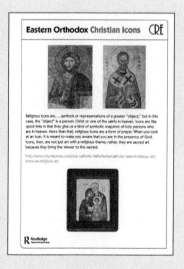

ACTIVITIES

Key activities:

- Reflection on pillars
- A think-pair-share on the links between the five pillars and the six key beliefs
- Truth exercise
- Watch video on the Shahadah
- A think-pair-share on what makes the Shahadah an initiation and not just a recitation
- A consideration of what they submit to in their lives
- A second video and related plenary

Resources:

- PowerPoint including videos

Lesson 4: Shahadah

Learning objectives

1. To understand the meaning of the Shahadah
2. To understand the importance of the Shahadah
3. To reflect on submission in our own lives

The aim of Lesson 4 is to introduce students to the five pillars and to elaborate on the first of these – Shahadah. The beliefs about Allah and Muhammad in the Shahadah are considered, along with the act of witnessing and the concept of submission. Thus, students will also consider who or what they submit to and how this differs from the Islamic community.

At the beginning of the lesson students should be shown a picture of a building with pillars at the front. They should be asked to consider why the key practices in Islam may be called the five pillars. Students should be briefly introduced to each pillar and should be asked to consider how they relate to the key beliefs of Islam.

Students should then be asked to write down a statement that they believe to be 100% true (starting with 'I believe'). Once they have done this they should be asked to reflect on what needs to be behind that statement for it to be valid (a genuine belief that it is true). Students should explore the idea of giving testimony and witnessing and compare this to recitation of the Shahadah. This provides a lead into an explanation of the Shahadah as a witness to beliefs which Muslims believe to be the truth at the heart of Islam. Both Sunni and Shi'a versions of the Shahadah can be presented via the PWP. Students will then answer questions analysing what the Shahadah says about the nature of God and the nature of Muhammad, and consider how these beliefs link to the six key beliefs.

Following this, students should watch a video in which a Muslim explains the importance of the Shahadah. Some key ideas are presented on the next PWP slide followed by the question of what it means to have a full understanding (intellectual, emotional and volitional) when stating the Shahadah. Students can think-pair-share on this question. They will then be asked to reflect on what authorities they submit to in their own lives (see PWP) and can write an answer to this in their books.

As a plenary, students can watch a second video which is a prank by some American Muslims who encourage strangers they meet to recite words they don't understand in Arabic and then try to convince them that they have become Muslims. The teacher should then state the Shahadah and ask they class whether this makes them a Muslim. Finally, students should consider whether they would recite the Shahadah themselves or not.

Lesson 5: Salah

ACTIVITIES

Learning objectives

1. To understand the practices of Salah and Wudu
2. To critically compare these to other religious traditions

Key activities:

- Discovering East
- Watching videos of practice
- Prayer positions activity
- Written work

Resources:

- PowerPoint including videos

The aim of Lesson 5 is for students to understand the practice of Salah and to relate this to Islamic beliefs. This lesson is largely phenomenological in nature as there are a number of features of Salah which we felt needed to be included for an authentic understanding.

A simple starter activity is to ask students to work out which direction is east and then to ask them why you've instructed them to do so. A short PowerPoint presentation could be given to introduce the nature and times of Salah and then a video clip of a Muslim performing Wudu could also be played. The teacher might ask students to consider why Muslims may wash in this way and what beliefs may be reflected by this practice. They could also ask students to consider their initial response to the practice and to compare this practice to other religious traditions.

Following this, students can watch a video clip of a Muslim praying during which they can note down similarities and differences between this form of Islamic prayer and that of their own tradition/one with which they're familiar. Students can then discuss the reflective questions on the PWP and feedback could lead into an introduction of Du'a as individual requests to God. It could also lead to a discussion on the utility of prayer from different worldview perspectives.

Towards the end of the lesson, students can be introduced to the various 'prayer positions' via a demonstration with a basic explanation of what the prayers associated with each position are about. This can also be turned into a game. Prayer positions can be numbered 1–10 whilst being demonstrated and then the teacher can call out a number and the students have to assume the correct position. The last person to assume the position is out. Following this, the teacher can ask students to consider how the different positions reflect Islamic beliefs.

Students should watch the video clip of a discussion between a Sunni Muslim and Shi'a Muslim and then be given an opportunity to briefly reflect on Sunni and Shi'a differences in practice. They could be encouraged to give a personal response to the nature and efficacy of prayer.

If there is more time, or as a homework activity, students could reflect on/discuss and write a response to the statement 'Muslims in Britain should be allowed time out of work to go and pray'.

ACTIVITIES

Key activities:

- Mexican wave
- Comprehension sheet
- Preparation for critical question
- Written task

Resources:

- Zakah and Sadaqah worksheet
- PowerPoint
- Christian attitudes to charity handout
- Humanist attitudes to charity handout
- Zakah and Sadaqah Special Educational Needs (SEN) worksheet

Lesson 6: Zakah

Learning objectives

1. To understand the Islamic practice of Zakah
2. To critically reflect on whether giving should be compulsory

The aim of Lesson 6 is for students to develop an authentic understanding of Zakah in order to be able to critically reflect on the concept of compulsory giving.

To start, students should be encouraged to stand in a circle and complete a Mexican wave – the wave is passed from one person to another. Explain that in Islam, it is worship (Ibadah) to both give and receive. Students can then read the information sheet on Zakah and answer the comprehension questions. An extension activity can be given in which students have to work out individual rates of Zakah.

If lesson time permits, or as a homework exercise, students should write a critical response to the question 'Should giving to those less fortunate than yourself be obligatory?' In order to prepare for this task, students can work in pairs or groups to come up with different critical responses to the question, which can be fed back to the class. An information sheet is available for students to use if desired. If the written task will be for homework this can be done as a plenary. If lesson time permits this can be done in the lesson and students can self or peer assess the work as a plenary activity. This question allows for a number of possible answers from different worldviews and relates to the issue of truthful living e.g. within a secular worldview there may be different answers which relate to different political stances and current issues. Furthermore, whilst Muslims would obviously say that it should be obligatory due to Zakah a nuanced understanding may also include reference to Sadaqah which is given out of choice.

Lesson 7: Sawm

Learning objectives

1. To understand the Islamic practice of Sawm
2. To critically compare it to other religious traditions

The aim of Lesson 7 is to develop an authentic understanding of Sawm and to compare this to other religious traditions. Again, as the content of this topic is vast, the lesson is largely phenomenological.

As a starter, the teacher can give out some wrapped chocolates. Students should be encouraged to open the chocolate and smell it before wrapping it back up again. This is to encourage empathy with Islamic women in traditional settings who have to cook food whilst fasting.

Students should then mind-map the reasons that people may fast. It should be considered which of these reasons may relate to Islamic beliefs. Students can then complete the comprehension sheet on Ramadan and Id-ul-Fitr.

When students have finished their comprehension activity they can be encouraged to eat the chocolate. The teacher can ask how their own experience in the lesson links to their learning.

As a plenary, students can discuss some critical questions in relation to Sawm. There is also an extension task available focusing on the experience of the Buddha who found fasting ineffective. Which perspective do the students agree with and why?

As a possible homework activity, students can devise a bulletin for staff about what to expect during Ramadan.

ACTIVITIES

Key activities:

- Chocolate temptation
- Comprehension exercise
- Critical comparison

Resources:

- Chocolates
- Ramadan and 'Id worksheet
- PowerPoint

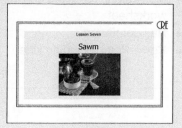

Lesson 8: Hajj

Key activities:

- Story with actions
- Hajj grid
- Testimony
- Ordering motivations
- Hajj dominoes
- Interactive Hajj

Resources:

- Map of Hajj
- Motivations for going on Hajj worksheet
- Hajj dominoes
- PowerPoint including video

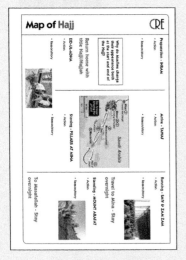

Learning objectives

1. To understand the Islamic practice of Hajj and how it reflects beliefs

Lesson 8 is the first half of a two-part lesson exploring Hajj. The first lesson is phenomenological, ensuring that students understand the links between belief and practice. The second lesson is then a critical exploration of one particular belief associated with Hajj.

To start, students are given four words and asked to make up an action for each of them. The teacher then tells a short story in which each of these words occurs multiple times and the students are to demonstrate the actions they have developed each time a related word is said. This is used to draw out the fact that often, in religious rituals, actions have a specific explanation behind them.

Students then watch the video introducing what happens on Hajj. Students use this to complete a Hajj Map exercise, comparing the actions which Muslims do on Hajj with their meanings. Following this, students read testimonies on the blog *Hajj Stories*, for example 'The journey of forgiveness' (see PWP). In order to empathise further with the Islamic experience of Hajj, students then consider some different reasons for embarking on the pilgrimage. They order the possible motivations, given on the sheet, in terms of importance from their own perspective.

Finally, to consolidate learning, students play Hajj dominoes. The student with 'Start' stands up and reads the first question. The student who has the answer then stands up and reads out their answer followed by the next question and so on until the student with 'End' reads their answer. This can be timed and repeated to see if students can complete it faster the second time/at the start of the next lesson etc.

Another effective consolidation/empathetic activity is to participate in a 'pilgrimage' around the school buildings and to mark off associated actions as you go (e.g. climbing to the top of the school building and drawing out the associated activity in Hajj (climbing Mount Arafat) or running between set points in the playground (running between the hills of Marwa and Safa). Whether this is possible, however, is dependent on the school context, ease of movement around the building and lesson time allocated.

Lesson 9: Hajj and equality

Learning objectives

1. To critically discuss whether the Hajj demonstrates equality

---

The aim of Lesson 9 is to critically discuss a claim made about the Hajj from an Islamic perspective – that it demonstrates equality. Students will already be aware of this belief from the previous lesson but now they will have the opportunity to consider to what extent it is true.

As a starter, students should watch a clip of Malcolm X discussing the need for segregation between Black and White Americans before he went on Hajj. The content of this is both emotive and challenging so the teacher will need to draw out from the students and consolidate with them the key points being made.

Students should then read a testimony from Malcolm X once he returned from Hajj. Draw out from the students that Malcolm X's experience on Hajj helped him to view human beings as equal. Mark this up in a chart on the board/in the students' books as a reason for believing the Hajj does demonstrate equality alongside other aspects from the previous lesson (e.g. wearing white, giving money to the poor at Id-ul-Adha etc.).

Following this, show the students the guidelines for women on Hajj (link in PWP). Discuss whether these demonstrate inequality between men and women (it is important to ensure that students consider the reasons behind the different rules as part of this discussion). Ask the students to consider other reasons why some may say that Hajj does not promote equality (e.g. only Muslims are allowed in Mecca during Hajj) and mark these on the chart also. There is an anecdote from a non-Muslim traveller reflecting on his experiences which could be used here.

As a plenary or homework task, depending on time, ask students to critically respond to the statement 'the Hajj demonstrates equality'. If completed in lesson time student can then peer/self-assess as a plenary. If completed at home, the plenary could be to ask for students' opinions, with explanations, given the learning in the lesson.

ACTIVITIES

Key activities:

- Malcolm X clip
- Malcolm X testimony
- Information sheet on women
- Drawing up a chart
- Written task

Resources:

- PowerPoint including video
- Malcolm X letter from Mecca handout
- Non-Muslims in Mecca handout

Lesson 10: Muhammad: religious, political and military leader

Key activities:

- List political figures
- Watch videos on Muhammad's military campaigns
- Group work on sources
- Analysing the last sermon

Resources:

- PowerPoint including videos
- Muhammad's last sermon handout
- Highlighters
- March on Mecca source worksheets

Learning objectives

1. To critically reflect on Muhammad's role as a political and military leader
2. To analyse the last sermon of Muhammad

The aim of Lesson 10 is to introduce Muhammad as a political and military leader. Muhammad differs from many religious leaders as a result of these roles. Muslims are often reported to insist that Islam is a peaceful religion, but some scholars find it difficult to accept this given Muhammad's example. Sources present Muhammad differently with regards to his military campaigns and thus it is important for students to consider differing opinions relating to this, especially as it is relevant when critically analysing the Lesser Jihad later on in the scheme of work.

The lesson starts with students being asked to make a list of political leaders who have been involved in wars. Students should then discuss what the public perception of these people is. Use this as a way in to explain Muhammad's role as a political and military figure. Students can then discuss what they saw in the video from Lesson 1 about wars in which Muhammad was involved. You could also use excerpts from the History Channel's production of 'The Life of Muhammad' (see PWP - key excerpts at 31–35; 37–39).

Following this, students should be split into four groups. Each group should be given an historical 'source' relating to the march on Mecca. These sources offer different levels of challenge so think carefully how you organise your groups. Students should discuss and then write down answers to the questions on the sheet. Each group should then elect a student to feedback to the class.

Students can be presented with the last sermon of Muhammad and some highlighting pens. They should read the sermon and highlight phrases which they think are key in pointing to Muhammad's priorities and intentions for the Islamic community after his death. Ideas can be fed back to the class.

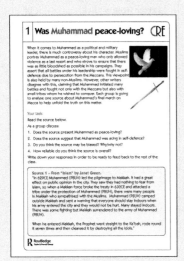

Lesson 11: the Sunni and Shi'a split

Learning objectives

1. To identify differing groups within Islam
2. To compare and critically discuss beliefs and practices within Islam
3. To recognise the impact of history and context on these groups

The aim of Lesson 11 is to begin to understand variations within the Islamic tradition. Often, schemes of work on Islam only present Sunni interpretations of the tradition and it is important to acknowledge that in fact there are many areas of belief and practice about which Muslims disagree. This is especially important given that these differences date all the way back to the death of Muhammad. In general, the scheme of work focuses on Sunni interpretations as these are the majority view. However, by introducing Shi'a variations at this stage of the scheme of work, students are made aware of important differences which can then be raised again in critical discussion in later lessons.

As a starter, students are given 'voting cards' with information on them about Abu Bakr and Ali (these should ideally be in contrasting colours). Students are to read the cards and to consider who they think Muhammad would have wanted to succeed him as leader of the Islamic community after his death. Students can discuss this in pairs and should then be encouraged to vote by holding up one of their cards. They can then be called upon to explain their choice.

This can be followed by a PowerPoint presentation on the Sunni/Shi'a divide in the world today, concentrating on where variations are most commonly practiced. As in the previous lesson, students should then be split into groups and allocated areas of belief and practice where Shi'a Muslims deviate from the Sunni tradition. Students should complete the task sheets in their groups and feedback to the class.

As a plenary, students can reflect on the last sermon of Muhammad and consider what Muhammad would have made of the split in the Islamic tradition. There are also various other activities which would be complimentary to this lesson or the scheme of work if practitioners have extra time or homework allocations. For example, a good homework task could be for students to research Sufism. Furthermore, it may be beneficial for students to look at newspaper articles relating to the Sunni/Shi'a divide in the world today and to understand current issues relating to this.

ACTIVITIES

Key activities:

- Voting
- Group work on Sunni and Shi'a variations
- Reflection – relate back to Muhammad's last sermon

Resources:

- Voting cards handout
- Sunni and Shi'a differences – resources
- PowerPoint

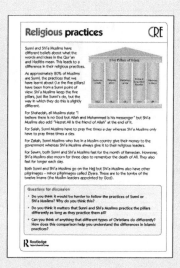

Lesson 12: Shari'ah law

Key activities:

- Robin Hood clip
- What happened next task
- Information sheet on Shari'ah law
- Clips relating to debate on Shari'ah law in the UK
- Critical discussion

Resources:

- PowerPoint including videos
- Shari'ah law handout

Learning objectives

1. To identify areas of the world where Islam is practised today
2. To consider the legal systems in some majority Muslim countries
3. To critically reflect on the concept of Shari'ah law and critically discuss whether Shari'ah law should be allowed in Britain

The aim of Lesson 12 is to consider how Islam is practiced in the modern world, focusing on areas of the world in which Shari'ah law is practiced and on Britain. The earlier lesson on different groups within Islam should also be drawn upon as much as possible throughout.

To start, students should watch the introductory scene of Robin Hood Prince of Thieves in which Robin is to have his hand chopped off (2.05–3.30). Ask students how they think this might relate to Islam and use this to introduce the 'Hadd offenses' in Shari'ah law.

Following this, students should complete the 'What happened next' activity on the PowerPoint in which they are given three, real life, scenarios and asked what they think the penalties might have been for these offenses under Shari'ah law if the penalty for stealing is the chopping off of a hand. The teacher then explains what the penalties technically are for these offenses, followed by what actually happened. The latter introduces students to the fact that the context of the offenses is very significant in Shari'ah law and, often, it cannot be enforced for this reason.

Students should then read the handout on Shari'ah law which explains the different levels of enforcement etc. of it in the world today. It is key to draw out here that it is not enforced in most countries and that even in some countries where it is enforced, the Hadd penalties do not apply. This can lead into a critical discussion about whether and to what extent it should be applied in different contexts.

Finally, students should apply the issues directly to their own context by considering whether Shari'ah law should be allowed in Britain. Students can watch clips relating to different opinions on the issue and should then discuss/debate their responses as a class. This can be developed into a written exercise if time allows.

Lesson 13: Western perspectives on Islam

Learning objectives

1. To reflect on your own responses to Islam
2. To consider reasons behind general Western perspectives on Islam

Key activities:

- Silent PowerPoint activity
- Activity sheet
- Critical discussion

Resources:

- PowerPoint
- Western perspectives on Islam worksheet

The aim of Lesson 13 is to consider Western perspectives on Islam, including the students' own. This follows neatly from the previous lesson in which students began to consider how the practice of Islam differs around the world. In this lesson, students consider how perspectives may differ and the teacher should draw out how these are influenced by the people and information around us.

To start, students are shown the PowerPoint presentation 'Western perspectives on Islam' and are asked to write down the first words or phrases which come into their heads as they watch the images on the slides, without speaking to anyone else. The teacher should explain that it is important that students are honest in their responses and that these will not be judged as right or wrong. Music can be played in the background if desired. Students then spend time analysing their responses by working through the rest of the sheet 'Western perspectives on Islam'.

Following this, the teacher can take feedback from the sheet and lead this into a critical discussion on how our perspectives are formed and whether they can be justified. (N.B. The final question on the sheet which the students will have completed is whether there are any areas of Islam on which they feel they need more knowledge and understanding. In our experience, the two issues which come up most frequently are Hijab and Jihad. This is one of the reasons that these particular issues follow this lesson in the scheme of work. However, if your students highlight other areas in which they are interested and you have lesson time to spare, it is obviously worthwhile to dedicate time to these issues also.)

ACTIVITIES

Key activities:

- Video clip
- Mini silent activity
- Reading and analysing texts
- Sticky notes and discussion
- Reading news reports
- Written task

Resources:

- PowerPoint including video
- Women's veils handout
- Sticky notes

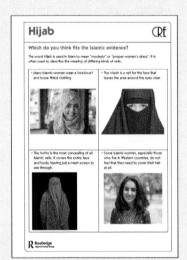

Lesson 14: Hijab

Learning objectives

1. To understand Islamic beliefs about gender and equality
2. To analyse Islamic teachings relating to hijab
3. To critically reflect on how Islamic women should dress and how this relates to our context

The aim of Lesson 14 is to critically discuss women's dress within Islam. This was selected over other ethical issues as it has been very controversial in the West and, as a result, there are numerous resources which can be drawn on. It is also a topic which the students are likely to have had some exposure to already without having had the religious literacy to form a truly critical response about it before.

To start, it is worth returning to the issue of equality between men and women in Islam. It is important for students to understand that, whilst the Islamic tradition claims that men and women are equal in value, this does not mean that the expectations on them are 'the same'. This use of the word 'equality' has created challenges for more conservative approaches to many ethical issues. Within the CRE classroom, the assumptions embedded within the common liberal use of 'equality' need to be challenged as much as more conservative interpretations. Ensuring that students understand a traditional perspective also avoids the entire lesson taking a tangent into discussion of sexism when this is only one issue relating to Islamic dress. It is very important that students can assess the issue from a position of inclusivity with regards to different positions. Thus, the lesson begins with a clip from an advert in which men and women are portrayed differently. Students should consider this portrayal and whether they agree with it. They can then be introduced to some traditional Islamic teachings regarding gender roles via the PowerPoint.

Following this, students should look at the four pictures of Islamic women on the PowerPoint and, similarly to the silent activity in the previous lesson, should note down their initial responses. The teacher should take feedback on this and then introduce the Qur'anic texts and texts from the Hadith to the students. Students should be handed the sheets with the various pictures on along with a sticky note and be asked to discuss in pairs which image they think most accurately portrays the Islamic teachings. Students should come to the front and place their sticky note on the image displayed on

Lesson 14: continued

the board which they think is most appropriate. This can lead into a class discussion on the issue.

To finish, students should consider some recent news relating to hijab in the West from the PowerPoint. They should then be asked to create a law on the issue for the British context in response to the learning from the lesson. Students should be able to justify their ideas in relation to both the context and Islamic teachings.

ACTIVITIES

Key activities:

- Student response and prior knowledge
- Introduction of terms
- Listing/mind-mapping Greater Jihad
- Exploring the Qur'anic sources
- Comprehension – Lesser Jihad
- Pictures – Greater or Lesser?

Resources:

- PowerPoint
- Qur'anic evidence for Jihad handout
- Lesser Jihad handout

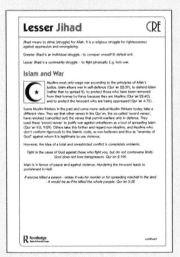

Lesson 15: Jihad

Learning objectives

1. To understand the concepts of Greater and Lesser Jihad

Lesson 15 is the first of two lessons exploring the concept of Jihad. As with hijab, it is likely that students have had some exposure to the Lesser Jihad at least but, as representations in the media are often inaccurate, they are unlikely to have an authentic or, in turn, truly critical view of it. The aim of Lesson 15 is thus to introduce Jihad and for students to make a distinction between the Greater and Lesser Jihad. This will set them up for critical discussion surrounding the Lesser Jihad in the following lesson.

To start, students should be asked whether they have heard the word 'Jihad' before and what they think it might mean. Following feedback, the teacher should introduce the concepts of Greater and Lesser Jihad without saying which is which. Students should be asked which they think may be Greater and which may be Lesser and should explain their responses.

Students should make a list of actions which may be considered as part of the Greater Jihad, drawing on all prior learning. This can be fed back and mind-mapped on the board. This works well as a revision activity in the lead-up to assessment. Students should then be given Qur'anic sources relating to Lesser Jihad and should consider when they suggest a Lesser jihad is acceptable. This understanding will be consolidated through the information sheet on Lesser Jihad and students should answer the questions.

To ensure understanding of these terms is secure, as a plenary, students should look at the images on the PowerPoint and ascribe each as 'Greater' or 'Lesser' Jihad, explaining their reasons. There may be a couple of images which they will ascribe as 'neither' as a result of their learning on Lesser Jihad.

For homework, students should research the situation in Israel and Palestine and answer the questions: 1. Are Muslims oppressed in Palestine? 2. Does this count as a Lesser Jihad?

Lesson 16: Jihad debate

The aim of Lesson 16 is to critically reflect on the Lesser Jihad.

As a starter, students should be asked how many of the rules for Lesser Jihad they can remember from the previous lesson. Students will then begin to apply the rules for jihad via the worksheet which can be completed individually or in pairs before opening up to the whole class for discussion. As a class, discuss whether each of the scenarios on the sheet is an example of Lesser Jihad. Use this to lead into a critical discussion on whether the Lesser Jihad can ever justify terrorism.

Students should then work in pairs to compare the research they did for their homework and the conclusions that they came to. This should be fed back as a class and may lead to a critical discussion.

Following this, students can consolidate and extend their understanding of Lesser Jihad by reading through the information sheet and discussing the questions at the bottom. This can be done in pairs or as a class but we do suggest that, if completed in pairs, ample time is allowed for feedback as the questions are quite challenging.

The teacher should then ask the question: 'Should Muslims ever use violence today?' After a brief class discussion, the students should debate this via RE boxing (see Chapter 3). Each student should write down five points which could contribute to each side of the debate. Then they should move in the room to which side of the debate they most agree with (if this is very uneven, teachers can move some students onto the other side). Students on each side can pool their ideas and then RE boxing can take place. The teacher should facilitate the debate and keep score.

ACTIVITIES

Key activities:

- Lesser Jihad consolidation sheet
- Scenarios
- Homework comparison/ discussion
- Formal debate

Resources:

- PowerPoint
- Sticky notes
- Students' homework
- Lesser Jihad consolidation worksheet
- Applying the rules of Jihad worksheet

Lessons 17–18: assessment and feedback

Key activities:

- Constructing an essay/ dialogue to demonstrate understanding
- Completing self-assessment

Resources:

- PowerPoint
- 'What is Jihad?' assessment guidance for students
- 'What is Jihad?' mark sheet

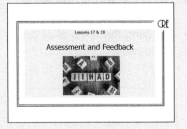

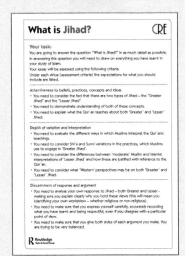

Learning objectives

1. To demonstrate your learning on the topic
2. To receive feedback on your progress
3. To self-assess your response to the topic

The assessment question 'What is Jihad?' was chosen as it is a question which allows students to demonstrate the breadth of the knowledge they have gained over the course of the scheme of work. Given that the Greater Jihad is to strive or struggle for God, the whole Islamic tradition could potentially be relevant in answer to the question. In addition, the question can also be viewed as evaluative – students can critically discuss what counts as a Lesser Jihad as part of their answer or could even critically evaluate ethical or denominational issues. As suggested in the introduction for the scheme of work, an understanding of Jihad necessarily involves an understanding of numerous other factors within the Islamic tradition and thus is a fitting culmination for the scheme of work.

As the assessment question is so open, students can also respond to the question on a number of levels. Under the old eight level framework, students were able to respond in an explanatory, comparative or evaluative manner as was fitting of their target level at the time. Within our own framework, there is guidance on the assessment sheet as to how students may wish to respond in order to demonstrate their academic virtues most effectively. The question is so open that it could be translated into different levels of response whatever framework your school or department is using.

How you decide to structure this assessment will depend on your school setting. Here we suggest a lesson for students to complete the assessment (in written or other form) and a lesson for feedback with the possibility of planning for their assessment as a homework task. Ensuring that your students receive proper feedback is vital for good practice in any framework. For CRE reflection time is particularly important as the learning process and the application of judgemental rationality are always ongoing. Students also need lesson time to consider how they have responded to the scheme of work by completing the 'responsibility' section on the assessment sheet.

References

Hella, E. and Wright, A. (2009). Learning 'about' and 'from' religion: phenomenography, the Variation Theory of Learning and Religious Education in Finland and the UK. *British Journal of Religious Education* 31, no.1, 53–64.

Marton, F. (2015). *Necessary Conditions of Learning*. New York: Routledge.

Smart, N. (1968). *Secular Education and the Logic of Religion*. New York: Humanities Press.

CHAPTER 5

Critical Religious Education and philosophy

An exemplar scheme of work for teaching science and religion (Year 9)

CRE and philosophy

'Isn't CRE just turning RE into philosophy?' This is a question that we have been asked on numerous occasions, to which the answer is 'no'. Replacing RE with philosophy would relegate religious questions to the periphery, viewing theological topics as just one of a number of topics that philosophy might investigate. In contrast, these questions take centre stage in CRE. Philosophical analysis is just one (particularly useful) tool for engaging in CRE. It is to be used alongside other tools which would *not* find a home in philosophy departments, such as detailed textual analysis of scripture.

However, we can easily understand the motivation for the question, for CRE and philosophy share a number of commonalities. Both:

● are interested in 'ultimate questions'
● adopt a rigorous methodology which aims at approaching the truth
● draw on a common language (for example, both talk of 'assumptions', 'arguments', and 'consistency')
● encourage drawing on other disciplines in order to reach informed judgements about reality.

These shared aims and methods mean that topics traditionally viewed as coming under the 'philosophy umbrella' fit naturally into the CRE classroom.

This chapter aims to explain what is distinct about a CRE approach to philosophy. It outlines what might go wrong in attempting to do philosophy in RE and how to avoid these potential shortcomings. It explains the benefits and importance of a rigorous introduction to doing philosophy; in particular, preparing students to be adept in their use of 'philosophical tools' so that they can apply them to topics elsewhere in the RE curriculum. It sets out a general method for planning a philosophy scheme of work, before talking through a detailed exemplification of this planning process in the form of a Year 9 science and religion scheme of work.[1]

A non-CRE approach to philosophy

There has been a general trend towards growth in the study of philosophy in schools. Typically, philosophy makes a sudden appearance at Year 9, as a very different type of topic to the 'world religions' studied in Year 7 and Year 8. This is often to prepare students for studying the exam specifications. (For some time, philosophy of religion and ethics have been the most popular options taken by schools at GCSE and A Level.) Unfortunately, popularity does not guarantee that philosophy will be taught well. We suggest that there are a number of potential problems with the way in which philosophy is currently approached in some schools.

First, in some school contexts there does not seem to be a clear rationale for the combination of world religions and philosophy. Why does the KS3 curriculum so often move from one to the other? In CRE, there is a clear relationship between the two: they are both concerned with truth claims about reality. This relationship is not so clear in other pedagogical models. Without this clarity, there is a danger of skewing the boundaries between the disciplines of philosophy and theology / religious studies and of not treating them appropriately as distinctive areas of academia. However, if the links are made explicit to students, this problem may be overcome, and the transition between the disciplines appears more natural.

Second, students are often expected to engage in tricky philosophical topics (e.g. the cosmological argument) without having been given the tools with which to do so. There is a popular myth that 'everyone can do philosophy', which in a sense is true – everyone can engage in thinking critically about ultimate questions. However, it is true in a similar way to the way that 'everyone can do art' is true. Everyone can 'have a go' at expressing themselves by drawing a picture or making a sculpture. But to produce the artwork that best represents reality, generally some formal training is required. It is the same in philosophy; there is more chance of reaching truthful, wise judgements if one engages in philosophy having been equipped with key skills.

Third, there is sometimes a misplaced focus on the *process* of philosophising as an end in itself, rather than viewing philosophy as a *means* to the end of pursuit of truth. In order to explain this difference in approach, it will be instructive to look at Philosophy for Children (P4C) as an example that contrasts with the CRE approach to philosophy in RE.

P4C[2] has been particularly popular at primary level. Teachers are trained in P4C methods and run these either as discrete sessions or as activities within the existing curriculum. In some cases, external 'facilitators' come into schools to run discrete philosophy sessions.[3] Philosophy as a separate subject is rare at secondary level. Some secondary RE teachers adopt P4C methods as an approach to classroom discussion, and plan P4C activities into their lessons. There have been some attempts to implement P4C independently.[4]

The aim of P4C has been summarised by one research study as being "to help children become more willing and able to ask questions, construct arguments, and engage in reasoned discussion" (Philosophy for Children, 2015, p.3). The approach encourages 'communities of enquiry', where the group thinks together in a positive and supportive group atmosphere. The enquiry usually begins with a stimulus, such as a piece of music or a picture. Students then suggest questions relating to this stimulus, and they vote on which of these they would like to discuss. The teacher acts as a 'facilitator', encouraging students to exhibit the four Cs (caring, collaborative, creative and critical) in their discussion.

Research studies suggest that P4C can have many positive effects on student learning. These effects seem particularly notable amongst the most disadvantaged students. For example, one study reported that P4C positively influenced "pupils' confidence to speak, listening skills, and self-esteem" (Philosophy for Children, 2015, p.3). Significant media attention accompanied the publication of this research study. This included new calls for more philosophy in schools, based on the finding that undertaking P4C improved progress in maths and literacy (Adams, 2015).

We welcome these positive outcomes for students, which no doubt also accompany the practice of good CRE. However, our concern is that the development of skills is the *focus* of P4C, rather than a welcome by-product. This focus affects the classroom practice and the learning outcomes. For example, a student may leave a P4C discussion with better communication skills and more understanding of the different opinions of their peers. Yet at the same time, they may leave with no more insight into what view they should take on how to answer the critical question under consideration. As for understanding how this answer should then relate to their own life and behaviour, the student is probably no better off than before the discussion.

In contrast, in a good CRE lesson that engages in philosophical enquiry, students should leave the discussion with more insight as to the *answer* to a critical question. This does not mean that they will leave with a firm answer; the insight may simply be that the matter is more complex and difficult than they initially thought! The discussion has a clear end-point, which is a more informed personal judgement about the matter under discussion. Additionally, unlike with the standard model for a P4C enquiry (especially enquiries where the students choose the question), students of CRE will have an authentic understanding of the core knowledge required for an *informed* discussion of the topic.

An example might help bring out the contrast here. We might imagine a P4C enquiry which begins with the stimulus of a sea shell and results in the question 'How was this made?' The enquiry could bring up lots of interesting issues, including disagreements amongst the students about whether such a beautiful, patterned object could result from purely natural causes. However, without knowledge of evolutionary theory or an understanding of what different religious people say about creation, it would be hard for students to make an intelligent, informed judgement on the question. A teacher of CRE might choose to adopt the community of enquiry approach at the beginning of a topic, to spark the debate using the shell as a stimulus, and this could work well. Alternatively, and perhaps more fruitfully, if P4C techniques were used *after* studying the topic, the students would come at the discussion from an informed angle. Although the discussion would resemble in many ways a discussion on the same question in the P4C setting, the student contributions will have greater depth as a result of their prior studies. It is therefore important to get right the order of your scheme of work, so that P4C elements that you choose to incorporate in your teaching are most profitable.

In order to overcome the issues discussed above, our exemplification of a philosophy scheme of work begins with analysing arguments, so that students are more equipped from the start to think rigorously through philosophical problems. Again, we see the importance of ordering the scheme of work so that it layers up the skills and knowledge required for making a discerning judgement about key critical questions. Ideally, your students will also have completed the Introductory Scheme of Work (see Chapter 3) and so will have reflected on what tools are most effective for exercising judgmental rationality. If students have been doing CRE since the beginning of Year 7, then they will have got into the habit of using philosophical tools such as judging an argument for its consistency. Moving on to a philosophy of religion scheme of work in Year 9 is thus a natural move for CRE.

A CRE approach to philosophy

The discussion above should already have provided some insight into the way that a CRE approach to philosophy might differ from a non-CRE approach. In this section, we explicitly highlight some key differences, and provide an example to show how rigorous philosophical argumentation can be usefully applied to theological questions.

If you have looked ahead to our exemplar scheme of work, you may have thought that there is not a great deal of difference in terms of *content* from a non-CRE scheme of work on the same topic. Even if this is so, there are some important differences in *approach*:

- **Variation**. There is an expectation that students fully engage with variations to their own view. This is set up throughout the scheme of work. For example, a variety of responses to the Genesis creation account are considered and students are expected to engage critically with these. This is in contrast to the tendency (encouraged by the old GCSE) for students to be presented with a variety of viewpoints or arguments and then asked to pick a view, without having fully engaged in the 'tussle' over truth. With that approach, students are free to regurgitate their own belief, without it having been 'touched' by the new information. In a CRE approach, there is no expectation that students *change* their belief, but they should be better able to justify *why* they hold their view. They should also be able to respond to basic objections to their view, having attained a more authentic understanding of the issue.
- **Order**. The scheme of work is ordered so that it begins with analysing arguments, which can later be applied to philosophical content. This way, from the start, students are equipped to use rigorous thinking when encountering philosophical problems. Relevant subject knowledge is taught *before* engaging in philosophical debate, so that the debate is suitably informed.
- **Aimed at truth**. The focus on truth influences the path taken by the scheme of work. It begins with students expressing their viewpoint on questions such as 'How did we get here?' This is not for the sake of affirming each other's personal views, but is so that students develop awareness of their own starting-point and that of others. Through the scheme of work students are encouraged to question their own beliefs. (Note, 'question' does not mean *give up* beliefs; it can be developing a deeper understanding and faith, via questioning.)

  The concern with truth leads to some distinctive subject content. For example, Lesson 2 on 'Fact vs. Belief' encourages students to reflect on what it might mean for religious statements to be true: do religious statements make claims that are true for everyone, or that are just true for the believer?

  The overarching aim of the scheme of work is that through consideration of scientific theory, different religious interpretations of scripture, and different philosophical arguments, students exercise judgemental rationality to reach a *more truthful judgement* on the question of how we got here.

- **Ensuring theological depth**. Within a CRE framework, the inclusion of both philosophy and theology in RE makes a great deal of sense. These disciplines give different (although sometimes interlinked) ways of grappling with the reality in which we exist. When particular topics make use of both disciplines, it is necessary that the material is approached in an appropriate manner. 'Philosophical' schemes of work on the relationship between science and religion will often involve reflection on examples of religious texts which have been brought into question by scientific discoveries. This is to be encouraged. However, if there is only a cursory examination of the texts, there is a danger that they will be misinterpreted. If, for example, students are only exposed to a literal interpretation of Genesis, then they may (reasonably) conclude that the Biblical account of creation can be written off since it so clearly conflicts with scientific evidence. There are significant differences of interpretation within the religious traditions that include the Genesis stories in their holy scriptures. Students must learn about these alternative interpretations if they are to be able to give an informed appraisal of the evidence. Thus, where theological content is included in philosophy schemes of work, it is vital that appropriate theological depth is achieved.

- **Applying philosophical argumentation to theological content**. Students are encouraged to analyse theological statements using philosophical argumentation.

As we show in the example below, using philosophical methods benefits RE by enabling better critical engagement with theological content. In their research into student views on religion and science, Billingsley, Taber, Riga and Newdick (2013, p.1729) comment that "What students seemed to lack were the intellectual tools needed to explore the dilemmas in any depth." By starting this scheme of work by teaching students how to use philosophical tools, this challenge is answered.

An example of how philosophical argumentation can be used to analyse theological content:

"God does not exist, because of the Big Bang."

This is a statement we have heard voiced by both students and adults. Here, a reason (the Big Bang) is being given for a belief (God does not exist). However, it remains to be seen whether this is a *good* argument.

At its simplest, we can state this 'argument' as a single **premise** (premises are denoted by 'Ps' below) and a conclusion (conclusions, including 'interim conclusions' are denoted by 'Cs' below):

> **Premise**: A statement assumed to be true for the purposes of the argument. Premises are the 'building blocks' of arguments.

(continued)

(continued)

    P   Big Bang theory
    C   God does not exist

However, as soon as we state it like this, we see that it is not clear how we get the move from P to C. At least a few premises are missing. By encouraging students to rigorously think through the reasoning process underlying this statement, they are better able to evaluate the argument. Once the argument is broken down into a series of steps, we see that the statement relies on a series of inferences, which although valid, depend on hidden assumptions which are ripe for debate and questioning.

Here is one way that the missing steps might be filled out.

Inference 1

    P1   Big Bang theory is true.
    P2   If Big Bang theory is true, then the Genesis creation accounts are false.
    C1   The Genesis creation accounts are false.

Inference 2

    P3   The Genesis creation accounts are false. (C1)
    P4   If the Genesis creation accounts are false, then the Bible is not the word of God.
    C2   The Bible is not the word of God.

Inference 3

    P5   The Bible is not the word of God. (C2)
    P6   The Bible being the word of God is the only evidence for God's existence.
    C3   There is no evidence for God's existence.

This is just one way of setting up the possible inferences. The student who makes this claim might have had in mind a different reasoning process, such as the Big Bang showing that there is no need to posit a 'creator' to explain the world. Whatever series of inferences lies behind the thought, going through the process can help expose premises that are particularly shaky. Using the philosophical apparatus of validity and soundness helps us to assess whether the argument is a good one.

Valid: An argument is *valid* if it is logically correct. That is, if the premises are true, the conclusion will definitely be true.

As set out above, all the inferences are **valid**; they are logically correct. However, whether the arguments are *successful* is dependent on whether they are **sound**. It is far from clear that this is the case. A proper evaluation of the argument will critically discuss each of the premises.

Evaluation of some of these premises is covered in the scheme of work. For example, Lessons 4–6 (on the notion of myth and on different interpretations of Genesis) show that we need not necessarily accept P2. It may be that Genesis should not be read literally. If so, scientific evidence suggesting the literal falsehood of Genesis need not imply that Genesis be rejected wholesale as devoid of truth. (This is not to say that P2 is false, merely that P2 is not as obvious as it first seems and can (at the least) reasonably be questioned.)

Going back to our initial statement "*God does not exist, because of the Big Bang*", we can now see that what initially looked like a 'justified belief' (and perhaps by some mark schemes, would be judged as one), actually needs further work in order to be a clear argument. Additionally, the premises in the argument need more thought and justification in order to be convincing.

> **Sound**: An argument is *sound* when it is valid AND the premises are true. (So, if an argument is sound, then the conclusion is true.)

This method of exploring exactly what lies behind a statement can be utilised in future lessons as a tool for analysis of other controversial statements. Going through this process allows students to see what makes for a good argument, and through practice and experience, teaches students the art of giving strong justifications.

Planning a philosophy scheme of work

Our exemplar scheme of work is on the topic of science and religion. However, the principles used to plan our scheme of work could equally be used to plan other topic areas (for example, another popular philosophy of religion scheme of work is 'arguments for and against the existence of God').

A general approach to planning a philosophy scheme of work underpinned by CRE should keep in mind the following key points:

1) **Question**. Start by identifying what critical question you want your scheme of work to investigate. For example, in our exemplar scheme of work, the question 'How did we get here?' best captured the tensions between religion and science, as well as having a good *number* of *deep* variations. (See Chapter 4 for discussion of how to select the best critical questions.)

2) **Content**. Content should be selected primarily for its potential to shed light on the critical question. Picking the *right variations* is of particular importance. In the case of philosophy schemes of work, this might simply be a question of examining the most appropriate counter-arguments, in the appropriate depth. What counts as 'appropriate' is likely to be highly dependent on the class you are teaching. For example, looking at Hume's objections to the cosmological argument based on his doubts about causation may be suitable for A Level teaching, but is unlikely to be the right variation for GCSE level or younger. At these earlier stages, it is more appropriate to

simply look at whether we need a 'first cause' at all, and whether or not the Big Bang 'fits the bill' for this 'first cause'.

3) **Order**. The lessons should proceed in a logical order, so that students are adequately prepared for critical discussions that take place later in the scheme of work. Additionally, there is obviously no point looking at counter-arguments *before* the arguments themselves.

As we have emphasised elsewhere in this book, teachers possessing good subject knowledge is of paramount importance to getting all three of the above right. For example, deciding on the most salient critical question and on what variations are appropriate requires a good understanding of the surrounding debate.

Rationale: why choose science and religion as an example topic?

'Religion and science' has been chosen as a prototype 'philosophy of religion' scheme of work for several reasons. First, it is an area of genuine controversy, and one of practical and political significance. For example, there is often discussion in the media of whether it should be compulsory for evolutionary theory to be taught in schools (see, for example, Humanists UK, 2014). Second, there is clear overlap with other curriculum subjects, and this sort of interdisciplinary approach to truth-seeking is encouraged by CRE. Third, philosophy is brought in as a tool to help untangle the issue of the relationship between religion and science, rather than being brought in as a different subject. Fourth, it forms an ideal introduction to popular topics at GCSE and A Level. Fifth, the way that students tend to understand the relationship between religion and science (discussed below) suggests that a rigorous scheme of work that introduces students to important variations is necessary and important.

There is a tendency amongst students to view science according to one of two extremes. At one extreme, science is viewed as possessing unquestionable authority and as 'having all the answers'. (One might term this 'scientism', the view that science is the sole route to knowledge (see Billingsley et al., 2013, p.1716).) At the other extreme, science can be viewed as highly suspicious, due to its apparent conflict with sources of religious authority (cf. Hanley, Bennett and Ratcliffe, 2014, p.1220). Both these views, held by *some* atheists and *some* theists respectively, view science and religion as inherently in conflict. Indeed, research has suggested that a common view amongst students is that science and religion are 'rivals' that need to be compartmentalised in order to be made sense of (Billingsley et al., 2013, p.1729). There is little evidence of students having awareness of alternatives to the 'conflict' view of the relationship (Billingsley et al., 2013, p.1728; Easton and Billingsley, forthcoming). This scheme of work reacts to this tendency by introducing variations to the 'conflict' view and bringing the different views of the relationship between religion and science under critical scrutiny.

Particularly in the context of classrooms where the majority of students are non-religious, there is a tendency to treat science as the 'gold standard' by which to judge all other claims to truth. Trevor Cooling, who has taught both science and RE at secondary schools, has suggested that teaching about religion poses a "unique epistemological challenge" (2008, p.88). Whereas in science lessons, Cooling's scholarly knowledge was generally respected, he found that in his RE lessons, religious content was often dismissed as "just an opinion".

A recent small-scale research study by Easton (2019) reports similar findings. In focus group discussions, students tended to view it as 'improper' to question scientific theory, due to the presence of empirical evidence. At times, students equated 'science' with 'certainty' (for example, by labelling mathematical statements such as '2+2=4' as "scientific"). In all focus groups, students stated a requirement for *empirical verification* in order to be able to assign a truth-value to a statement. That is, students felt that to be able to say whether a statement was true or false, there needed to be some sort of physical evidence for or against that statement. It was also found that students had a narrow interpretation of 'proof', as *'scientific* proof'. For example, one student said about the statement 'There is no God' that "it can't be proven in any way", despite the fact that she had discussed at least some arguments for and against God's existence in her RE lessons. These findings

> **Empirical verification**:
> Being checked by means that are accessible to the senses, of the sort provided by the traditional sciences.

support the conclusions of Billingsley et al. that students tend not to have reflected on the nature of science and scientific method and that "students need more opportunities to consider and compare the natures of science and religion" (2013, p.1729).

These research findings provide further impetus for the scheme of work, which addresses some of the student tendencies that have been observed. It does so by:

1) Developing a more inclusive notion of 'evidence'. The understanding of 'evidence' developed in the scheme of work goes beyond purely *empirical* evidence to also include (for example) argumentation, personal experience and revelation. All these types of evidence can be subjected to critical scrutiny and evaluated to be either good or bad evidence (or as is often the case, somewhere in between).

2) Inviting students to explore the nature of science and scientific method. This includes questioning whether scientific theory amounts to *certainty*, through developing an understanding of how inductive reasoning works and of the concept of theory.

3) Inviting students to question whether empirical verification is essential for meaning and truth.

4) Inviting students to question whether the supposed conflict between religion and science is insurmountable – is it really impossible to believe in both science and religion?

Aims of the scheme of work

The scheme of work deals with some general philosophical issues that are relevant to the relationship between religion and science. It looks at the implications of these issues by eventually inviting students to make a responsible, informed personal judgement on the question 'How did we get here?'

CRE aims to create religiously literate individuals who hold their beliefs responsibly. Thus this scheme of work invites students to explore their own beliefs about creation and humanity more deeply, to consider variations to their own beliefs, as well as a critical evaluation of the arguments for these variations.

The intention of the scheme of work is *not* to take students towards a 'middle way' where scientific consensus is accepted alongside religious belief. (This view is given detailed consideration in Lessons 7 and 8, since it is an important variation of Christian belief.) In all likelihood, most students will retain the beliefs that they held before commencing the scheme of work. However, they will be better informed about the alternatives, and will have changed from a dogmatic or passive understanding of their beliefs to a more personal, active understanding. As John Stuart Mill pointed out, "a living belief" (2006, p.46), held in a manner such that it can be defended against objections, is far more likely to "acquire a real mastery over the conduct" (2006, p.47). The belief will have more of an impact on the person's behaviour, and so will be more likely to result in **truthful living**.

> **Truthful living**: Living out your life in a way that fits with the beliefs you hold.

As always, CRE is concerned not just with questions of truth, but looking at the implications of different purported truths for *how we should behave*. This will often involve thinking about questions of *purpose.* CRE encourages students to ask: 'If X is the truth, what does that mean for me?' 'What are the implications of X for how I should behave?' For this scheme of work, examples of such questions are as follows:

- If there is no pre-designated purpose for creation, does this mean I can behave in any way that I feel like?
- If it is true that humanity results from a godless process of evolution, what implications does this have for whether we should care for weaker members of society?
- If God created humans by a process of evolution, how should I treat non-human animals?

Although the scheme of work does not deal directly with questions of purpose and ethics, you should make the link explicit and encourage your students to make links between their decisions about truth and how they behave in their own lives. These links should be made throughout the scheme of work, but (as always) the relationship between the topic and truthful living is explicitly considered in the assessment.

Note that although this scheme of work draws largely on the Christian tradition, this is purely because of the predominant influence of Christianity in the UK. The scheme of work could easily be adapted so that the focus switches to another religion.

The remainder of this chapter is taken up with the details of the suggested scheme of work. We begin with an overview, before giving a more detailed explanation of the reasoning behind the lessons (as well as explaining some of the trickier aspects of subject knowledge). This is then followed by a closer look at each of the individual lessons within it. For each lesson there are learning objectives and a set of key activities, which are explained in a short paragraph. Potential resources are provided for each lesson. Ideally teachers should use the entire scheme of work as it stands, but it is possible that particular lessons or even individual resources could be used by teachers within other complementary units of study.

The subject content involved in this scheme of work may seem tricky in places, and you may find that you need to read up on areas that you are less familiar with. It is an important requirement of CRE that the material is an authentic representation of what people believe. Similarly, it is important that the fruits of other disciplines are brought to bear on questions of truth. (For example, Lesson 2 draws on discussions in philosophy over whether empirical verification is a necessary condition for statements to have meaning.) This does put extra pressure on the already-busy teacher, but ensuring that you are adequately prepared in terms of your subject knowledge is of paramount importance.

Overview of the scheme of work

Sequence	Lesson title	Learning objectives
1	Introduction: student views and philosophical arguments	To reflect on existing views on religion and science To begin to understand how philosophical arguments are constructed and analysed
2	Fact vs. opinion	To critically reflect on the distinction between fact and opinion To understand the influential philosophical stance of logical positivism and be able to critically evaluate this
3	Scientific explanations	To know the basics of Big Bang theory and evolutionary theory To understand induction as part of the scientific method To understand the controversial nature of scientific theory
4	Myth	To understand the concept of myth To compare creation myths and consider their purpose
5	Genesis: the Biblical accounts	To understand the nature and differences of the creation stories in Genesis 1 and 2 To begin to reflect on one's own interpretation of Genesis

(continued)

Sequence	Lesson title	Learning objectives
6	Genesis: Christian theological responses	To understand different theological positions regarding the Biblical creation stories and the reasons for these positions To critically analyse the creation stories in Genesis in light of theological interpretations – which position is most appropriate?
7	The cosmological argument	To understand a simple form of the cosmological argument for the existence of God To critically reflect on its success To consider the argument that God created the Big Bang
8	The teleological argument	To understand a simple form of the teleological argument (Paley) To critically reflect on its success To consider other forms of the teleological argument To consider the argument that God designed the world through evolution
9	Science vs. religion?	To bring together what has been learnt in order to begin critically answering the question of 'How did we get here?'
10 & 11	Assessment and feedback	To demonstrate your learning on the topic To receive feedback on your progress To self-assess your response to the topic

The scheme of work explained

In this section we aim to give a more thorough overview of the scheme of work than is given in the table above. In particular, there is extra guidance given for Lessons 1 to 3. These lessons contain some complex ideas which may be new to some RE teachers, but which are necessary for the study of science and religion within a critical realist framework.

With any topic, it is important to begin with the students' own views, for the understanding that the students bring to the classroom will affect what material it is appropriate to present to them. Thus the scheme of work begins in Lesson 1 by asking students to think about their own views on some of the 'ultimate questions' that will be tackled during the scheme of work: How did we get here?

What is the purpose of life? Can you believe in both science and religion? The majority of the first lesson is then spent learning how to construct philosophical arguments and how to evaluate these as valid / invalid and sound / unsound. The purpose of this abstract discussion of philosophical arguments is two-fold.

First, it gives the students a new tool in their toolkit for critically evaluating arguments. Explain to your students that this is something that they can use in their other subjects too. They can even use it at home when arguing with their parents! This could be demonstrated to your students in the following example.

P1 If you don't do your homework, your parents will be angry at you.

P2 You do your homework.

C Your parents will not be angry at you.

This is an **invalid** argument: even if it is true that 'if you don't do your homework, your parents will be angry with you', it doesn't follow that if you do your homework, they won't be angry at you. You could then argue that your parents will probably still find something else to be angry about, so really there's not much point in doing your homework! Students tend to find thinking through arguments in this way both empowering and enjoyable.

Second, this discussion of argumentation makes the students aware that there are ways to offer support for a statement other than by experience or scientific evidence. It introduces students to the idea that arguments can be presented as a type of 'evidence' too – and that arguments can (and should) be subjected to critical analysis, just as with all types of evidence.

Lesson 2 aims to get students thinking about whether there is a difference between fact and opinion and what this difference might be. Students often assume that because religious statements are controversial and uncertain, they cannot be true in the same way that scientific statements are true. Our experiences of teaching the starter activity serve as a good example of this. In the starter, students are given two handouts (or 'sides'), each with a different set of statements. Side A contains statements which are commonly viewed as 'opinion', such as 'Chocolate is the best flavour of ice cream' and 'Cats are the nicest animals'. Side B contains statements that are usually viewed as 'fact' such as '2+2=4' and 'Copper conducts electricity'. Students are then given cut-up statements to sort out, and asked to place these on the most appropriate side. Some of these statements are religious in nature (e.g. 'God does not exist'), some are scientific (e.g. 'Cheetahs can run faster than lions') and others are moral (e.g. 'Hitler was an evil man'). Different students will divide up the statements in different ways, but in general we have found that students tend towards putting religious and moral statements on Side A (alongside subjective opinions) and scientific statements on side B (alongside objective facts).[5]

If 'God wants us to pray five times a day' is the same kind of statement as 'Blue is the best colour for decorating bedrooms' then it is a *subjective* truth, one about which there can be only limited debate. If we take this view of religious and moral truth, then there is little need or impetus to justify our religious or moral beliefs, since such statements are expressions of mere subjective preference and can be true for one person but not for another. Opposed to this, CRE invites students to consider that there is a 'truth out there' (ontological realism) and encourages students to use a variety of means (e.g. argument, scientific evidence) to make a judgement about the truth of religious statements (i.e. to exercise judgemental rationality).

Therefore, to challenge these ideas, a class discussion follows this activity in which students are encouraged to discuss the difference between facts and opinions. A variety of views will be brought up by students when it comes to whole-class feedback from discussions, but if there are not sufficient variations in viewpoints for a good discussion, it may be necessary for you to add in one of these two contrary ideas:

1) Statements such as X – 'God does not exist' – could be true statements about the world, despite us lacking conclusive evidence for or against them. Just as the statement Y 'There are 2,433,093 million grains of sand on Blackpool beach' may be unprovable, it is still the case that the statement is either objectively true or objectively false. With both statements X and Y, we have arguments for and against (including pointers from empirical evidence) which shed at least some light on the truth of the statement, and enable at least a preliminary, cautionary judgement. *This is the viewpoint a critical realist is likely to hold.*

2) Religious statements could never be 'facts' about the world because there will always be disagreement about whether the statements are true or false. It is impossible to physically prove X and therefore the statement is neither true nor false – it depends on what the individual believes. *This is the viewpoint a postmodernist (as characterised in Chapter 3) is likely to hold.*

Verification Principle: a statement is only meaningful if it is analytically true or empirically verifiable.

Logical positivism: a philosophical movement popular in the early 20th century which confined the boundaries of knowledge to logical and scientific truths.

It is common to hear students voice a (simplified) version of the **Verification Principle (VP)**. This principle, initially proposed by logical positivists, asserts that a statement is only meaningful if it is analytically true (true by definition) or empirically verifiable. **Logical positivism** is a movement that arose in the 1920s which views scientific knowledge as the only kind of factual knowledge. If we accept the logical positivist view then religious statements such as 'God is good' and ethical statements such as 'murder is wrong' are meaningless. Like the statement 'my smoogel has pomped', such statements have *no* truth-value – they are neither true nor false.

You might have heard your students say things like 'there is no answer to whether God created the world, as there is no evidence'. Students often think that because we lack the *means* to find an answer to a question, that there is *no truth* of the matter. To think like this is to commit the **epistemic fallacy** by expecting reality to conform to the extent and limits of our knowledge (Wright, 2013, p.10). There is some debate as to whether to think like this is to commit a fallacy, but students should at least be encouraged to reflect on their reasoning here. This lesson invites students to critically reflect on whether a statement can be true or false *even where there is a lack of scientific evidence.*

Students are invited in small groups to consider whether they agree with the VP – initially with the only 'clue' of 'Can you think of any statements that *you* think are *true* that *can't* be proved empirically? This then leads into a class discussion. There are certain classic objections to the VP which can be raised by the teacher at the end of the discussion if they have not already been voiced by the class, for example:

a) VP rules out statements that most of us consider meaningful, e.g. 'I love you', or 'Harry Potter has a lighting-shaped scar'.
b) VP encourages us to take a narrow view of evidence that we don't usually take in everyday life. For example, usually we are willing to believe things based on testimony and philosophical argumentation. You might like to remind students of Lesson 5 within the Year 7 Introductory scheme of work (see Chapter 3) where we discussed the different tools and criteria one might use to make judgements.
c) VP fails its own test – it cannot itself be empirically verified, and so by its own standard is not meaningful!

For the plenary, students are asked to decide on the truth-status of statements displayed on the board. Students are required to either go and stand by 'true', 'false' or 'neither true nor false, like "blue is the best colour"'. On this occasion, 'I'm not sure' is not allowed, for the middle ground represents the viewpoint that the statement lacks a truth-value. Ideally, there should be few students in the middle of the continuum for all the statements. Most of your students should realise that just because something is controversial and not provable by scientific evidence, this doesn't mean that the statement is mere opinion, something arbitrarily decided upon or outside rational thought like 'chocolate is the best flavour of ice cream'. However, it is important to emphasise that clearing students from the middle of the room (away from a postmodern, relativist approach) is not an essential outcome, nor an ultimate aim of the lesson. To have this as an aim would be to indoctrinate students into a particular stance, which is against the principles of critical realism. Rather, students are being invited to reflect on some of their assumptions, which may or may not lead to a change of opinion.

If students are to be able to make informed critical judgements about the truth of Big Bang theory and evolutionary theory, then it is essential that they have a sound understanding of the basics of the theories. For this reason, Lesson 3 begins with examining the basic claims made by these theories. Students also need to understand that these theories are

theory (as opposed to **proof**). That is, they are widely accepted **hypotheses** that have substantial evidence. After studying the theories more thoroughly, the lesson moves on to looking at the difference between **deductive** and **inductive** arguments and theory and proof, to highlight to students that science falls short of complete certainty.

Hypothesis: a tentative explanation or statement, yet to be supported by adequate scientific evidence.

Proof: a set of evidence that establishes the truth of something *beyond doubt*. An example is the proof that the angles of a triangle add up to 180 degrees.

It is useful for students to have an understanding of inductive reasoning, since the scientific method is so dependent on this. Thus, students will be introduced to an inductive argument such as:

P1 Socrates was Greek.

P2 Most Greeks ate fish.

C Socrates ate fish.

Students should be able to identify that in the case of the inductive argument, it is possible that the premises be true, but the conclusion false. (In the above example, it could be that Socrates' mother had terrible vomiting from fish and so always kept Socrates away from it, thus he was one of a minority of Greeks who never ate fish.) Since all scientific claims are like this, they are never 100% certain. For example, the scientific claim that 'all metals expand when heated' is based on lots of instances of heating metals and them always expanding upon heating. The more evidence you have, the more probable the conclusion. Hence, it is a pretty safe belief to hold that 'all metals expand when heated'. It is, however, lacking the absolute certainty of a valid deductive argument or a mathematical proof.

Deductive arguments: if valid and if the premises are true, the conclusion is 100% guaranteed to be true. Valid deductive arguments constitute **proofs**.

In making the point that these theories are *theory*, it is worth making clear to students that there has been some debate *even within the scientific community* about the truth of these theories. The Big Bang theory was very slow to be accepted against rival theories such as the Steady State theory. (In fact, the Roman Catholic Church joined in the debate by *supporting* the Big Bang theory (Singh, 2004).) The fact that there is *disagreement* over religious claims is what leads many students to designate such claims as 'mere opinion', whereas scientific claims tend to be viewed by students as unquestionable and the subject of consensus (Easton, 2019). It is therefore important to emphasise the *controversial* nature of these scientific theories, so that students recognise that this is not just a feature of religious and moral claims.

Inductive arguments: unlike deductive arguments, the conclusion will never by 100% proven; it will only ever be *probable*. Scientific arguments are inductive. The more evidence there is, the more likely the conclusion is true.

To conclude the lesson, students are asked to reflect on what our purpose is, preparing them for the following lesson. Possible answers might include:

- Our purpose is to reproduce.
- There is no purpose.
- We can create our own purpose.

You may want to stretch more able students by asking them about the implications of these answers for ethics (see Chapter 6). For example, you could spark some controversial debate by asking: 'If the only purpose is to survive and reproduce, should the NHS be spending money on helping people with genetic diseases?'

Lesson 4 introduces students to the notion of myth by looking at a variety of creation myths. This is then put to use in Lessons 5 and 6, where attention is devoted to the Genesis creation accounts and discussion of how best to interpret these. The cosmological and teleological arguments for the existence of God are examined in Lessons 7 and 8, with particular focus on 1) putting to use the tools of philosophical analysis learnt in Lesson 1, and 2) reflecting on the extent to which science disproves these arguments. In Lesson 9, students are given space to reflect on the ultimate question 'Why are we here?' and are encouraged to draw together their thoughts from across the topic to conclude on what they believe to be the most truthful response. Students are then assessed in Lesson 10 and there is the opportunity for feedback and self-assessment in Lesson 11.

Key activities:

- Preliminary discussion of relevant ultimate questions
- Worked examples of philosophical arguments
- Construction of own valid arguments

Resources:

- 'How did we get here?' discussion cards
- Analysing arguments worksheet
- PowerPoint

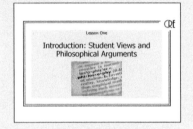

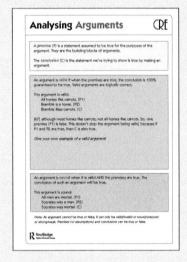

Lesson 1: introduction: student views and philosophical arguments

Learning objectives

1. To reflect on existing views on religion and science
2. To begin to understand how philosophical arguments are constructed and analysed

Give out discussion cards and ask students to 'think-pair-share' (TPS) in relation to these ultimate questions.

At this stage, this is about students hearing a variety of views on these questions and understanding the scope and purpose of the upcoming lessons. For the teacher, the discussion provides a valuable opportunity to listen to what views are present within their classroom.

The bulk of the lesson time is devoted to introducing philosophical arguments and the concepts of validity and soundness as tools for evaluating arguments. This is conceptually difficult material, and so needs modelling by the teacher through a variety of examples. Work through the examples on the PowerPoint (PWP) and take the opportunities indicated in the PWP for students to fill in their sheets whilst you check their understanding.

Note that students have not been asked on the handout to give an example of a sound argument. This is because it is very hard to do so. A useful extension exercise on the PWP is to ask students to try this, and to check whether the premises are in fact all true. If you are lucky, some students might point out that the examples that are both valid and sound don't say very much – they are uninformative. This leads nicely into the need for inductive arguments (much more common and much more useful!) which will be covered in future lessons.

Finally, as a plenary, students are asked to think back to the start of the lesson and see if they can think of an argument that was advanced (by themselves or others) and set this out in premises towards a conclusion.

Lesson 2: fact vs. opinion

Learning objectives

1. To critically reflect on the distinction between fact and opinion
2. To understand the influential philosophical stance of logical positivism and be able to critically evaluate this

---

The starter is a card sort, best done in groups of about 3 students. There are already some pre-arranged statements on handouts labelled 'Side A' and 'Side B'. As explained in the rationale above, Side A contains statements which are commonly viewed as 'opinion' and Side B contains statements that are usually viewed as 'fact'. The card sort itself includes statements that are religious, moral and scientific in nature. Students should arrange the cards as to whether they best fit on Side A or Side B. It is an open task; they can divide the cards in many different ways, e.g. by certainty, by whether there is agreement, etc. However, in our experience, most groups will end up dividing the cards by what they view as 'facts' and what they view as 'opinions'.

Having divided up the statements, students are asked to discuss with their group what they think the difference is between Side A and Side B. It is likely that the distinction between 'facts' and 'opinions' will be brought up, and often these will be distinguished by the former having empirical evidence, with the latter being more controversial. This is then put up for discussion in small groups, using the questions on the PWP.

A version of the Verification Principle is likely to have been voiced during this discussion, but a simplified version of the logical positivist belief is now introduced more formally by the teacher, and explained via examples (see PWP). Students are invited in small groups to consider whether they agree with this principle (see PWP). Critically evaluating an influential philosophical view is conceptually very hard, so you need to think carefully about your student pairings or groupings here. If you are short on time, you may want to skip straight to having some picture clues displayed on the board (see PWP). Following a whole-class discussion, introduce some of the classic objections that have not been considered by the class (see rationale above for guidance).

Key activities:

- Card sort
- TPS surrounding Verification Principle
- Human continuum plenary

Resources:

- Fact vs. opinion card sort
- PowerPoint

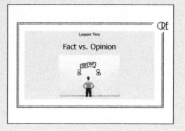

The plenary requires at least five, but ideally ten, minutes. A variety of statements are displayed one at a time, most of which are religious in nature (e.g. 'God created the Big Bang'). Students are required to either stand by 'true', 'false' or 'neither true nor false'. Students can question each other about where they are standing to help bring further understanding and critical evaluation. This gives the teacher a chance to assess whether students have understood the day's lesson content and whether any have changed their views in response to the material. It also provides a useful link with future lessons. For example, one of the statements is 'evolutionary theory has good scientific evidence for it', providing a direct link to next lesson on evolutionary theory.

Lesson 3: scientific explanations

Students are asked to 'think-pair-share' in answer to the questions 'What is the Big Bang?' and 'What is evolution?' The feedback from this will be useful for giving you an idea of where students are at in their understanding of these theories, as well as airing common misunderstandings (e.g. 'apes turned into a humans') so that these can be corrected.

Give students a clear but brief introduction to both theories. There are some excellent, short, introductory videos on YouTube (e.g. as part of the Stated Clearly series). A good kinaesthetic exercise to help students understand the idea of an expanding universe (important as key supporting evidence for Big Bang theory) is for students to draw marks on a balloon, approximate the distance between these, and then blow up the balloon. The distance between the marks will increase, just as the distance between galaxies is increasing. Make sure that there is discussion of what *evidence* there is in support of the theories, even if briefly, as we want the students to see that (just like religious claims), scientific claims must be accompanied by justification. You can check student understanding of both theories via structured pairs questioning. For example, one member of the pair could be asked to explain to their partner how evolution by natural selection explains why giraffes have long necks, and the other could explain why 'Big Bang' is a bad name for the theory.

Following this, you should introduce inductive and deductive arguments using the PWP and handout. The key point that students must recognise is that with inductive arguments (and thus the scientific method) it is possible for the premises to be true but the conclusion to be false. Explain that all scientific claims are like this – never 100% certain. Students are then introduced to simplified definitions of 'hypothesis', 'theory' and 'proof' (see handout). Ask students to identify which category 'evolution by natural selection' and 'Big Bang' come under. Students should

ACTIVITIES

Key activities:

- TPS on Big Bang / evolution
- Videos on Big Bang and evolution
- Discussion of inductive / deductive / theory / proof

Resources:

- PowerPoint including videos
- Balloon (optional)
- Inductive and deductive arguments worksheet

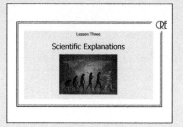

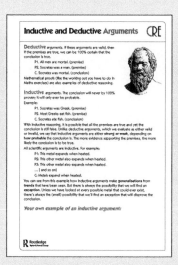

identify these as *theories* as opposed to proofs and, in turn, understand that whilst evidence in support of these ideas is strong, they are still contested.

Allow ten minutes for a plenary discussion that links the content of today's lesson with next lesson. Display on the board the question 'What do the Big Bang theory and evolutionary theory suggest that our purpose is?' and 'think-pair-share'. See the rationale above for suggested extension questions.

Lesson 4: Myth

ACTIVITIES

Learning objectives

1. To understand the concept of myth
2. To compare creation myths and consider their purpose

Computer room preferable

Many students, both atheist and theist, automatically take a literal approach to Bible stories. For example, a common first response to Genesis 1 might be 'But snakes don't talk!' This lesson invites students to consider that stories can be read in a different manner, as myth. Through looking at a variety of creation stories, the role of storytelling as providing answers to ultimate questions is brought out.

The lesson starts with a guided visualisation. Ask your students to close their eyes and imagine the following: 'You are living 10,000 years ago. You head down to the water-side to do some washing when suddenly you see this . . .' At this point, if you have the equipment, ask students to open their eyes and watch a video of a volcano erupting. (The one on the PWP is good as it fits with the story of watching from afar by the river, and there is no distracting sound). If lacking the technology, describe the loud and fiery explosion as vividly as you can.

After watching the clip, ask students to think-pair-share the questions on the PWP and then proceed to a whole-class discussion of their ideas. Perhaps one student might suggest as a possible explanation that there is a divine cause (e.g. the Gods are angry). If not, you can ask some additional prompting questions. The purpose of the exercise is to introduce students to the idea that stories might be told that help explain natural phenomena, which may not be literally true. However, there may be some deep metaphysical truths that lie behind the stories (e.g. that the Gods are involved with the physical world, or that God has power over nature).

The main part of the lesson requires individual work on the computer. Using the Big Myth website (see PWP), students choose four different myths to learn about. (If you cannot access computers, choose four myths and print the PDF scripts, available on the website either via the main page or in the teacher section.) Students then work through the handout. Towards the end of the lesson, take feedback on some of these questions (see PWP). In discussion, try

Key activities:

- Guided visualisation – volcano
- Comparison exercise using the Big Myth website – www.bigmyth.com

Resources:

- Computer room (or alternatively, scripts of myths)
- Big Myth website
- The Big Myth worksheet
- PowerPoint including video

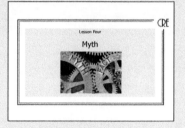

to bring out the idea that myths might provide answers to difficult 'why' questions such as 'why are we here?'

As a plenary, ask the students to work in pairs answering these two questions: 'What is a myth? What is the purpose of a myth?' Take feedback.

You could ask students to make up their own creation myth as a homework.

Lesson 5: Genesis: the Biblical accounts

Learning objectives

1. To understand the nature and differences of the creation stories in Genesis 1 and 2
2. To begin to reflect on one's own interpretation of Genesis

Key activities:

- Watching 'Noah' clip
- Class reading of Genesis 1
- Questions comparing Genesis 1 and Genesis 2
- Personal reflection

Resources:

- Bibles
- Genesis comparison worksheet
- PowerPoint including video

Two lessons are devoted to Genesis and its interpretation. One reason for this is that it raises important questions about how to respond to internal conflict (contradictions within the Bible) and external conflict (contradictions with science).

As a starter, show students the clip from the film *Noah*, which recaps the creation story as told in Genesis 1. (Start at 0.47; stop at 2.50 where it starts to merge the story with Genesis 2.) Ask your students to listen out for what happens on each day of creation. (If you don't have the equipment to do this, just move onto the next activity, which also makes for a good starter.)

Next, read aloud Genesis 1, asking students to clap their hands every time they hear something that is difficult to accept in light of modern scientific knowledge. (For example, a student might clap when they hear that the sun was created after the light, or when the moon is described as a separate 'light' to the sun.) Ask students to explain their clap, and discuss this as you go along.

Individually, students then read the different account in Genesis 2 and write down answers to the questions on the handout. (These are big questions, and so you should expect this written exercise and the subsequent discussion to take up the bulk of the lesson.) This is followed by a whole-class discussion of the questions from the handout. Next, ask students to reflect on how we should deal with the fact that the Bible seems to be giving an account that conflicts with both itself and with science (see questions on PWP). In response, some students may suggest that these problems indicate that the Bible should not be interpreted literally, which will lead nicely into next lesson, as well as linking with the previous lesson on myth.

Finish with students having a few minutes quiet reflection time on how they individually interpret Genesis (see PWP questions). For some students, the lesson may have raised fundamental questions about their own faith in the Bible, and so it is important to allow time for reflection on what this means to them. Students can share in pairs and with the class but this should be voluntary.

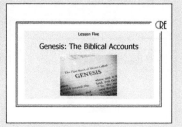

ACTIVITIES

Key activities:

- Teacher-led explanation of different interpretations of the Bible
- Evaluation of the arguments in the 3 videos and of different interpretations of Genesis
- Reflection on purpose

Resources:

- Theological interpretations worksheet
- PowerPoint including videos

Lesson 6: Genesis: Christian theological responses

Learning objectives

1. To understand different theological positions regarding the Biblical creation stories and the reasons for these positions
2. To critically analyse the creation stories in Genesis in light of theological interpretations – which position is most appropriate?

This lesson begins with the question 'Do all Christians believe in the Bible?' You should get a mixture of answers, since of course it is not a straightforward question – all Christians believe in the Bible, but this does not mean that every Christian accepts every word literally. Use the class feedback on this starter question to introduce a teacher-led explanation of different interpretations of the Bible within Christianity (see PWP and handout). Students are then invited to apply this new knowledge of fundamentalist, conservative and liberal interpretations to Genesis. Students can then turn over their handout, which provides a more detailed explanation of what these different groups might think.

The second part of the lesson is devoted to discussing three BBC Class Clips videos. These videos include an entertaining rap and cartoon, followed by a representative of each opinion being interviewed about their view: Taylor on creationism (6.13 min), McGrath on theistic evolution (7 min) and Dawkins on atheistic evolution (6.32 min). To consolidate understanding, ask your students to identify which of the Christian views introduced above are represented. (Check your students understand the missing view, which is the liberal view that the Genesis account should be treated as a myth.) These videos provide a rich resource for practising evaluating arguments. If you have time, you can take a particular section of the interviews and ask students to write them up into premises and conclusions and then evaluate these arguments.

The discussion ends by asking students which of the views of Genesis they found most plausible and why. Here students are being encouraged to exercise judgemental rationality. This part of the lesson should not be rushed. Allow time for personal reflection before the opportunity to share views in pairs or groups.

The lesson concludes with a brief discussion about purpose: what do these different views say about human purpose, and which of these views do you think is most satisfactory?

Lesson 7: the cosmological argument

ACTIVITIES

Learning objectives

1. To understand a simple form of the cosmological argument for the existence of God
2. To critically reflect on its success
3. To consider the argument that God created the Big Bang

Key activities:

- Exercise identifying cause and effect
- Watching dominoes and Faraday videos
- Pairs work evaluating the argument
- Human continuum

As a starter, ask students to fill in the blanks to check their understanding of 'cause' and 'effect'. This is a simple, accessible activity (with multiple possible answers) to get students going on a lesson that will involve some difficult conceptual thinking.

Show students the video of a domino chain and invite students to discuss in pairs: Can the dominoes start on their own? How do they start moving? Can you think of anything that has *no cause* for its existence? Explore the analogy with God and the world: Who is the boy? (God). What are the dominoes? (Tricky, but probably *events* happening in our world.)

Introduce the cosmological argument, reminding students that this is an *argument* and therefore will be set up as *premises* towards a *conclusion*. To check understanding of the argument, ask students to complete the 'fill in the gaps' sheet.

The bulk of the lesson is devoted to evaluating the argument. Using prompts on the PWP, students are asked to raise objections and think of possible replies to these objections. For example, one prompt asks students to identify a premise that they find plausible (e.g. 'everything that exists has a cause'). Another prompt asks whether the argument is valid and/or sound.

A central point for discussion given the scheme of work's focus on science and religion is on whether the Big Bang disproves the cosmological argument. One important variation of a response to this is demonstrated with a video clip (Faraday video). The clip is of a scientist explaining why he sees science as explaining *mechanism* (the way something works) but leaving open whether there is *agency* involved (whether someone made it). There are some further views on the PWP to prompt further critical exploration, which you can dip into if time allows.

As a plenary, students are asked to form a human continuum based on what (at this stage) they think is the most plausible answer to the question 'what caused the universe?'

You may wish to set the preparatory homework for next lesson.

Resources:

- The cosmological argument worksheet
- PowerPoint including videos

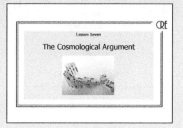

Lesson 8: the teleological argument

Key activities:

- 'Show and tell' with natural objects (or modelling clay)
- Discussion evaluating argument
- Video: Secular Believers
- Sorting exercise
- Stand up / sit down plenary

Resources:

- PowerPoint including video
- Intelligent design card sort

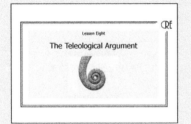

Learning objectives

1. To understand a simple form of the teleological argument (Paley)
2. To critically reflect on its success
3. To consider other forms of the teleological argument
4. To consider the argument that God designed the world through evolution

Use the starter to introduce what is meant by *design* and *purpose*. Set your students as a homework to bring in a natural object (e.g. a leaf, a pine cone) and ask them to explain how its features help it to fulfil its purpose. Alternatively, show the images on the PowerPoint (e.g. knife, chair, giraffe's long neck) asking students to identify the purpose. An alternative, kinaesthetic option as a 'way in' to design is to give out modelling clay and ask your students to design an object or living thing which has features that perform a specific function (e.g. a toothbrush would have bristles to allow it to clean all around one's teeth).

Introduce Paley's design argument using his example of the watch. Students are asked to evaluate this and one of the criticisms will almost certainly be that evolution disproves the argument. According to this criticism, the argument fails when it says that like the watch, the eye is designed. Watch the video clip with Dawkins objecting to Paley's argument and discuss using the questions on the PWP. Depending on your students and the time available, you could introduce them to subtleties within the debate such as the argument (in support of a designer God) from irreducible complexity, and how atheists such as Dawkins respond to this (see PWP slides).

Give out the worksheet which presents various facts about the universe. Students either tick or cross the boxes (or divide them into 2 piles, as a card sort) based on whether or not they support the idea of a designer God. (These are debatable and so as a pairs or group activity this should take at least 10 minutes.) Some of these facts illustrate the very specific conditions needed to create the universe. Use the feedback to introduce a second version of the teleological argument, based on the universe being 'fine-tuned' for life to exist. Evaluate this using the questions on the PWP as prompts.

As a plenary, students are asked to stand up / sit down based on their view on various controversial statements, e.g. 'evolutionary theory destroys belief in God', 'humans are designed'.

Lesson 9: science vs. religion?

Learning objectives

1. To bring together what has been learnt in order to begin critically answering the question of 'How did we get here?'

Although this lesson does function as a recap on the scheme of work's content, don't be tempted to drop this lesson if you are running behind. It is here that students are given space to draw together the strands of thought from across the scheme of work and put them together to develop what they think is the answer to the ultimate question 'How did we get here?'. Although students have been making critical judgements in prior lessons, here students are given time and space to reflect, to enable them to best exercise their judgemental rationality and really wrangle with the philosophical and theological issues that have arisen.

Begin the lesson with a revision exercise from the scheme of work. In the PWP, we suggest words for playing 'Just a minute'. Here students have to talk without hesitation, deviation or repetition on a key word to do with the topic (e.g. creation, science, design, purpose). (This is really hard, so if doing this with one person in front of the class rather than in pairs, we recommend picking confident students! Or, try reducing from a minute to 30 seconds.)

Organise your students into groups in a way that will enable them to get the most out of the activity. Give out the handouts and introduce 'thinking hats' to your students. (Note that it works equally well to replace the group work with an individual mind-mapping task and then have longer for whole-class feedback.) Each group is to work with *all* the hats in relation to the question. They should record their work by making a detailed mind map on their handout. (All students need this filled in so that they have it as a resource for their assessment.)

Feedback as a class in the last quarter of the lesson. Although each group will have worked with all hats, different groups can be responsible for feeding back on each hat. Ideally, you will hear from more than one group for each hat, to get suitable variation. You can make the feedback into a more active activity by arranging chairs according to different colours and students choosing a chair to sit in.

Key activities:

- Recapping learning through *Just a Minute*
- Thinking hats group work

Resources:

- 'How did we get here?' Thinking hats handout
- 'How did we get here?' worksheet
- PowerPoint

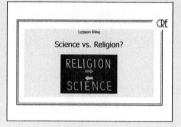

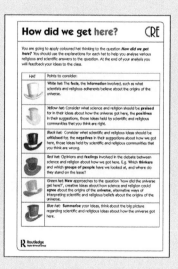

As a plenary, students are to write down a couple of sentences explaining what they plan their conclusion to be in their written assessment. Alternatively, you can ask your students to create an image that expresses and demonstrates their personal beliefs about how the world came to exist. (This also works as homework or as a replacement to the written assessment (see next lesson).)

Lessons 10–11: assessment and feedback

Learning objectives

1. To demonstrate your learning on the topic
2. To receive feedback on your progress
3. To self-assess your response to the topic

The assessment question 'how did we get here?' was chosen as an open question that enables students to draw on content from across the scheme of work. For example, a very able student can show knowledge of the scientific theories that purport to explain the world, but can criticise these by explaining how scientific evidence can only ever be inductive and therefore never amounts to certain proof.

As elsewhere in our schemes of work, it should be noted that although we have chosen an essay as the assessment, other forms of assessment are possible. You might, for example, choose to set the creative drawing task that formed a possible plenary for the previous lesson. If this is the formal assessment, then you would need to include oral or written explanation of the picture in order to obtain an informed view of student progress.

How you decide to structure this assessment will depend on your school setting. Here we envisage allowing the students a lesson to write out the assessment, and a lesson for feedback. (These do not need to be consecutive; we realise that you may not have completed your marking in time!)

As with Lesson 9, resist the temptation to think of the feedback lesson as 'buffer time' that you can use to catch up on subject content from earlier lessons. Having time to reflect on learning and performance on written work is important, especially given the emphasis placed on written assessment in our examinations system. Feedback and reflection time takes on an added layer of importance in CRE assessment, which should be a continuing conversation about how best to approach the ultimate question. Students also need lesson time to reflect on how well they think they have achieved the virtue of responsibility. They should fill in a comment and mark on the feedback sheet. In this topic, it may not be immediately obvious to students what this would involve, so you may need to prompt your students to think of the implications of their viewpoint for human purpose, and what that might mean for ethics (see PWP for suggested questions).

ACTIVITIES

Key activities:

- Constructing an essay, demonstrating virtues in relation to the topic of science and religion
- Completing self-assessment

Resources:

- 'How did we get here?' assessment guidance for students
- 'How did we get here?' mark sheet
- PowerPoint

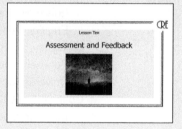

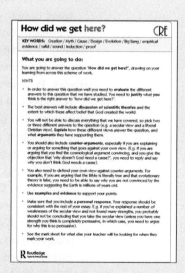

Notes

1 Although ethics is a branch of philosophy, we have chosen to separate ethics and philosophy of religion. See Chapter 6 for discussion of the distinctive issues presented by the teaching of ethics.
2 SAPERE (The Society for the Advancement of Philosophical Enquiry and Reflection in Education) is the major trainer and promoter of P4C. See SAPERE (2017) for information about the aims and methods of P4C.
3 For example, The Philosophy Foundation provides training for philosophy graduates, who then run sessions in disadvantaged schools (see Philosophy Foundation, 2017).
4 For example, P4C formed part of the Northumberland Raising Aspirations in Society Project (NRAIS). See SAPERE, 2016, p.4.
5 There is one notable exception: Students usually feel so certain of the truth of 'White and black people are of equal value', that they make an exception here and place on Side B.

References

Adams, R. (2015). Philosophical discussions boost pupils' maths and literacy progress, study finds. *Guardian*. 10/07/15. Available online at: https://www.theguardian.com/education/2015/jul/10/philosophy-for-children-pupils-maths-literacy (accessed 22/08/16).

Billingsley, B., Taber, K. S., Riga, F., and Newdick, H. (2013). Secondary School Students' Epistemic Insight into the Relationships Between Science and Religion—A Preliminary Enquiry. *Research in Science Education* 43, no.4, 1715–1732.

Billingsley, B., Brock, R., Taber, K. S., and Riga, F. (2016). How Students View the Boundaries Between Their Science and Religious Education Concerning the Origins of Life and the Universe. *Science Education* 100, no.3, 459–482.

Cooling, T. (2012). Faith, Religious Education and Whole School Issues. In *Debates in Religious Education*, ed. L. Philip Barnes, 88-97. Oxon: Routledge.

Easton, C. (2019). Truth in science and 'truth' in religion: An enquiry into student views on different types of truth-claim. In *Science and Religion in Education*, ed. B. Billingsley, K. Chappell & M. Reiss, London: Springer.

Easton, C. and Billingsley, B. (forthcoming). Conflict and confusion: An interview study of primary school children's perceptions of the relationship between science and religion.

Hanley, P., Bennett, J. and Ratcliffe, M. (2014). The Inter-relationship of Science and Religion: A typology of engagement. *International Journal of Science Education* 36, no.7, 1210–1229.

Humanists UK. (2014). Ofqual and exam boards collude with 'faith' schools to censor questions on evolution. Available online at: https://humanism.org.uk/2014/03/02/ofqual-exam-boards-collude-faith-schools-censor-questions-evolution/ (accessed 27/08/15).

Mill, J. S. (2006). *On Liberty*. London: Penguin.

Philosophy for Children (2015). Evaluation report and Executive summary. Available online at: https://educationendowmentfoundation.org.uk/uploads/pdf/Philosophy_for_Children.pdf (accessed 27/08/15).

Philosophy Foundation (2017). The Philosophy Foundation. Available online at: https://www.philosophy-foundation.org/ (accessed 18/04/17).

SAPERE (2017). Philosophy for Children. Available online at: http://www.sapere.org.uk/ (accessed 18/04/17).

SAPERE (2016). Research Highlights. Available online at: http://www.sapere.org.uk/Portals/0/SAPERE%20Research%20Brochure.pdf (accessed 22/06/16).

Singh, S. (2004). *Big Bang Theory*. London: Harper Perennial.

Warburton, N. (2001). *Freedom: An Introduction with Readings*. London: Routledge.

Wright, A. (2013). *Christianity and Critical Realism*. Oxon: Routledge.

Critical Religious Education and ethics

An exemplar scheme of work for introducing moral decision making (Year 9)

As with philosophy, 'ethics' is an area of academia which has been assumed under the religious education (RE) umbrella for many years and which is taught by the vast majority of RE departments across the country. However, our own experiences as teachers have led us to believe that it is often taught in a manner which is inappropriate given its rich academic history. This, we believe, is largely due to positivistic and postmodern philosophies which have influenced education for decades and which partially explain why RE is selected as the appropriate setting for ethical discussion.

As discussed in Chapter 5, the Verification Principle, one of the key assertions of the philosophy of **logical positivism**, suggests that statements are only meaningful if they are true by definition, (e.g. 'a bachelor is an unmarried man') or if they can be empirically verified (e.g. 'water boils at 100°C'). According to this principle, statements which do not fall under one of these categories cannot be ascribed as 'true or false' – they are meaningless. Most logical positivists would thus consider all theological and ethical statements to be meaningless. The influence of logical positivism at least partially explains why theology and ethics are often categorised as 'subjective'[1] areas of study in which opinion, as opposed to fact, is investigated. In contrast, science and maths are seen as objective and factual and are thus placed at the top of the knowledge hierarchy. Thus, logical positivism is arguably one of the leading causes for the devaluing of theological and ethical study in the UK education system. This philosophical stance is largely outdated but continues to influence much educational policy and practice today.

With regards to ethics in particular, one of the leading proponents of logical positivism in Britain – A. J. Ayer (1936) – famously claimed that all moral statements are simply emotive. When we say something is right or wrong, we are actually just saying 'I approve of this' (like saying 'Hurrah!') or 'I don't approve of this' (like saying 'Booooo!'). We are not making a meaningful statement about the way the world actually is but are simply stating a personal feeling or preference. This meta-ethical theory is known as **emotivism** (nicknamed the boo-hurrah theory (Bunnin and Yu, 2004)). It has given further impetus for ethics to be viewed as, and in turn studied as, subjective.

Similarly, **postmodernism** – here defined as the philosophical assertion that we construct truth ourselves and that we can have no 'true' knowledge

Meta-ethics: a branch of philosophy which questions the nature of morality itself, e.g. by asking 'Is there such a thing as "right" and "wrong"?'

of anything outside of ourselves – has also influenced educational theory and policy for many years. Whilst this philosophy actually arose as a rebuttal of positivism, its effects on RE and ethical study have been similar. As there is no 'truth' outside of ourselves, we are only discussing our own perceptions and nothing 'objective'. This philosophy has also influenced much RE pedagogy so that questions of truth are either avoided in the RE classroom or discussed in a manner which lacks consistency (see Wright, 2004).

Thus, in many RE classrooms, ethics, alongside much other RE content, is implicitly presented as subjective, at least prior to KS5. In addition, whilst students may be introduced to differing opinions on ethical issues at KS3 and KS4, there is rarely proper consideration of the historical or meta-ethical origins of ethical standpoints (especially those outside of a religious tradition), the consistency between ethical stances taken by the same group or individual, or, ultimately, of the 'truth' with regards to these differing perspectives. Hence, historically a GCSE evaluative answer would be considered good even if it simply explained two different perspectives and then the student's own perspective, without there being any real critical engagement in the answer (see Chapter 7 for a more critical approach to GCSE).

Our vision for the teaching of ethics throughout secondary education is different. We are not, of course, saying that ethical statements are definitely objective, nor are we saying that either positivism or postmodernism are definitely wrong. We would not claim these things within a CRE framework due to the premise of epistemic relativity which deems all conclusions limited and contingent. CRE is necessarily inclusive of all standpoints. What we are saying is that to teach ethics with an implicit background assumption of either positivism or postmodernism is confessional of these particular philosophies and thus does a disservice to thousands of years of ethical study which has offered significant alternatives. Whether ethical judgements are objective or subjective, right or wrong, is up for debate within the critical realist community and thus needs to be up for debate in the CRE classroom. This begins to happen at A Level in many schools, where students are introduced to ethical theories and asked to evaluate them, but we suggest that any meaningful ethical study needs to begin this process much earlier in a student's school career. Recent research suggests that students are already influenced by the prevalence of positivist and postmodern thinking with regards to ethical statements, regarding them as subjective and relative (Davis, 2014, p.38). It is a concern to us that, for the majority of students who do not take RE at A Level, this may never be challenged. Thus, rather than having students discuss and debate ethical issues at KS3 and KS4 without any grounding in ethical theory, we suggest that it is best to introduce differing ethical theories *before* teaching about ethical issues.

When ethics is taught properly, as a branch of philosophical study, it is entirely appropriate to ask whether the ethical positions which students encounter are true or false. This is especially important in CRE given that one of the intended outcomes of the approach is 'truthful living'. By this we mean that consistency is demonstrated between the judgements you come to about reality and the way in which you live. If, for example, a student comes to the conclusion that eating meat is wrong as a result of their critical discussion surrounding it, one would hope that they would cease to eat meat. This cannot be enforced, of course, and it must be acknowledged that achieving ethical consistency in our own lives is very difficult (see, for example, Wolff, 2011, p.32). However, within CRE this consistency is certainly an ideal and something which we should aspire towards, as is demonstrated in our framework for assessment (see Chapter 9).

In most contexts the teaching of stand-alone ethics schemes of work begins at Year 9. Therefore we have developed an introductory scheme of work for ethics from a CRE standpoint, aimed at Year 9 students. This, we suggest, should be taught prior to other schemes of work which fall into the ethics bracket. If this is not possible, at the very least it is necessary to present ethics as a branch of philosophical study in which ethical standpoints are grounded in ethical theories. Students should be encouraged to scrutinise the ethical theories being drawn on alongside the ethical issues being considered. If ethical issues are studied without any reference to ethical theory, any judgement about the truth or falsity of moral assertions will lack critical rigour.

Developing the scheme of work

Ethical study is vast and ethical theories numerous, thus our first task in developing this scheme of work was to consider which ethical theories to prioritise. Our immediate response was that, as this scheme of work would be taught in a RE setting, it was necessary to ensure that the scheme of work included a reasonable exploration of religious approaches to moral decision making. However, given that CRE also starts with the views of the students, and that religious affiliation is rapidly declining amongst young people in the UK (Lee, 2011), it was clear that secular approaches to moral decision making also needed to be granted exposure. In CRE the views of the atheist and the agnostic are as important as those of the theist. However, the atheist and the agnostic also have to consider the internal consistency of their own positions to the same degree as the theist. This doesn't just require the refutation of theistic perspectives by claiming that they are built on something which doesn't exist or isn't true, but also requires reasonable explanation of where their own standpoints come from and a defence of these in light of theistic claims. Thus we decided that it was important that both theistic and non-theistic approaches were given the same amount of coverage in order that both could be evaluated appropriately.

We have chosen to order the scheme of work around the divide of 'theistic' and 'non-theistic' approaches given that 'God' is an obvious variable with regards to authority in ethical systems. In theistic systems 'God' is the lawgiver and various forms of guidance are believed to be mediums through which we understand God's will. However, in non-theistic systems there is no such lawgiver and thus the question of who or what has authority to define what is right or wrong becomes all the more apparent. Thus, dividing the scheme of work in this way also ensures that meta-ethical questions are asked as part of the evaluation of particular ethical systems.

We have chosen to use the terms 'theistic' and 'non-theistic' rather than 'religious' and 'secular' for this scheme of work in order to be as inclusive as possible. The term 'theist' was necessary in order to divide systems which take authority from God from those which do not. However, to separate 'theist' from 'secular' is non-inclusive of Buddhism which is religious but atheistic. Whilst we did not highlight this example for Year 7s in the introductory scheme of work as we felt it would be over-complicated, it seemed necessary at Year 9 given that Buddhism will likely have been studied prior to this. Similarly, we could not create a simple divide between 'theistic' and 'atheistic' as many students identify as 'agnostic'. These students may not have rejected theism intellectually but are likely to live according to atheistic rather than theistic models. Thus, the term 'non-theistic' allows for this without labelling the agnostic as an 'atheist'.

Most theistic ethical systems include guidance from God as communicated through various sources of authority – holy books, holy laws, religious leaders and the conscience. Thus these have all been included in the content of the scheme of work. However, the weighting put on each of these elements often differs amongst adherents within the same religious tradition, causing divides on ethical issues (e.g. divides on clothing within Judaism). It is thus important that students consider the strengths and weaknesses of combining forms of guidance in ethical systems. They should also contemplate the internal consistency of different positions with regards to this guidance. Furthermore, it should be highlighted that religious traditions may also make use of non-religious ethical systems at times. Many Christians, for example, will use a form of **utilitarianism** when making ethical decisions on which there is no clear guidance elsewhere. The consistency of such combinations should thus also be considered. Hence, there are 'reflections on theistic/non-theistic guidance' lessons intended precisely for these purposes.

> **Utilitarianism**: an ethical theory which (broadly speaking) suggests that what is right is what creates 'the greatest good for the greatest number'.

With regards to non-theistic ethical guidance, we have attempted to select theories or systems which we consider to be the most influential in our current context. Given the prevalence of utilitarianism this clearly needed to be included. We have also included Humanism given its prevalence in recent discourse surrounding RE (see Juss, 2016), as well as Buddhism which is non-theistic as discussed above. **Egoism** is an interesting ethical system to include, as in our experience, most students will consider it to be wrong initially, but they begin to identify with it more once they have worked through a number of scenarios. This, in itself, is an interesting discussion point with regards to ethical consistency.

> **Egoism**: an ethical theory which suggests that it is right to act in your own self-interest.

Finally, **cultural relativism** has been included as it is often used to justify our current lack of interference in the political affairs of other nation states. The inclusion of cultural relativism also provides an opportunity to discuss a more general ethical relativism. It is worth noting here that we have incorporated discussion of **human rights** into the lesson on cultural relativism. Human rights are frequently referenced by students when they explore ethical issues. This is unsurprising given that our current legal system accepts these as 'correct' and there is frequent talk of human rights issues in the media. However, there are meta-ethical questions relating to human rights which require discussion. It can be argued that they are pure constructions and do not have sufficient philosophical grounding to be seen as truly objective. Furthermore, there are potential inconsistencies in the way in which human rights are approached. For example, many governments uphold human rights as objective whilst using a form of cultural relativism as a reason not to interfere in the affairs of

Cultural relativism: an ethical theory which suggests that what is right or wrong is dependent on the culture in which you live. There are no 'objective' rules which apply to all cultures.

other nation states, even when human rights are being violated. These sorts of inconsistencies need to be challenged in the CRE classroom.

Developing schemes of work on ethical issues

This scheme of work is 'standalone' in that it is intended as a springboard from which to move into the study of ethical issues. It does not provide the reader with a model on which to build further ethics schemes of work in the same way as the Islam scheme of work does for world religions or as the science and religion scheme of work does for philosophy of religion topics. Thus, below are a couple of pointers for planning schemes of work on ethical issues.

Generally speaking, the same rules should apply to an ethics scheme of work as a philosophy scheme of work.

1) QUESTION. Start by identifying what critical question you want your scheme of work to investigate.
2) CONTENT. Content should be selected primarily on its potential for shedding light on the critical question. Picking the right **variations** is of particular importance.
3) ORDER. The lessons should proceed in a logical order, so that students are adequately prepared for critical discussions that take place later in the scheme of work.

Selecting a question which you are trying to answer is fundamental to the CRE process. It may be controversial to claim that, when studying ethical issues, we *are* trying to find truthful answers with regards to how we should actually behave (if we conclude these answers exist). However, the sorts of ethical issues which are typically discussed in the RE classroom lend themselves perfectly to a CRE approach. Indeed, those who would oppose such a search for truth in ethics may wish to ask themselves the following questions: Why study ethical issues at all if not to acknowledge that there is disagreement surrounding the 'correct' answers? Why would there be disagreement on ethical issues if people didn't believe that there were right and wrong answers? Why study social issues which students may well be faced with if not to prepare them for making decisions in those situations? Our intention is that a CRE approach would equip students to both tolerate and support others and make informed and wise decisions on ethical issues for themselves. This is what truthful living is all about – acknowledging that we live in a real world and that the way we respond to it matters. Thus, carefully thinking about the question(s) that you want students to answer is paramount in the planning of any ethics scheme of work.

Similarly, the content of a scheme of work and the order in which it is presented is just as important in ethics as philosophy (see Chapter 5). The most relevant variations should be selected for study and the most organic rebuttals of these positions should follow them, so as to encourage logical thought. It is also important that students are introduced to the scope of the topic before being exposed to different opinions about it. For example, a scheme of work on abortion should necessarily begin with an introduction to the issue which includes explanations of what an abortion is, what the law says about abortions, etc. Without this, students may fail to understand arguments about viability, etc. which are likely to be raised later on. The more informed the students are on the issues, the more fruitful their learning will be.

The scheme of work below on moral decision making provides students with 'ethical tools', but if for any reason students study ethics before an introduction to philosophy, philosophical tools (as discussed in Chapter 5) should also be introduced. Ethics is, after all, a branch of philosophy. Ethical arguments can be assessed as sound, unsound, valid or invalid and, in fact, this can be a useful way of highlighting the relationship between the ethical theory being applied and the assertions on ethical issues which groups or individuals are making.

Evidence and examples in support of ethical assertions are fundamental.

Moral realism: a meta-ethical view which suggests that morality is objective and independent of us.

Whilst we believe that the postmodern and positivistic agendas have significantly influenced perceptions of ethics in education, it remains the case that when most people make ethical assertions, they try to justify their opinions with evidence, examples or logical reasoning, implying a **moral realism**. Such evidence and examples should be highlighted in ethics schemes of work. Ethical assertions can be supported by 'examples' from current issues, historical cases or personal experience. Similarly, they can be supported with textual evidence – from academic resources or, indeed, from religious texts. **Ethical naturalists** even claim that empirical evidence can be used to support ethical claims. Understanding, identifying and applying examples and evidence is vital to the exercise of judgmental rationality. Thus the study of relevant evidence and examples should be fundamentally incorporated into the scheme of work. (This is also true of all schemes of work, but is particularly important to point out with regards to ethics and world religions due to the specific influence of the philosophies already discussed.). Ethical assertions which engage with concepts of 'right' and 'wrong' but which

Ethical naturalism: a meta-ethical position which (broadly speaking) suggests that we can work out what is 'right' and 'wrong' by looking at the natural/physical world.

are not appropriately supported by examples or evidence require an appeal to **intuitionism** which, whilst plausible, needs to be supported with logical reasoning.

> **Intuitionism**: a meta-ethical theory which suggests that we know whether something is right or wrong by intuition.

Given that the unique subject matter of RE is the transcendent or religions, we would particularly encourage the use of religious texts in the process of ethical study. As with philosophical schemes of work, theological content needs to be covered in sufficient depth for students to be able to analyse it critically. The best schemes of work will therefore include considerable study of religious texts with regards to the ethical issue under scrutiny. For example, for a student to simply identify that some Christians will disagree with abortion as the Bible says 'Do not kill' whereas other Christians will think it is okay as the Bible also says 'Do not judge', is a gross oversimplification and ignores the complexity of interlinked passages and systematic Biblical study. Clearly a balance is needed, as Year 9 students (for example) are not expected to be seasoned theologians, but a lack of systematic study will lead to uninformed and uncritical judgements which make the learning fruitless. To argue intelligently why one view may be more truthful than another requires a deep engagement with authoritative sources and not a tokenistic gesture towards them. As with world religions, a deep understanding of certain religious views in relation to ethical issues is always preferable to a shallow, descriptive understanding of a wider range of views.

The inclusion of current issues from the news etc. should similarly be encouraged. Advocates of CRE claim that we live in a real world and deal with real issues. This is never more apparent than when looking at situations in the world around us. Thus the more practical application of ethics the students can be exposed to and the more they can relate their learning to events in the world, the more meaningful, relevant and ultimately real the learning will be.

Finally, as discussed above, it must be emphasised that CRE does not exclude the possibility of students positing and upholding a postmodern or positivist viewpoint and this should not be discouraged. What is important is that students understand that if they suggest that, for example, all ethical musings are subjective (postmodernism) or meaningless (positivism), they need to acknowledge that this therefore applies to any of their own ethical assertions too and living this out with integrity provides its own challenges.

An overview of the scheme of work

Sequence	Lesson title	Learning objectives
1	How do we make moral decisions?	To understand what is meant by 'morals' and 'ethics' To understand that there are different approaches to making moral decisions To begin to reflect on how you make moral decisions and how consistent this is
2	God as lawgiver?	To identify different theistic approaches to ethics To understand that in theistic systems God provides guidance for what is 'right' and 'wrong' To understand what is meant by autonomy and how this can be seen to be in conflict with God as lawgiver To reflect on where morality could come from without God as lawgiver
3	Holy laws	To understand the concept of holy laws To identify differing types of holy law To begin to evaluate 'holy laws' as a source of moral guidance
4	Holy books	To identify various holy books To understand different theistic approaches to holy books To begin to evaluate the strengths and weaknesses of holy books as a source of moral guidance
5	Religious leaders	To identify various religious leaders To understand how these people influence others To evaluate the strengths and weaknesses of religious leaders as a source of ethical guidance
6	The conscience	To identify the conscience as a form of ethical guidance for theists and secular believers To evaluate the conscience as a form of ethical guidance in both theistic and secular settings
7	Reflections on theistic guidance	To understand the relationship between different forms of theistic guidance To begin to prioritise them

8	Buddhist ethics	To identify various non-theistic ethical approaches
		To understand some Buddhist ethical principles
		To compare Buddhist ethics to theistic ethics
		To begin to evaluate Buddhist ethics
9	Humanism	To understand the concept of 'Humanism'
		To understand how humanists make moral decisions
		To begin to evaluate humanist ethics
10	Utilitarianism	To understand a simple form of utilitarianism
		To evaluate utilitarianism
11	Egoism	To understand egoism as an approach to moral decision making
		To evaluate egoism
		To reflect on our motivations to be 'good'
12	Cultural relativism	To understand cultural relativism
		To consider the relationship between human rights and cultural relativism
		To begin to evaluate cultural relativism
13	Reflections on non-theistic guidance	To consolidate learning on non-theistic guidance
		To discern between/order different forms of non-theistic guidance
		To begin to reflect on what the most truthful approach to ethics is overall
14	Ethical consistency	To identify moral issues surrounding sexual relationships
		To consider how useful each approach is when making decisions about sexual relationships and other issues
		To reflect on consistency in moral decision making
15 and 16	Assessment and feedback	To demonstrate your learning on the topic
		To receive feedback on your progress
		To self-assess your response to the topic

Lesson 1: how do we make moral decisions?

Key activities:

- TPS Hardest decision
- Definitions
- Group activity – who should get the liver?
- Moral dilemmas

Resources:

- Making moral decision cards
- Moral dilemmas worksheet
- Moral decision making handout
- PowerPoint

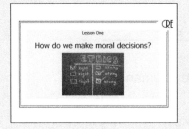

Learning objectives

1. To understand what is meant by 'morals' and 'ethics'
2. To understand that there are different approaches to making moral decisions
3. To begin to reflect on how you make moral decisions and how consistent this is

The aim of Lesson 1 is to introduce students to the study of ethics and to reflect on the process of moral decision making. The lesson begins with a think-pair-share activity – 'What is the hardest decision you've ever had to make?' Ideas can be fed back to the class. The teacher uses these ideas to lead into introducing the key words 'ethics' and 'morals'.

The main activity for the lesson is a group activity in which students pretend that they are doctors with four patients, each of whom is in need of a liver transplant. The doctors have only one donated liver and thus have to decide who it should be given to. In order to make these decisions students are given snippets of information about each of the patients which build up as the lesson progresses. There are three layers of information and after each is given out students should discuss in their groups who they liver should go to and should then write down a justification of their own individual decision before the next set of information is revealed. The second and third time round students could also write down why they have/haven't changed their minds. At the end of the activity the teacher can lead a whole-class discussion on whom the liver should be given to and whether students' answers changed over time.

The point of the main activity is for students to reflect on the process of moral decision making and they should be encouraged to consider how they personally came to the conclusions they did – what were the key factors for them? To build on this students should complete the sheet 'moral dilemmas' for homework, considering what they would do in a set of scenarios and which ethical theory this most closely mirrors in each case. In preparation for that, as a plenary, the teacher can introduce the differing ethical theories to be studied (using the moral decision making handout) and ask students to identify which they were most closely akin to during their moral decision making in the main activity.

Lesson 2: God as lawgiver?

The aim of Lesson 2 is to introduce God as the author of morality in theistic ethical systems and to consider meta-ethical questions relating to this. The lesson begins by drawing out what students already know about God as lawgiver. Students should have two minutes to mind-map/list ways which religious people believe they get guidance from God. This should be fed back and the result will hopefully resemble the outline of the first half of the scheme of work on theistic guidance. The teacher should use this to introduce the first half of the scheme of work. Either before or after the starter, the teacher should also take feedback on the 'moral dilemmas' homework and draw out from the students how consistent they were regarding what guidance/ethical theories they were using in each case. Point out that one aim of the scheme of work is to develop consistency in our moral decision making.

Following this, students should be given the chart and should simply tick or cross whether they believe each of the activities are innately wrong (N.B. explain that this means that we know it instinctively, without being told). Use this to introduce the moral argument. Students should then discuss in pairs whether they think that a) the moral argument is valid and b) the argument is sound. This, along with feedback from the chart activity, can lead into a discussion on where morals come from – Are they from God? If not where do they come from? Can they be objective without a 'lawgiver'? etc.

To finish the lesson, students should be given a definition of the word 'autonomy' and should be asked to consider, based on what they've already learned in the lesson, whether theists can be said to have autonomy over ethical decisions.

ACTIVITIES

Key activities:

- Mind-map – religious guidance
- Feedback from homework
- Moral argument
- Discussion – objective morality?
- Consider autonomy

Resources:

- Moral argument chart worksheet
- PowerPoint

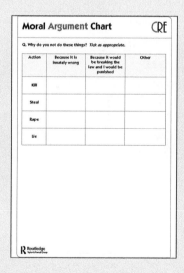

ACTIVITIES

Key activities:

- Name the Ten Commandments
- Group activity – are the commandments relevant?
- Other types of holy law
- Pick and choose?

Resources:

- Evaluating the Ten Commandments worksheet
- PowerPoint

Lesson 3: holy laws

> **Learning objectives**
>
> 1. To understand the concept of holy laws
> 2. To identify differing types of holy law
> 3. To begin to evaluate 'holy laws' as a source of moral guidance.

The aim of Lesson 3 is for students to identify holy laws and to begin to consider how relevant these are today/how useful they are as a source of moral guidance. The lesson should start with a competition – how many of the Ten Commandments can you name? Once all ten have been identified ask the students which of the world religions comply to these holy laws.

Students should then work in groups to evaluate the Ten Commandments individually. Each group will be given two of the Ten Commandments and will be asked to discuss of each; 1) What does the commandment mean in practice? 2) What is good about the commandment? 3) What could potentially be bad about the commandment? 4) How relevant is the commandment today (students should be encouraged to consider both to what extent it IS followed and to what extent it SHOULD be). One student from each group should then feed back to the class and, during this time, students can complete the chart using their classmates' ideas. Allow a short time after each group feeds back for other students to question or further what is said.

Students should then be encouraged to consider other types of law which could be incorporated under 'holy laws' e.g. Shari'ah law, Church law (Catholicism) with Natural Law as a possible extension. Much of this material may have been covered previously so how this is done will depend on context. This can lead into a discussion about whether these laws are revealed or manmade.

To finish students should be asked to think about the question; 'If you have a set of holy laws, is it appropriate to follow some and not others?' They can write an answer to this question or feed it back to the class.

Lesson 4: holy books

Learning objectives

1. To identify various holy books
2. To understand different theistic approaches to holy books
3. To begin to evaluate the strengths and weaknesses of 'holy books' as a source of moral guidance

Key activities:

- How many holy books?
- Context activity
- Interpretation activity
- List the positives
- Human continuum

Resources:

- Bibles
- PowerPoint
- Sati in scripture worksheet

The aim of Lesson 4 is to introduce holy books as a source of moral guidance for theists and to begin to consider strengths and weaknesses of these as sources of authority in moral decision making. The starter begins this process automatically. Students are asked to list as many holy books as they can think of from their previous studies. They should then be asked – what is the problem with this? Use this to lead into a discussion about whether it is possible for different holy books to all be true/the word of God. Further this by considering how we might differentiate between holy books if they give different ethical guidance.

Following this, students will work in pairs to consider two more potential problems with using holy books for moral guidance. For the first activity, students will read extracts from different holy books and discuss whether this ethical guidance is still relevant today. This can be fed back to the class. There is also an extension activity on sati in scripture in relation to this which can be used if desired. For the second activity each pair of students will be given two different Bible passages to look up which, on the face of it, give different guidance on the same ethical issue. Students should discuss what the problem is and feed it back to the class. The teacher should use this to draw out the issue of interpretation and to introduce students to the terms 'liberal' and 'conservative'.

To counter-balance these activities, students should then have an opportunity to consider what is positive about using holy books for moral guidance. Use the PowerPoint to introduce the different types of moral guidance within holy books – why is this useful? Students can then make an interactive list of other strengths on the board. You should find that many of the strengths are direct counter arguments to the 'weaknesses' e.g. 'It doesn't change over time' and 'some ethical guidance is contextual and no longer applies'.

To finish the students should complete a human continuum – 'Holy books are useful for moral guidance'. Students who strongly agree should go at one end of the room and students who strongly disagree at the other with students who are unsure placing themselves at a suitable distance in between to reflect their stance. The teacher can call upon any student to justify where they are standing in the room.

ACTIVITIES

Key activities:

- Role model
- Group work activity 'Religious leaders'
- Revisit your role model

Resources:

- PowerPoint
- Group resources – religious leaders

Lesson 5: religious leaders

Learning objectives

1. To identify various religious leaders
2. To understand how these people influence others
3. To evaluate the strengths and weaknesses of 'religious leaders' as a source of ethical guidance

The aim of Lesson 5 is to consider a variety of religious leaders and how useful it may be to follow the example of important people when making moral decisions. To start therefore, students should be asked to consider three questions; 1) Who is your role model? 2) Why do you think it is good to follow this person's example? 3) Has this person ever actively influenced one (or more) of your decisions?

Students should be introduced to some of the key reasons for believing that religious leaders can give us guidance, via the PWP. They can then discuss as a class whether we should trust the teachings/testimonies of religious leaders based on this.

The majority of the lesson is based around a differentiated group work activity in which small groups of students consider the example of one 'religious leader'. Each group will read about the religious leader and then discuss a number of questions about them. Each group will then feed back what they've learned to the rest of the class. Once all groups have fed back about their religious leader and their discussion, the class can discuss the questions; 1. Why is it useful to have religious leaders as examples to us? 2. Does it matter if our role models or religious leaders do things which we consider to be wrong? Can they still be examples to us about how to live?

At the end of the lesson students should return to thinking about their role model. Is this person a good role model when it comes to making ethical decisions? Why/why not?

Lesson 6: the conscience

Learning objectives

1. To identify 'the conscience' as a form of ethical guidance for theists and secular believers
2. To evaluate the conscience as a form of ethical guidance in both theistic and secular settings

Key activities:

- Jiminy Cricket
- Mind-map – what is the conscience
- Individual dilemma
- Pair discussion on problems relating to conscience
- Class discussion – conscience as voice of God?
- Sentence starters

Resources:

- PowerPoint including video

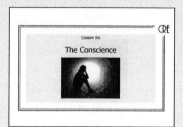

The aim of Lesson 6 is to examine the concept of 'the conscience' and to evaluate it as a source of moral guidance in both theistic and secular frameworks. To start, students should watch the song 'Always let your conscience be your guide' from Pinocchio, considering the question 'What is the conscience according this clip?' This can lead into a mind-mapping activity on the conscience – What is it?/Where does it come from? Possible answers are displayed on the PowerPoint.

Students should then consider the dilemma on the PowerPoint (What would you do if you were given too much change in a shop?). Take feedback from the class and use it to draw out the fact that our 'consciences' seem to tell us different things. Discuss why this is, relating back to the mind-map. Is this a problem?

Ask the students to think-pair-share on the questions: 1) Does conscience lead to morality in society or does morality in society lead to conscience? and 2) Does the conscience stop you from doing bad things or does it make you feel guilty when you've already done them? Students can write answers to these questions explaining their ideas if there's time. All of these activities should be used to help the students understand that it is very difficult to define 'the conscience' and that experts disagree on what it is, what its function is and whether it even exists.

Following this, return to/introduce the idea that theists often believe the conscience is the voice of God. As a class discuss whether this solves any of the problems raised or creates more of them. Explain that many Christians believe that 'the conscience' is the Holy Spirit speaking to us (whilst accepting that there are also other psychological factors in play) and, again, discuss whether this is a help or a hindrance to the concept.

To finish students should complete the sentences 'I think the conscience is . . .' and 'It is/is not a reliable guide for making moral decisions because . . .'.

ACTIVITIES

Key activities:

- Card sort – ordering forms of guidance
- Liberal/Conservative/Catholic
- Medical ethics discussion
- Shari'ah law discussion
- Return to card sort

Resources:

- Theistic guidance card sort
- Shari'ah guidance worksheet
- PowerPoint

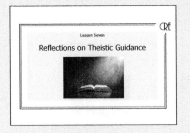

Lesson 7: reflections on theistic guidance

Learning objectives

1. To understand the relationship between different forms of theistic guidance
2. To begin to prioritise them

The aim of Lesson 7 is for students to consolidate their learning on theistic moral guidance and to begin to understand the relationship between the different forms of guidance. Students need to recognise that different theistic believers, even within the same religion, give more weight to some forms of God's guidance than others and they should begin to make judgements about which should be given the most authority for themselves.

To start students should be given cards with the different forms of theistic guidance on them. They should be asked to order these from the most to the least reliable. They should then write their lists down with an explanation of their choices. Students will return to this at the end of the lesson.

Following this the teacher should display the PowerPoint slide showing the differences between liberal protestants, conservative protestants and Roman Catholics with regards to how the forms of guidance are ordered (acknowledging this is a generalisation). Students should discuss in pairs which they agree with most and why. Take feedback and use this to lead into a class discussion on whether it's appropriate for theists to prioritise different forms of guidance at different times e.g. sometimes the Bible is the most important but at other times it is the conscience. Can this be consistent? Use the PowerPoint slide on medical ethics to further the discussion – what should a theist do about issues on which there is no guidance from the usual sources?

Return to the concept of Shari'ah law using the handout provided. Students can discuss these questions in small groups or pairs or can answer them individually, depending on preference. Take feedback.

To finish, students should return to their card sort. Would they still put the forms of guidance in the same order? Can they justify this further now? If it has changed, why is this? Students should note down their answers.

Lesson 8: Buddhist ethics

> **Learning objectives**
>
> 1. To identify various non-theistic ethical approaches
> 2. To understand some Buddhist ethical principles
> 3. To compare Buddhist ethics to theistic ethics
> 4. To begin to evaluate Buddhist ethics

Key activities:

- Meta-ethical questions
- Recap Buddhist ethics
- Discuss 'karma'
- Compare Buddhist and theistic ethics
- Enlightenment instead of God?

Resources:

- PowerPoint including videos

The aim of Lesson 8 is to introduce the second half of the scheme of work on non-theistic approaches and, in particular, to consider Buddhist ethics as a bridge between 'religious' and 'secular' frameworks.

To start, students should be asked to think back to lesson two in which they considered arguments for and against 'God' as the author of morality. Ask the students whether they have thought any further on the questions of where morals might come from without God and whether they can be objective if God is not part of the equation? Use this to introduce the second half of the scheme of work. Then explain that today you will be looking at Buddhism and ask why this wasn't covered under 'theistic' moral guidance. Students are likely to have studied Buddhism prior to Year 9 and thus hopefully will be reminded that Buddhism is an atheistic religion.

The teacher should then spend some time recapping/introducing Buddhist moral teachings with/to the students. If Buddhism was studied relatively recently, students could be encouraged to complete a mind-map on Buddhist ethics. Alternatively, students could watch introductory videos to the Four Noble Truths, the Eightfold Path and the Five Moral Precepts – Buddha bits are short animated videos which do this very well for a young teenage audience.

The concept of 'karma' in Buddhism should also be recapped/introduced. The PowerPoint includes different conceptions of karma within Buddhism. Use the questions on the power-point to discuss as a class how this concept may motivate Buddhists – this will feed into discussion on motivation for moral behaviour in a later lesson.

Following a recap/introduction to the core moral teachings of Buddhism, students should be asked to Think Pair Share on the question 'How is Buddhist moral guidance similar/different to theistic moral guidance?' The chart on the PowerPoint can be a visual aid. Take feedback from the students. Use this to lead into a plenary in which the students return to the meta-ethical questions from the beginning of the lesson and discuss whether the Enlightenment of the Buddha provides a viable alternative to 'God' as lawgiver.

Lesson 9: Humanism

Key activities:

- That's Humanism video
- Highlighting the definitions
- 'What makes something right or wrong'? video
- Humanist dilemmas
- Golden rule sheet
- Humanism and meta-ethics discussion

Resources:

- PowerPoint including videos
- How do Humanists deal with moral dilemmas?
- Humanism definitions handout
- Highlighters
- Humanism – The Golden Rule handout
- Humanist moral dilemmas worksheet

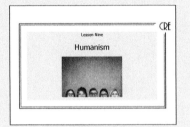

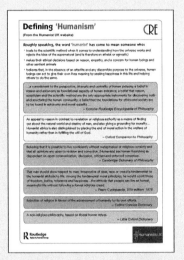

Learning objectives

1. To understand the concept of 'Humanism'
2. To understand how humanists make moral decisions
3. To begin to evaluate humanist ethics

The aim of Lesson 9 is to introduce Humanism and to consider a humanistic framework for ethics. Thus, to start, students can be shown the video 'That's Humanism' for a simple overview of the humanist tradition.

Students should then be given the sheet with different definitions of Humanism on it and asked to highlight what guidance each gives with regards to 'ethics'. (There is an optional extension activity of unpacking a particularly tricky definition which can be used if some students finish before others and/or for discussion as a class. Alternatively, this could be added in to the meta-ethical discussion at the end of the lesson.) Students can then watch the second animated video 'What makes something right or wrong?', noting down key ideas.

Following this, the teacher can recap the key principles that humanists rely on using the PowerPoint from Humanists UK and can ask students to consider a couple of the dilemmas on it in order to try to apply humanist teaching. This is also available in worksheet form if it is more convenient in your setting.[2] After having used these resources, pose the following questions to the class: Does everyone agree on the right answers? What issues might this raise for Humanism?

Students can be given the Humanists UK sheet 'The Golden Rule' and be asked to read it in pairs. Is this a good rule? Why?

To finish students should consider meta-ethical questions relating to Humanism. Watch the section of the video 'What is Humanism?' entitled 'How can Humanists live ethical lives without religion?' (starts at 2.04). Are the answers given satisfactory? What about the rest of our learning from the lesson? Where do humanists say morals come from? Are they suggesting that morals are objective or not? What do we think of their answers? (N.B. A major criticism of Humanism is that its ethical framework is not entirely clear – is it objective or subjective, why are certain principles accepted? etc.)

Lesson 10: utilitarianism

Learning objectives

1. To understand a simple form of utilitarianism
2. To evaluate utilitarianism

The aim of Lesson 10 is to introduce a simple form of utilitarianism and begin to evaluate it. Thus, to start, students should be introduced to the 'Hitler dilemma' (see PWP), being asked the question; "If you could have killed Hitler before World War II, would it have been right to do so?" Ask students to discuss their answers in pairs and then feed back to the class. Use their answers to draw out the two key ideas of utilitarianism; 1) The greatest good for the greatest number – what is good is what benefits the majority 2) It is the consequences of an action which make the action right or wrong. (N.B. This is obviously a simplified version of 'utilitarianism' but in most contexts would likely be more appropriate for a Year 9 audience than introducing 'Act', 'Rule', 'Preference' Utilitarianism etc. though the teacher can of course include these differences if they see fit.)

The main body of the lesson is made up of compiling a chart of the strengths and weaknesses of a utilitarian approach. This will be done by the class as a whole via feedback from pair or small group discussions on two dilemmas ('conjoined twins' and 'Torture' – see PWP), designed explicitly to draw out these strengths and weaknesses. In each case, the teacher should allow the students to discuss their responses to the dilemmas and then to feed back to the class. Relevant ideas from the discussion should be added to the chart. You should find that many of the 'strengths' have an opposing 'weakness' e.g. 'It is good because it benefits the majority' vs 'It is bad because it ignores the minority' or 'It is good because it focuses on the consequences' vs 'Consequences are always unknown'. Any relevant ideas from the starter activity can also be added to the chart.

To finish students should be encouraged to return to the meta-ethical questions from the previous lesson and to relate them to utilitarianism – if we say utilitarianism is correct, what makes it right? Can it be objectively right? As an extension to the plenary you could explain to the students that J. S. Mill tried to go further than many humanists and 'prove' that cultivating maximum happiness was good. Show them his proof on the PowerPoint. Does this work?

Key activities:

- Hitler dilemma
- TPS on two scenarios
- Chart construction from feedback
- Return to meta-ethics and J. S. Mill

Resources:

- PowerPoint

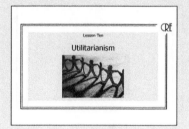

ACTIVITIES

Key activities:

- Harry Potter's invisibility cloak
- TPS selfish
- Egoism sheet
- Friends clips
- Karma vote

Resources:

- Egoism worksheet
- PowerPoint including video

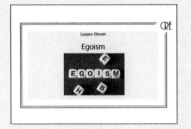

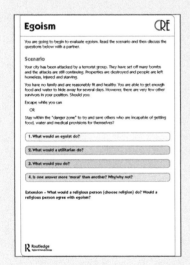

Lesson 11: egoism

Learning objectives

1. To understand egoism as an approach to moral decision making
2. To evaluate egoism
3. To reflect on our motivations to be 'good'

The aim of Lesson 11 is to consider egoism as an ethical approach and to compare this to other approaches with regards to motivation.

For the starter, students should be asked to write down what they would do if they had Harry Potter's invisibility cloak for a day. Take some feedback and then ask students to consider their motivations for doing those things.

Following this, ask the think-pair-share questions 'Is it good to be selfish?', 'Why/why not?' Take feedback again and then draw the tasks together – aren't we often driven by selfish desires? Is it any different with morality? Use this to introduce egoism. It may be useful here to return to the moral dilemmas homework as one of the scenarios on that – the burning houses – often elicits an egoistic response. Is this wrong?

Students should be given the 'Egoism' activity sheet and asked to complete it individually. The teacher should then take feedback. Use the answers to lead into the 'Friends' clips in which Joey and Phoebe discuss whether it is possible to perform a selfless good deed – Do the students agree with Joey's premise? Why/why not? What examples could they give against it? (N.B. A really good answer to this question requires strong theological literacy. On the surface for example one could say a Christian's motivation to do good would be to get into heaven but this would be inaccurate for many Christians who believe we are not saved by our actions but rather we do them out of gratitude).

To finish students should 'vote with their feet' on the statement 'Acting correctly because you believe in karma is essentially egoism'. Those who agree should stand up. Those who don't should sit down. Have a critical discussion on the statement.

Lesson 12: cultural relativism

Learning objectives

1. To understand cultural relativism
2. To consider the relationship between human rights and cultural relativism
3. To begin to evaluate cultural relativism

The aim of Lesson 12 is to introduce ethical relativism, specifically in the form of cultural relativism. To start students should look at the different ethical 'issues' displayed on the board. They should spend a few minutes discussing with a partner what they think about three of those issues and why. Ask the class – did you and your partner agree on all issues? If not is one of you right or can you both be right?

Students should then work in the same pairs to discuss the questions on the PowerPoint regarding changing opinions and should then be encouraged to write down individual answers. Take feedback.

The teacher should then organise students into groups and give them the resource sheet 'human rights'. As discussed above, these are important to consider with regards to cultural relativism but, as the content is relatively complex, we suggest you ask a confident student to be the group leader, to lead the discussion and feed back to the class at the end of it.

To finish, students should look at the current issues on the PowerPoint and discuss the related questions as a class.

ACTIVITIES

Key activities:

- Ethical issues
- Changing times questions
- Human rights
- Current issues

Resources:

- PowerPoint
- Human rights worksheet

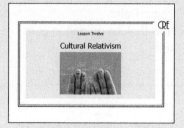

ACTIVITIES

Key activities:

- Card sort
- Balloon activity in groups
- Discursive feedback
- Return to card sort
- What would the theists say?
- Individual response and class debate

Resources:

- PowerPoint
- Non-theistic guidance card sort

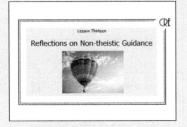

Lesson 13: reflections on non-theistic guidance

Learning objectives

1. To consolidate learning on non-theistic guidance
2. To discern between/order different forms of non-theistic guidance
3. To begin to reflect on what the most truthful approach to ethics is overall

The aim of Lesson 13 is to consolidate learning from the second half of the scheme of work and begin to make critical judgements about what the most truthful ethical approach is overall.

To start, as in Lesson 7, students should be given cards with the different forms of non-theistic guidance on them. They should be asked to order these from the most to the least reliable. They should then write their lists down with an explanation of their choices. Students will return to this towards the end of the lesson.

Students should then be split into five groups and assigned the titles 'Buddhists', 'Humanists', 'Utilitarians', 'Egoists', 'Cultural Relativists'. Set up the main activity by introducing the hot air balloon scenario. The groups then have to discuss what the correct actions would be according to their ethical approach. Give students a short amount of time to do this and then take feedback from a nominated person from each group. During the feedback allow members of the other groups to pose challenges or ask questions of the group feeding back. The group feeding back need to defend their position.

Ask the students to go back to their individual card sorts and to check whether they still agree with their ordering. Then ask students to explain their responses in their books. If they still agree with their ordering can they justify it further? If they think it should be changed, why is this? Take feedback as appropriate.

Following this, the students should be asked to think back to their learning in the first half of the scheme of work. In pairs, they should discuss what guidance each of the theistic approaches may give on the balloon dilemma. As an extension, students could consider what individuals may do e.g. the liberal Christian, the conservative Christian, the Hindu etc.

To finish, ask students to reflect on what their own response to the dilemma would be. Ask them to identify which approach they are using. If there's time, you could open up for debate what the 'correct' course of action would be in that scenario.

Lesson 14: ethical consistency

Learning objectives

1. To identify moral issues surrounding sexual relationships
2. To consider how useful each approach is when making decisions about sexual relationships and other issues
3. To reflect on consistency in moral decision making

The aim of Lesson 14 is to consider the consistency of our moral decision making and prepare for an assessment on the question 'How should we make moral decisions?'

To start, students should look at the images linked in the PowerPoint 'Sex in the media' and should write down their instinctive responses to each picture, without talking to anyone else (N.B. Teachers may wish to download these images before the lesson for efficiency). Take feedback on the students' responses and discuss the questions: 1. What does this suggest about our attitudes towards sexual relationships? 2. What influences these attitudes? 3. Are our individual attitudes consistent with a particular ethical approach?

Students should then work individually to complete the chart on how useful each approach is to the issue of sexual relationships. Encourage students to complete this in as much detail as possible, e.g. giving examples, specific teachings, etc.

Following this, students should be asked to identify another moral issue which they feel passionate about. They should then repeat the process of applying each ethical approach to the issue and considering how useful it is in relation to that issue. If students finish early they can repeat this process for numerous ethical issues.

Once students have completed their charts, they should be encouraged to reflect on whether any of the approaches was deemed to be useful in relation to both issues. Were any not useful in both cases? If one approach was useful for one issue but not the other, can it be complimented by another approach without being internally inconsistent (e.g. a Christian may use a utilitarian framework in some scenarios if there is no obvious guidance from the Bible/their religious leaders)? Take feedback.

To finish, students should feedback their ideas on what the most truthful approach is overall. You may also want to set up the assessment for the next lesson using the 'useful guidance' on the PowerPoint for the next lesson.

Key activities:

- Immediate responses
- Chart on approaches and sexual issues
- Chart on approaches and other issues
- Consistency of approaches

Resources:

- PowerPoint
- Sex in the media (weblinks)
- Useful guidance chart worksheet

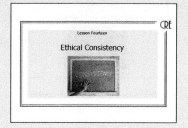

Key activities:

- Constructing an essay/dialogue to demonstrate understanding
- Completing self-assessment

Resources:

- PowerPoint
- 'How should we make moral decisions?' assessment guidance for students
- 'How should we make moral decisions?' mark sheet

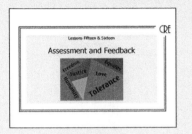

Lessons 15 and 16: assessment and feedback

> **Learning objectives**
>
> 1. To demonstrate your learning on the topic
> 2. To receive feedback on your progress
> 3. To self-assess your response to the topic

The assessment question 'How should we make moral decisions?' was chosen as it is the critical question upon which the scheme of work is based. To ask how people DO make moral decisions would be to invite simply explanatory or comparative answers. To ask 'What is the best approach to moral decision making?' would allow for more evaluation but ultimately only asks for students to suggest a preference. The imperative 'should' focuses the question on what CRE is aiming at; the truth of the matter.

The question requires students to evaluate the different ethical guidance/theories which they have studied over the scheme of work and to justify why one particular source/theory or combination of sources/theories is most likely to provide us with the right answers. The best answers will likely include meta-ethical discussion as part of the evaluative process. Students should use examples to support their evaluative points and these can be drawn from the charts which they compiled in the previous lesson alongside other learning form the scheme of work. It is important to ensure that students do not fall into the trap of discussing the ethical issues which should be used as examples rather than the ethical theories themselves. Thus there is guidance on our assessment sheet as to what the students might include in their answers to exemplify their academic virtues most effectively. If however you are using a different assessment framework, it is suggested that the materials you are using or at the very least the teacher's own guidance when setting up the assessment, is very clear about this.

How you decide to structure this assessment will depend on your school setting. Here we suggest a lesson for students to complete the assessment (in written or other form) and a lesson for feedback with the possibility of planning for their assessment as a homework task. Ensuring that your students receive proper feedback is vital for good practice in any framework. For CRE reflection time is particularly important as both learning and the application of judgemental rationality are always ongoing. Students also need lesson time to consider how they have responded to the scheme of work by completing the 'responsibility' section on the mark sheet.

Notes

1 'Subjective' is being used here as per its typical use in the English language and not to denote ethical subjectivism, which is an ethical theory in its own right.
2 All of the Humanists UK resources used in this lesson have been taken from http://understanding humanism.org.uk/uhtheme/ethics/?age=11.

References

Ayer, A. J. (1936). *Language, Truth and Logic*. London: Victor Gollancz Limited.

Bunnin, N. and Yu, J. (2004). The Blackwell Dictionary of Western Philosophy. Available online at: http://www.blackwellreference.com/public/tocnode?id=g9781405106795_chunk_ g97814051067953_ss1-90 (accessed 26/08/16).

Davis, C. (2014). Looking for answers? An investigation into student responses to religious and moral issues. Unpublished Master's thesis. King's College London, UK.

Juss, S. (2016). High Court Ruling on Religious Education: Legal guidance on what it means for local authorities, academies, schools, teachers, Agreed Syllabus Conferences, and SACREs. Available online at: https://humanism.org.uk/wp-content/uploads/2016-04-28-FINAL-High-Court-ruling-on-Religious-Education-legal-guidance.pdf (accessed 25/08/16).

Lee, L. (2011). Religion: British Social Attitudes 28. Available online at: http://www.bsa.natcen. ac.uk/latest-report/british-social-attitudes-28/religion.aspx (accessed 11/08/16).

Wolff, J. (2011). *Ethics and Public Policy: A Philosophical Inquiry*. Oxon: Routledge.

Wright, A. (2004). *Religion, Education and Post-modernity*. London: Routledge Falmer

CHAPTER 7

Critical Religious Education and GCSE Religious Studies

New GCSE RS specifications were brought in for teaching from 2016, for first examination in the summer 2018. In this chapter we will explore these specifications and consider the opportunities they offer. We will suggest how they can be planned and delivered using a critical pedagogy.

Introducing the specifications

The rationale behind the development of the new GCSE specifications was one of increased academic rigour. The content to be covered was decided by the DfE and Ofqual, but the task of how the specifications were formulated and organised, was given to the exam boards.

The new specifications are offered as long or short courses (although the popularity of the short courses has waned, arguably because they no longer count for the purposes of school league tables (National Association of Teachers of Religious Education, 2016)). If you have some students taking the short course and some are 'topping up' to the full course, the specifications are designed to allow you to teach them alongside each other; they are 'co-teachable'.

Significant changes

The most significant changes are as follows:

- All students are required to study two religions.
- Opportunities for philosophy and ethics remain but they make up a smaller portion of the specification. Various themes are offered and students are required to explore these in relation to either one or both of the religions being studied.
- There is an option to study a religious text.
- Non-religious worldviews (NRWVs) have been omitted (though not a change as such, there was an opportunity to include these, which was not taken).

The impact of the 'two religions' requirement, has been felt most acutely by faith schools which have traditionally chosen to study their own faith solely as the path most compatible with the school's mission statement. Catholic schools have been directed by the Catholic Bishops' Conference to teach Judaism as their second religion (Catholic Education Service, 2016), whilst the Chief Rabbi has encouraged Jewish schools to choose Islam as their second religion (The Jewish Chronicle, 2016). However, the legal requirement for Agreed Syllabuses to 'reflect the fact that the religious traditions in Great Britain are in the main Christian' (HM Government, 1996) also needs to be met in the exam specifications. This means that if non-Christian faith schools (such as Jewish schools) teach their own faith plus another, but choose not to study Christianity, then there will still be a requirement for students to show some knowledge of Christianity. This has been received with concern within the Jewish press.

Whilst the legacy specifications gave no opportunity to systematically study a non-religious worldview, many were hoping, even presuming, that they would feature in the new specifications. This never happened and many were disappointed. Following a High Court ruling, this omission was declared unlawful; the judgement stated that "statutory RE in schools without a religious character must be 'objective, critical and pluralistic' and a syllabus that covered religions in detail but did not give students the opportunity to learn similarly about a non-religious worldview such as Humanism would not meet this requirement" (Juss, 2016, p.2). The DfE responded that the judgement did not "directly affect the detailed content of our reformed GCSE" (Department for Education, 2016). Given the incongruity between this and the judgement of the court, it is likely that this ruling will be subject to further challenge (Pells, 2016). In the meantime, the new specifications do provide students with the option of bringing in non-religious responses to philosophical and ethical issues in the themes studied, and indeed, for some specifications, this is a requirement (e.g. AQA Specification A, Theme C: The existence of God and revelation).

Choosing your specification

The decision about which specification to choose is not an easy one. You may be concerned about the increase in the volume of content to be taught, but don't let this push pedagogical issues lower down the agenda. You have a great opportunity to consider not only your choice of what to teach, but also how you intend to teach it.

You will need to decide: Short course or long course? Option or compulsory? Once this decision is made in your school, you will have the task of choosing which exam board specification to follow:

For faith schools, it is likely that the choice will be made between:

- Specifications which allow for a more significant focus on one primary religion (50%), a second religion (25%) and themes/texts (25%) – consider Edexcel A (allows for a choice between Christianity, Roman Catholic Christianity or Islam as the primary religions) and AQA Catholic Christianity (allows for a second religion of Judaism or Islam).
- Specifications which allow for a focus solely on beliefs and practices: Eduqas Route B (Catholic theology (37.5%) and applied RC theology (37.5%) and Judaism (25%).

Non-faith schools will make their decision informed by the choice and weighting of the two religions and the themes and/or texts:

- Those who want to focus more on one faith may choose a 50% primary religion option: Edexcel A (primary religion 50%, second religion 25%, themes/ texts 25%). The primary religions offered are Christianity, Roman Catholic Christianity and Islam. The textual papers offered are St Mark's Gospel or the Qur'an. The inclusion of textual papers is interesting as it enables exploration of one religion in significantly more depth, which from a CRE point of view is to be welcomed.
- Arguably the most popular route will be the one which provides a balanced weighting between the two religions studied, with each religion weighted at 25%, with a total 50%. The themes occupy the remaining 50% with a choice of philosophy and ethics, and/or texts. All boards offer this option: Edexcel B creatively integrates the themes and the religions. Each of the three themes (from which two are chosen) considers both beliefs and practices (coined as 'living the religious life') and then uses these to interpret and inform responses to ethical and philosophical issues. This approach offers an organisational framework, which may be attractive for some teachers.

How does the new assessment work?

The exams are linear, being examined by end of course exams. There are some differences in the length of the exams; however most routes will be examined by two exams, two hours in length each.

The specifications use the new grading structure 9–1. Note that the grade boundaries of the new numerical grades do *not* match those of the old lettered grades:

- Grade 4 is the equivalent of the bottom of an old C grade.
- Grade 5 is the equivalent of the top 1/3 of a C and the bottom 1/3 of a B. The expectation is that the government will make this the new benchmark by which schools are assessed.
- Grade 6 is the top 2/3s of a B.
- Grade 7 is the bottom of an A.
- Grade 8 is the equivalent of the A*/A boundary.
- Grade 9 is higher than the current A*.

Assessment objectives (AOs) are set by Ofqual and are the same across all GCSE RS specifications and all exam boards. All GCSE RS exams will measure the extent to which students have achieved the following:

AO1: Demonstrate knowledge and understanding of religion and beliefs including:

- Beliefs, practices and sources of authority
- Influence on individuals, communities and societies
- Similarities and differences within and/or between religions and beliefs

AO2: Analyse and evaluate aspects of religion and belief, including their significance and influence.

These assessment objectives are weighted equally.

What are the opportunities for a critical pedagogy?

Two faiths not one

To become religiously literate you need to explore a variety of responses to those ultimate questions of life, to which religions provide specific if varied answers. To gain a rich understanding of any religion, one needs to understand both the diversity within the faith and the ways in which it differs from other worldviews. To understand a faith position is to understand what it is, what it is not and the nature of both differences and similarities. Thus the requirement to study two religions is a change to be welcomed, and one which many schools already embrace.

The assessment objectives can work with CRE

The assessment objectives can work with a critical pedagogy. They specifically allow students to demonstrate knowledge and understanding of religion and beliefs, showing similarities and differences within religions and beliefs (internal variations) and between religions and beliefs (variations between different worldviews). They also require students to analyse and evaluate significance and influence. They do not specifically require the depth of engagement which CRE is seeking, but nor do they preclude it.

What are the potential problems for a critical pedagogy?

The content of the specifications is paradoxically too heavy and too light

One problematic factor is that the GCSE specifications are content *heavy* (meaning there is lots of it) and of course your primary concern will be to cover everything so your students are prepared for the examination. This may mean that students' understanding could consequently be *light*. However, for CRE ensuring coverage of the content in sufficient depth is a primary objective when curriculum planning.

There is also a concern that the nature of the content (i.e. the topics included in the specifications) is also *light*. By way of example, consider the subject content for GCSE Christianity, as provided by the Department for Education and Ofqual to the exam boards (Department for Education, 2015).

Christianity

1. Beliefs and teachings

- The nature of God, such as omnipotence, the problem of evil/ suffering and a loving and righteous God
- Creation, including the role of Word and Spirit, with textual references to John 1 and Genesis 1–3
- The Trinity, including the oneness of God: Father, Son and Holy Spirit
- The person of Jesus Christ, including beliefs and teachings relating to his incarnation, crucifixion, resurrection and ascension
- Salvation, including law, sin, grace and Spirit, the role of Christ in salvation, and the nature of atonement
- Eschatological beliefs and teachings, including the importance of resurrection and life after death, judgement, heaven and hell

2. Practices

- The significance of different forms of worship including liturgical, informal and individual
- The role and meaning of the sacraments in Christian life, including baptism and eucharist
- The place of prayer, including the Lord's Prayer, set prayers and informal prayer
- The role and importance of pilgrimage and celebrations, including at least two contrasting examples of Christian pilgrimage (such as Walsingham, Taizé, Iona) and celebrations
- The place of mission, evangelism and church growth
- The role of the church in the local community and living practices
- The importance of the worldwide church including working for reconciliation, the persecuted church and the work of one of Christian Aid/Tearfund/Cafod

3. Sources of wisdom and authority

- The Bible, including its development, structure and purpose (Old Testament: law, history, prophets, writings; and New Testament: gospels, letters), its unity as the Word of God, and two contrasting interpretations of its authority
- Jesus as the Word of God and the role of Jesus in modelling practices such as love for others, forgiveness, servanthood, reconciliation and social justice, and in establishing the Kingdom of God
- The growth of the Church, including belief in the Church as the body of Christ; the development of different churches: Catholic, Orthodox, Protestant and Pentecostal/Charismatic
- Leadership in the Church, including the Pope, bishops / priests / ministers/pastors; the role of women in leadership

(continued)

(continued)

- The role of the individual, including religious experience, reason and personal conscience
- The use of the Bible in worship and in personal and ethical decision making by Christians

4. Forms of expression and ways of life

- The significance and meaning of at least three forms of art, drawn from:
- Icons; drawing/painting; sculpture; music; drama e.g. the mystery plays; literature.
- The use of symbolism and imagery in religious art including Christian symbols such as ChiRho, Cross, fish, Alpha and Omega, symbols of the four evangelists
- The use of different styles of music in worship, including: psalms, hymns and worship songs

If you compare this content to the expectations for the KS3 programmes of study from the National Curriculum Framework for Religious Education (The RE Council, 2013), you will see that it is likely that much of the content identified for the GCSE specifications will already have been covered. Whilst the NCFRE does not specify content, the intentions for learning are clearly outlined. At KS3 students are expected to have the opportunity "to explain and interpret a range of beliefs, teachings and sources of wisdom and authority including experience, in order to understand religions and worldviews as coherent systems or ways of seeing the world" (p.11). If you were to teach Christianity at KS3 to meet these requirements it is difficult to conceive of a curriculum, which wouldn't include much of the content listed above. There is a need for more meaningful progression, so as to ensure content is not merely repeated in more detail, rather than offering carefully targeted theologically challenging explorations of doctrine. This problem with the content being paradoxically too heavy and too light is perhaps an inevitable outcome of RE not being part of the National Curriculum and not having prescribed curriculum content allowing exam boards to assume a certain baseline of knowledge.

There is limited opportunity for explicit dialogue about truth claims

The organisation of the specifications is unhelpful. The religion-specific papers suggest that each religion should be discreetly and systematically explored. This enables foundational knowledge to be secured and for internal diversity within each religion to be explored. However, in order to offer the most meaningful and enriching opportunity to develop religious literacy, the different religions studied must engage with each other, to be understood through dialogue with each other. Such dialogue embodies the Variation Theory of Learning: "for learning to take place students must experience variation in the educationally *critical aspects* of the 'object of learning'" (Hella and Wright, 2009, p.59). The way the GCSE specifications are organised and assessed does not require such dialogue in relation to each religion's fundamental beliefs about the nature of reality. The opportunity given in the specifications to juxtapose different beliefs is only given as students explore the philosophical and ethical themes; this involves the students applying their understanding of particular beliefs to particular ethical issues or philosophical questions. This still does not afford them the opportunity to consider *directly* the underpinning and conflicting truth claims.

The exam questions do not appear more challenging

The ambition behind the development of the new specifications was to provide more rigorous and challenging learning. Yet if you consider the types of questions and the mark schemes of the new specifications, it seems apparent that little has changed. There is a danger that in preparing students for the exams you will be concerned to train them to be alert to the expectations of examiners, embodied in the mark schemes, and so will be careful not to go too far 'off piste'. However, we have yet to see the impact of the new 9–1 grading, and it is possible that this could discourage formulaic responses, and allow students to excel in showing innovative answers.

Consider an example of a 12 mark question from the specimen AQA Christianity practice paper (AQA (2016)):

- 'The best way for Christians to reach an understanding of God is by practising prayer.'
- Evaluate this statement. In your answer you should:

  o refer to Christian teaching
  o give developed arguments to support this statement
  o give developed arguments to support a different point of view
  o reach a justified conclusion

[12 marks]

Consider the mark scheme:

Arguments in support

- Some forms of prayer are a direct contact between the individual and God, so their understanding of God is personal to them and not based on other people's ideas which could be wrong.
- The believer focuses on the feeling of being in God's presence/ this is sometimes described as a feeling of 'awe and wonder' at the greatness of God.
- God is beyond description because the words get their meaning from the human and natural world around us/so God cannot be understood by reading about him or hearing other people talk about him.

(continued)

(continued)

Arguments in support of other views

- Not everyone can have this kind of prayer experience so they do not feel the presence of God through prayer.
- The Bible as the inspired word of God is his presentation of himself to human beings, so an understanding of God can come from reading what he says about himself / for example, the creator of the world and Father in heaven.
- Study of nature can also lead to an understanding of God, because it is God's creation and God expresses himself through it.

The question requires students to '**refer to Christian teaching**' but the mark scheme appears to expect little in terms of specific biblical understanding. It has weak theological grounding. Christians would agree that the answer to the question of how to reach an understanding of God is found in the Bible, but it is what is said within it which is important for students to understand. It needs to be opened and read! It is difficult given the nature of the mark scheme to visualize what a Level 9 answer would look like, but it would surely go beyond the guidance given in both depth and breadth.

The question requires students to '**give a developed argument**', but the specific mark scheme is only expecting an understanding of Christianity, even though this may have been informed by the insights students have from other religions. The generic guidance to examiners does encourage them to award marks beyond the mark scheme, where this is warranted, but it is possible that the mark schemes may themselves be a limiting factor to how the specifications are taught. Whilst internal diversity within Christianity is required, if students have considered prayer in both Christianity and Islam, for example, a comparison of the different theological understandings of prayer in these different religions would be important and insightful.

The question requires students to '**reach a justified conclusion**' and this is a really important change. The legacy 'e' questions previously asked for discussion rather than justification. There are two points to consider here. First, this requirement positively provides the students with an opportunity to engage with and interweave different points of view. It encourages students to evaluate the strengths and weaknesses of arguments. In this way they are expected to present a coherent response to the viewpoints explored, rather than just stating arguments for and against and then expressing a preference, in a formulaic manner. This depth of engagement, at least theoretically, embodies the process of judgemental rationality, the third principle of CRE. Second, the legacy evaluative questions explicitly asked students to offer personal views. The new specifications neither require nor preclude this. CRE pedagogy expects students to be simultaneously reflecting on and evaluating new knowledge presented to them alongside their own commitments. Thus it is entirely appropriate to encourage students to include in any justified conclusion, an expression of their own viewpoint. This personal element is also an essential part of judgmental rationality.

This expectation of justification, then, is to be welcomed. But this opportunity needs to be grasped and teachers need to have a clear idea as to what such justification entails. For CRE, getting this right is vital. The mark schemes provide some limited guidance as to what is expected. We have included an example here of what we believe a justified answer could look like for an evaluation question. You need to encourage your students to answer with attentiveness, depth, discernment and responsibility.[1]

"If humans have rights, so should animals."

Evaluate this statement.
   In your answer you:

- should give reasoned arguments in support of this statement
- should give reasoned arguments to support a different point of view
- should refer to religious argument
- may refer to non-religious arguments
- should reach a justified conclusion

Some would disagree with this statement because they regard animals as substantially less intelligent than humans. *The weakness of this argument* is that the boundary between species doesn't seem to be that clear-cut. For, although it's beyond doubt that animals don't attend school or write essays, recent scientific research has shown that chimpanzees perform better at some memory tests than humans.

In reply, one could point to distinctively human qualities such as self-consciousness, rationality, moral awareness and the ability to make plans for the future. However, *this argument falls down when* we consider that humans in a persistent vegetative state also lack these qualities but don't lose their rights as a result. Surely logic demands that we extend the same rights to animals rather than being (what Peter Singer has called) 'speciesist'? Isn't the key point that both animals and humans feel pain? *This is a strong argument*: after all, no-one would ever argue for rights for non-sentient beings such as rocks and rivers.

In response, a Christian would point to the Bible. Humans alone are created in the image of God (Genesis 1.27) and are instructed by God to rule over all other species (Genesis 1.28). *Yet this argument depends upon* the Bible being reliable: written by humans, it could be biased against other animals. However, *the argument is unconvincing* even if we accept biblical authority: for we read at Genesis 9.9–10 that, after the Flood, God made a covenant with "every living creature" rather than with humans alone. We should respect that covenant and give them rights.

In conclusion, it seems to be inconsistent to give rights to humans but not to animals. Because I don't believe in God, I think that avoiding pain and promoting pleasure is what morality is all about. Therefore, given that animals are sentient, I think that they, too, should have rights. _____

Phrases in italics signal where EVALUATION is about to take place: this means assessing how STRONG or WEAK the arguments are.

The themes are not grounded firmly enough in theological consideration

In the theme papers, philosophical and ethical issues are explored in relation to the two religions studied in the religion-specific papers. This requirement is to be welcomed. However there is a danger that students will apply beliefs and textual evidence in a formulaic way, as they may have had insufficient opportunity to explore and evaluate the nature of the truth claims of each religion studied, particularly as they relate to each other.

Consider a 12 mark question from one of the theme papers:

'War is never right.'
    Evaluate this statement.
    In your answer you:
- should give reasoned arguments in support of this statement
- should give reasoned arguments to support a different point of view
- should refer to religious argument
- may refer to non-religious arguments
- should reach a justified conclusion

Consider the mark scheme:

Students may include some of the following evidence and arguments, but all relevant evidence and arguments must be credited:

Arguments in support

- Teaching about the sanctity of life – the belief that it is wrong to take life, and that by doing so a believer is disobeying religious commands.
- Arguments in favour of pacifism (both religious and non-religious) – violence breeds violence and does not bring about peace and stability.
- Modern warfare targets innocent civilians through use of weapons of mass destruction. Modern warfare is therefore morally wrong.

Arguments in support of other views

- Idea of Just War – criteria include - started and controlled by a properly instituted authority/just cause/last resort/not involve suffering to innocent civilians/protect trees, crops, animals/not act of aggression or to gain territory/aim to restore peace and freedom/ enable release of prisoners of war/must be winnable/proportionality.
- War can be the lesser of two evils: It can be justified if its purpose is to: stop atrocities/depose a dictator/to defeat terrorists/stop spread of weapons of mass destruction. If the consequences of war are better than the consequences of not fighting, then war is justified.
- People have a right to self-defence.

Consider the expectations for evidence from Buddhism and Christianity:
  Buddhism

- Dhammapada 270: "A man is not a great man because he is warrior and kills other men, but because he hurts not any living being he is in truth called a great man."
- the first precept not to take life, oppose warfare
- concept of Ahimsa (non. violence)
- will defend their lands if it is seen as having the right motivation
- Buddhists have fought in war e.g.in the 14th century Buddhist fighters led the uprising that evicted the Mongols from China.

Christianity

- Matthew 5v9: "Happy are those who work for peace."
- Matthew 5v44: "Love your enemies and pray for those who persecute you."
- Matthew 5v38–48 – do not take revenge, if anyone slaps you on the right cheek, let him slap your left cheek . . .
- Matthew 22v39: "Love your neighbour"
- Romans 12v17–21: "Jesus taught peace, forgiveness and overcoming evil with goodness"
- Matthew 10v34: "but he did use force in the temple because it had become 'a den of thieves.'"

There is a real danger that the texts identified on the specification will be lifted out of context and used simply to 'evidence' different religions' responses to ethical issues. If this happens deep understanding is forfeited, as the texts are dislocated from the necessary grounded theological understanding. The aim of CRE is to develop religious literacy and this is not primarily met through gaining an understanding of particular ethical issues or philosophical issues (though these are obviously important in their own right). The primary purpose of such learning is to enhance the students' understanding of the religions being studied. Thus for CRE it is vital for students to engage in theological exploration of text, in order to meaningfully explore the different answers each religion offers to the nature of ontological reality. This is a necessary prerequisite if students are to understand why religions and worldviews respond as they do to philosophical and ethical questions.

Thus it is not enough for students to learn how to apply structures for answering exam questions, and to learn to link, for example, conservative and liberal views on some issue to quotes from scripture. This feels like some sort of 'colour-by-numbers' task! Instead it is important for students when presented with ethical or philosophical issues to be able to speculate and explore different responses from a position of knowledge and understanding. Students need to understand the context of the textual evidence used and the reasons why the conservative or liberal would choose to use it to explain and justify their positions. If the frequently used Point Evidence Explanation Link (PEEL) paragraph structure were removed, could the students still answer effectively? Could they still engage? Whilst structures for answering questions can be useful, if students are dependent on them, and are unable to think independently of them, there is a problem! Religious literacy can be assessed on a basic level by the ability to engage thoughtfully and independently with the religious, ethical and philosophical questions posed.

In summary the specifications present positive opportunities:

- Students must study two religions.
- The assessment objectives do not preclude a CRE pedagogy.
- Dialogue between the religions studied is expected in response to philosophical and ethical issues.
- The new grading system may work to acknowledge independent thinking and flair.

And difficulties to overcome:

- There is more content than before and this may lead to superficial coverage.
- The religions studied are not required to be in dialogue regarding belief and practice; the explicit exploration of truth claims is not the central concern.
- The exemplar exam questions do not appear more challenging; the mark schemes appear limited.
- The themes are in danger of being dislocated from a grounded theological understanding.

Public exams have always ended up setting limits; this is nothing new. The content, exam questions and assessment objectives do not go as far as CRE expectations. They do not require exploration of the implications, ambiguities and controversies embodied within competing truth claims. However, this does not stop teachers from exploring the content at the deeper level which CRE requires. Dealing with these new specifications give us an exciting opportunity to consider learning theory and pedagogy and to enhance our students' levels of religious literacy. The question is how to organise the curriculum, the teaching and the learning, in order to enable a CRE pedagogy to be implemented.

Applying a CRE pedagogy to GCSE specifications

It is possible to organise the specification content differently from the way it is presented in its published form in order to embody CRE pedagogy. You will need to plan carefully to create an innovative structure in order to facilitate this.

How should I prepare myself to get started?

When writing schemes of work to teach the GCSE specifications, the planning elements and tools exemplified in the writing of the KS3 schemes of work can be applied in the same manner. The key elements for planning are authenticity, coherence and variation, and the key tool is critical questioning.

Authenticity

The specification you choose will dictate the content to be taught. It is important to ensure that you have a depth of knowledge beyond the outlined specification content. This will enable you to make accurate and authentic representations of religions, prioritising both the core foundational beliefs shared across a faith and the internal diversity of belief and practice.

Coherence

In seeking coherence, you will need to present fundamental beliefs and their nuanced and often complicated relationships with religious practices and ethical standpoints. This process of seeking coherence may itself reveal inconsistencies within the lived realities of religions. Acknowledging the inevitable 'messiness' of religious belief and practice is all part of this process of accurate representation.

Variation

You will need to explicitly explore the truth claims of the two religions being studied. This will mean encountering the variety of beliefs and practices within and between the religions, in order to understand and respond to their truth claims. It is important for you to begin such exploration with the core beliefs at the heart of each religion, and not just at the point of their application to the ethical and philosophical themes. Enabling the students to gain a solid theological foundation is vital and the way you choose to juxtapose variations should allow students to explore the ambiguities, controversies, and implications of the beliefs and practices. Remember the criteria to bear in mind when making the choices of variation to explore:

- Look for the obvious
- Look for this within the specific material being studied
- Look for breadth and depth of variation.

Critical questioning

We have seen that the essential tool for effective planning is critical questioning. Three layers of critical questions were identified in the KS3 schemes of work:

a) those relating to truth claims which the tradition makes in and of itself
b) those relating to disagreements within a tradition
c) those relating to disagreements between traditions

Which religions shall I choose?

As we have seen the legal requirements for RE are confusing, particularly given the freedoms given to academies and the lessening influence of SACREs.

The requirement by law for RE to reflect that "the religious traditions in Great Britain are in the main Christian" remains (HM Government, 1996, section 375.3). As all schools (including faith schools) are required now to teach two religions at GCSE, it seems fair to assume that a majority of schools will choose to teach Christianity at GCSE alongside another faith. The choice of a second religion may be influenced by many factors, including the expertise of teaching staff, the demographics of the students, the expressed interests of students, and the nature of the KS3 curriculum. In relation to CRE, you should also consider what choice of religion or worldview provides the most interesting and powerful variations for the students to explore.

Which board should I choose?

Once the decision of short course vs. long course and option vs. compulsory is made, you will have the task of choosing which exam board to follow. Scrutinise the specifications carefully, think about the expertise and preferences of teaching staff and engage with insights from the wider RE community. All of the boards meet the DfE subject requirements and all have been accredited. All have textbooks written to accompany the courses. All have central support provided by the exam boards. And yet teachers often develop affiliations to particular boards, and have clear ideas of what they like and what they don't. The new specifications do provide a unique opportunity to re-evaluate what is on offer.

What should I do about non-religious worldviews?

As we have seen, non-religious worldviews (NRWV) were not included as a specific option alongside the religions for study in the new specifications. However secular views are essential to include and will almost definitely be represented in the demographic of your KS4 classes, for such views arguably represent the default position of wider society. Using CRE pedagogy will make the exploration of non-religious worldviews inevitable if you have non-religious students in your class. In the unlikely event that this isn't the case, it will be important to choose NRWV as a significant variation when exploring the content of your chosen specification. Check this carefully as some of the theme papers usefully make direct reference to non-religious responses (for example, AQA Specification A, Theme C).

How does the GSCE fit in with the KS3 programme of study?

Having chosen a specification, your first task is to consider carefully its content and identify what has already been covered at KS3. If we consider Christianity, it is very likely that you will have taught some topics already at KS3. So it is important to see the KS3 curriculum as a steppingstone to the GCSE. The value of the spiral curriculum has been clearly evidenced in the work of Jerome Bruner (1977) introducing a generic learning theory and by Trevor Cooling (1994) specifically for RE. In his booklet 'Concept Cracking', Cooling talked about achieving progression through curriculum organisation, using analogies of an onion and a jigsaw. In the first method "rather like peeling away the layers of an onion until you reach its heart" (Cooling, 1994, p.13) you facilitate an "ever deepening exploration of the same material". In the second method beliefs are envisaged as consisting of different 'jigsaw' pieces, some of which are easier than others to understand and will have been introduced earlier in a student's education. As the different jigsaw pieces are joined together they will provide an increasingly "comprehensive picture" of Christian belief (p.14). Using these simple but useful analogies, you will need to consider what you have already taught in the KS3 curriculum. Identify what you will need to re-visit to deepen students' understanding and engagement, and what you have not yet covered which will need introducing to ensure a more "complete and coherent" understanding (p.14). So what needs deepening and what needs introducing?

Teaching CRE at KS3 would be a really positive preparation for your students at GCSE. Consider the example of the Year 8 Islam scheme of work introduced earlier in this book. There is a depth of understanding reached through the teaching and learning which would ensure that students studying any religion in this way at KS3, would be very well prepared to take on the expectations of the new specifications.

Whatever religions you decide to choose for GCSE, you would definitely be at an advantage if you had studied these systematically at some point in KS3. Students will then begin their GCSE study with significant prior knowledge and understanding. Some teachers begin the teaching of the GCSE in Year 9 and this is one option to ensure that you have sufficient time to explore the specifications in the depth CRE requires. However as long as the progression between the KS3 programme of study and the GCSE is carefully thought through, the specifications can be taught effectively within the two years.

How do I organise the content of my specification?

The most pressing dilemma we are faced with in organising the GCSE specification for teaching is what variation to bring in, and how and when to do this. You will be very concerned to ensure a solid foundation of core knowledge and understanding of each religion studied and may feel conflicted when thinking about bringing in other variations, particularly external ones. However, we have already seen that CRE requires variation and is underpinned by variation theory, which argues that variation is necessary for learning. We are therefore committed to creating opportunities for the students to explore those truth claims which the tradition makes in and of itself, and to enrich this exploration by introducing both internal variations/disagreements within the religion, external variations/disagreements between religions and the variations/disagreements provided by the students' own worldviews.

Let's begin with students' own worldviews, as these constitute the most obvious variation which exists in any classroom. As your students are engaging with each religion, they will simultaneously be making sense of these in relation to their own worldview. As teachers we must plan carefully to ensure that students have an opportunity to express and articulate their initial responses to what is being learnt, and then to reflect how their thinking develops in light of engagement with the topic studied. This means that immediately a plethora of possible worldviews will be articulated in the classroom.

For the pragmatic purpose of organising the content, we suggest that each religion should be studied systematically. This will include the introduction of the internal variations. We are given some expectations and guidance by the specifications, as some specific denominational differences are identified for study. Remember, too, the guidance from Chapter 4: you are seeking obvious variations, which arise directly from the material being studied and that are useful to create a depth of engagement. You will be concerned to focus on the content, but don't shy away from bringing in any obvious variations, which are either new to them or with which they are already familiar, as these can be a significant tool to deepen their understanding.

There will inevitably be opportunities for external variations to be explored as they arise when you cover the content, with the students identifying links from within their own worldview and their pre-existing knowledge, particularly from their KS3 studies. However once you have systematically covered each religion it is important to explicitly juxtapose the two religions in order to enhance students' understanding of the different beliefs about ontological reality at their heart. This will take significant curriculum time and the outcomes in learning will go beyond specification requirements, but we believe that the enrichment will be invaluable. It also constitutes the best possible revision opportunity, embedding deep learning rather than just re-visiting content. Students will be required to show the quality of their understanding of both religions studied, as they juxtapose them to explore the ambiguities, controversies and implications raised. In this way their own worldviews, those of other students, and the two religions being studied are all brought into dialogue. Expect 'cognitive conflict'! Piaget used this concept to identify the mental discomfort experienced as students are presented with new knowledge which challenges their existing understanding (Piaget, 1975). This is exactly what is needed; remember to be attentive to their questions and to the way they articulate their understanding. They will learn to respond confidently as their knowledge will be very secure, and they will develop their ability to engage thoughtfully and independently. In this way, students will be in a strong position to answer the more narrowly defined questions on the exam paper.

Having studied each religion systematically building on prior knowledge from their KS3 studies, and having juxtaposed these to consider specific truth claims, the themes will then be explored, allowing the students to apply their understanding of each religion to philosophical and ethical issues. This is a rich opportunity to use the exploration of these issues to throw even more light on the fundamental truth claims that drive the religions' responses. Remember the *raison d'être* is to seek truth.

Exemplification

What follows is an example of how we would go about organising the specification content for teaching in our hypothetical RE Department. With the key elements and tools kept firmly in mind, we have chosen to exemplify the AQA Specification A with Christianity and Buddhism as the religions to study. This choice of religions was informed by the existence of significant variation between these two worldviews. For example, in relation to the ontological question of the nature of reality, the answers given by Christianity and Buddhism provide a rich dialogue since they are so very different. The requirements for Christianity include understanding Protestant, Catholic and Orthodox beliefs and practices. For Buddhism the requirements include understanding Mahayana, Theravada and Pure Land traditions. Both the core shared beliefs and the internal diversity of each faith are identified and explored.

We begin with some assumptions which will impact how we plan. We are assuming that Christianity and Buddhism will both have been explored in some way at KS3. We are aware therefore that at least some of the topics included in the specification have already been covered, and will seek to revisit these, 'unpeeling the onion' in a new and enriched way to consolidate and deepen understanding. Other topics will be new and will need to be explored as new 'jigsaw pieces', to mix the metaphors! We are aware of the need to ensure that non-religious worldviews are included. We have 2 lessons of 50 minutes each week. We are planning to teach the beliefs, teachings and practices of Christianity and Buddhism in schemes of work which will have 24 lessons each. This will allow for flexibility.

What follows is an organisational framework; we have not attempted to identify the specifics of lesson plans, resources, or activities, other than the briefest of suggestions.

Autumn term Year 10

Christianity

The systematic study of Christianity begins with several foundation lessons. These require a little explanation. The first lesson will revise and deepen the students' understanding of worldviews, focusing on the relationship between the ontological questions of the nature of ultimate reality, the nature of humanity and the implications of how to live in light of these. Students can be encouraged to (re-)articulate their own worldviews. This is an important starting point in CRE pedagogy. The second and third lessons will provide an overview of the Christian story of salvation history. Wright (2007) argues that there is "enormous pedagogical value in approaching the worldviews of the religions and their secular counterparts in narrative terms" (p.175). The intention of such an overview is to sketch out the outlines of the Christian worldview. In doing so we begin the process of providing students with "a coherent vision of the tradition as a whole" (p.175). Having such an overview will allow students in subsequent lessons to locate the 'parts' of new knowledge, to gain a deeper and grounded understanding of the 'whole'. This is also a useful opportunity for revision and for ascertaining what they already know and can remember! The fourth lesson will focus on Christianity as evident in the world today, and in particular the key denominational differences required by the specification, providing historical and geographical context. The fifth lesson will enable students to make an initial response to the worldview of Christianity.

In subsequent lessons we have chosen to **use critical questions as organisational tools** to explore the content at a deeper level and to raise the key interpretations and variations. These questions are posed at the different levels described below:

a) those relating to truth claims which the tradition makes in and of itself
b) those relating to disagreements within a tradition
c) those relating to disagreements between traditions

As you work through the questions, all the specification content will be covered; the relevant content is identified question by question. It is important that you ground these questions in an exploration of Biblical text. You will also need to make clear reference to the Catholic, Protestant and Orthodox theological variations required, and variations within these denominations too.

Foundation lessons

Lesson 1

Introduction: understanding worldviews

You could use a version of the Year 7 questionnaire on ultimate questions as a starter and then re-visit Lesson 6 introducing the worldviews. You could introduce them to the ontological question triangle – What is the nature of ultimate reality? What is the nature of humanity? How then should we live? These three questions can provide a broad framework for teaching the specification. Think about visually representing this triangle on a display.

Lesson 2 and 3

Christian worldview:

> "The Christian story tells of the Trinitarian God who creates the universe out of nothing, and responds to the reality of the fall of this creation through the redemptive incarnation of the Son and regenerative activity of the Spirit to bring about the final consummation and perfection of creation." (Wright 2007, p.175)

Salvation history: an overview

God

Creation: Humanity: Sin

Covenant: Restoration: The History Of The Jews

Jesus: Salvation: Atonement

Holy Spirit

The Church: Denominations: History

End Times: Judgement And Final Restoration

There are many ways you could teach these lessons. One idea is to produce a chronological representation using the Bible from Genesis to Revelation, a timeline with specific reference to the text. Another idea is to analyse the Creed. Again it is useful if this is visual and you can come back to it and refer to it as you go along.

Lesson 4

Understanding Christianity in the world today

> The Church
>
> Denominational theological differences

Again there are many ways of doing this. Images are really useful, so students again have visual representations of different denominations. You could include leaders, places of worship, important geographical locations. You could organize this as a concept-mapping task in groups for different denominations. The grid in the appendix is really useful to explore (albeit simplistically) the nature of different denominations and branches within the Christian Church.

Lesson 5

Initial responses:

Re-visit the ontological question triangle and allow your students the opportunity to articulate their initial understanding of Christianity and to provide an initial response to this from a personal point of view. Discuss differences, similarities, questions and responses in class, using critical questions to explore the content.

Lessons 6 and 7

Specification content: the nature of God

How can a monotheistic God be three in one?

- the oneness of God and the Trinity: Father, Son and Holy Spirit
- different Christian beliefs about creation including the role of Word and Spirit (John 1:1–3 and Genesis 1:1–3).

Lessons 8, 9 and 10

Specification content: humanity, Jesus, salvation

Jesus: 'mad, bad, God' or something else?

- the incarnation and Jesus as the Son of God
- the crucifixion, resurrection and ascension.

Is humanity sinful by nature?

- sin, including original sin
- the means of salvation, including law, grace and Spirit
- the role of Christ in salvation including the idea of atonement.

Is Jesus the only way to God?

- different Christian beliefs about the afterlife and their importance, including: resurrection and life after death; judgement, heaven and hell.

Lessons 11 and 12

Specification content: theological responses to suffering

If God is good why does He allow evil and suffering?

- God as omnipotent, loving and just, and the problem of evil and suffering.

Lessons 13, 14 and 15

Specification content: how to live as Christians together – the Church

Is there a right way to worship?

- different forms of worship and their significance:

    o liturgical, non-liturgical and informal, including the use of the Bible
    o private worship

- the meaning of sacrament
- the sacrament of baptism and its significance for Christians; infant and believers' baptism; different beliefs about infant baptism
- the sacrament of eucharist (Holy Communion) and its significance for Christians, including different ways in which it is celebrated and different interpretations of its meaning.

How can a Church which appears so divided be effective?

- the importance of the worldwide Church including:

    o working for reconciliation

- how Christian churches respond to persecution.

Lessons 16, 17 and 18

Specification content: how to communicate with God

Does prayer work?

- prayer and its significance, including the Lord's Prayer, set prayers and informal prayer.

Does going on pilgrimage have some special effect?

- the role and importance of pilgrimage
- two contrasting examples of Christian pilgrimage: Lourdes and Iona.

Lessons 19 and 20

Specification content: how to live as Christians in the world

Why are there rich Christians in a world of poverty?

- the role of the Church in the local community, including food banks and street pastors
- the work of one of the following: Catholic Agency For Overseas Development (CAFOD), Christian Aid, Tearfund.

Lessons 21 and 22

Specification content: how to live as Christians in a multifaith world

Are Christmas and Easter for everyone in Britain?

● the role and importance of celebrations including:

    ○ the celebrations of Christmas and Easter, including their importance for Christians in Great Britain today.

Should Christians try and convert people?

● the place of mission, evangelism and Church growth.

Lesson 23

Assessment

Students to sit the relevant part of a past exam paper.

Lesson 24

Reflections and feedback

Re-visit your students' initial responses to the worldview of Christianity as explored in week 5. Use the virtues assessment framework (see Chapter 9) to explore your students' engagement and responses.

Spring term Year 10

Buddhism

We begin with the same process of sketching out the worldview, this time the Buddhist one:

> Buddhism tells the story of human beings entrapped in the cycle of karma, of the Buddha as one of a series of enlightened beings, and of a path of deliverance from the universal experience of suffering, through which the attainment of nirvana – the cessation of desire and the absorption of the self into the infinite – becomes a possibility.
>
> (Wright, 2007, p.175)

We then create a snapshot of the variety of Buddhist practices in the world today with geographical and historical perspectives. Critical questions have then been devised to organise and focus the learning for the rest of the content. Some aspects of the specification should definitely have been covered at KS3, for example, the Buddha and the Four Noble Truths, so begin with these thus ensuring the effective use of a spiral curriculum.

Foundation lessons

Lessons 1, 2 and 3

Reminder of the worldview's ontological question triangle

The Buddha and the Four Noble Truths (revision)

The Buddha's life and its significance:

- the birth of the Buddha and his life of luxury
- the Four Sights: illness, old age, death, holy man (Jataka 075)
- the Buddha's ascetic life
- the Buddha's Enlightenment.

The Four Noble Truths:

1. suffering (dukkha) including different types of suffering
2. the causes of suffering (samudaya); the Three Poisons, ignorance, greed and hate
3. the end of craving (tanha), interpretations of nibbana (nirvana) and Enlightenment
4. the Eightfold Path (magga) to nibbana/nirvana; the path as the Threefold Way: ethics (sila), meditation (samadhi) and wisdom (panna). Dhammapada 190–191.

Lesson 4

Understanding Buddhism in the world today

> The Sangha
>
> Denominational differences

Lesson 5

Buddhist worldview and initial responses

Having revised the Buddha and the Four Noble Truths, re-visit the ontological triangle, to explore with your students their initial understanding of the Buddhist worldview. What is the nature of ultimate reality? What is the view of humanity? How should we then live? Allow them to apply their learning from the previous lessons and then to make an initial response to the Buddhist worldview from the point of view of their own worldview. Record this in some way as it will be useful to re-visit.

Using critical questions to explore the content

Lessons 6 and 7

Specification content: the Dharma

Is it possible to understand Dharma without an understanding of dependent arising?

- the concept of Dhamma (Dharma)
- the concept of dependent arising (paticcasamupada).

Lessons 8 and 9

Specification content: the nature of humanity

Are the three marks of existence self-evidently true?

- the Three Marks of Existence:
  - impermanence (anicca)
  - no fixed self (anatta)
  - unsatisfactoriness of life, suffering (dukkha).

- the human personality, in the Theravada and Mahayana traditions:
  - Theravada: the Five Aggregates (skandhas) of form, sensation, perception, mental formations,consciousness
  - Mahayana: sunyata, the possibility of attaining Buddhahood and Buddha-nature.

Lessons 10 and 11

Specification content: human destiny

Should all Buddhists seek to become bodhisattvas?

- different ideals in Theravada and Mahayana traditions: Arhat (a 'perfected person') and Bodhisattva ideals
- Buddhahood and the Pure Land.

Lessons 12 and 13

Specification content: how to practice Buddhism

Does meditation work?

Is Western mindfulness the same as Buddhist mediation?

- Meditation, the different aims, significance and methods of meditation:
  - Samatha (concentration and tranquility) including mindfulness of breathing
  - Vipassana (insight) including zazen
  - the visualisation of Buddhas and Bodhisattvas.

Lessons 14 and 15

Specification content: how to practice Buddhism

Does it matter how you worship in Buddhism?

- Puja, the significance and role of puja/devotional ritual in the home and in the temple, including chanting, both as a devotional practice and as an aid to mental concentration, mantra recitation, use of malas
- Festivals and retreats and their importance to Buddhists in Great Britain today, including the
- Celebrations, origins and significance of Wesak and Parinirvana Day.

Lessons 16 and 17

Specification content: how to practice Buddhism

Are Buddhist places of worship holy?

- The nature, use and importance of Buddhist places of worship including temples, shrines, monasteries (viharas), halls for meditation or learning (gompas) and their key features including Buddha rupa, artefacts and offerings.

Lessons 18 and 19

Specification content: how to practice Buddhism

Does belief in rebirth fuel self-interest?

- The practice and significance of different ceremonies and rituals associated with death and mourning in Theravada communities and in Japan and Tibet.

Lessons 20, 21 and 22

Specification content: implications for how to live

Why value human life if it is illusory?

Can a Buddhist be a successful banker?

- The five moral precepts: do not take life; do not take what is not given; do not misuse the senses; do not speak falsehoods; do not take intoxicants that cloud the mind
- The six perfections in the Mahayanan tradition: generosity; morality; patience; energy; meditation; wisdom, including how the individual develops these perfections within themselves
- Ethical teaching: kamma (karma) and rebirth; compassion (karuna); loving kindness (metta).

Lesson 23

Assessment

Students to sit the relevant part of a past exam paper.

Lesson 24

Reflections and feedback

Is Buddhism a religion or a philosophy?

Re-visit your students' initial responses to the worldview of Buddhism as explored in Week 5. Use the virtues assessment framework to explore your students' engagement and responses.

Summer term (first half) Year 10

Juxtaposing Christianity and Buddhism

This half term is the really important one for CRE. The students have now explored the worldviews of Christianity and Buddhism, with the narratives and truth claims, and the beliefs, symbols and practices embedded within them. But the exploration and understanding of each religion needs to go even further:

> Critical Religious Education must attend to the process of making informed critical judgements between conflicting truth claims.
>
> (Wright, 2007, p.206)

So the students must be given the opportunity to explore the conflicting truth claims, not shying away from controversy and ambiguity. This they can do through seeking to answer a series of critical questions:

Lessons 1 and 2
- Is there God or no God?

Lessons 3 and 4
- Is life linear or cyclical?

Lessons 5 and 6
- Who are we as Humans?

Lessons 7 and 8
- Are we accountable?

Lessons 9 and 10
- Is the purpose of human life salvation or enlightenment?

Lessons 11 and 12
- Is there life after death?

Lessons 13 and 14
- What impact do our beliefs have on the way we live?

With two lessons on each question, a SOW can be developed which will consolidate existing knowledge and raise misunderstandings organically as students attempt to grapple with these questions. This will also work as an excellent revision opportunity.

Having covered the specification content for Christianity and Buddhism and having grounded the students' understanding using the key ontological questions as a conceptual framework, it is time to move on to consider the philosophical and ethical themes. Christianity and Buddhism will give different answers the questions raised by the themes. It is worth spending a revision lesson mind-mapping the key differences between the two religions in relation to their answers to the key ontological questions, and making it clear that it is important to always have these in mind when exploring the issues. When planning the schemes of work for the philosophical and ethical themes, please refer first to Chapters 5 and 6 of this book.

Summer term (second half) Year 10

Theme C: The existence of God and revelation

This considers philosophical arguments for the existence of God and explores the nature of knowledge of the divine and revelation, which links to the principle of epistemic relativity. Students are required to focus on contrasting beliefs in relation to visions, miracles and nature as general revelation. Students should consider Christianity and non-religious worldviews such as atheism/humanism. It will be important also to bring in Buddhism as a significant variation.

Philosophical arguments for and against the existence of God

Lessons 1–4

Do philosophical arguments for the existence of God help a person believe?

- The Design argument, including its strengths and weaknesses
- The First Cause argument, including its strengths and weaknesses
- The argument from *miracles*, including its strengths and weaknesses, and one example of a miracle.

Lessons 5–6

Is the existence of evil and suffering enough to prove that God doesn't exist?

- Evil and suffering as an argument against the existence of God.

Lessons 7–8

Does science make God redundant?

Does atheism take as much faith as Christianity?

- Arguments based on science against the existence of God.

The nature of the divine and revelation

Lessons 9–11

Is it ever possible to say that you have knowledge of God?

Can scriptures really reveal God?

- Special revelation as a source of knowledge about the divine (God, gods or ultimate reality) including **visions** and one example of a vision

- Enlightenment as a source of knowledge about the divine
- General revelation: **nature** and **scripture** as a way of understanding the divine.

Lessons 12 and 13

Is it possible to describe God using human language?

- Different ideas about the divine that come from these sources:
  - omnipotent and omniscient
  - personal and impersonal
  - immanent and transcendent.

Lessons 14–16

Are all miracles explicable to some extent by science?

Are all religious experiences as valid as each other?

- The value of general and special revelation and enlightenment as sources of knowledge about the divine, including: The problems of different ideas about the divine arising from these experiences
- Alternative explanations for the experiences, and the possibility that the people who claimed to have them were lying or mistaken.

Autumn term (first half) Year 11

Theme B: Religion and life

This is chosen because it gives an opportunity to explore three specific ethical issues which raise the question of origins and value and respond to very different cosmologies. The theme also allows students to consider how a western scientific view relates to Buddhism, atheism/humanism and Christianity. The students are required to focus on abortion, euthanasia and animal experimentation. These will need to be explored individually to explain contrasting beliefs held by Christians, Buddhists and Atheists.

Origins and value of the universe

Lessons 1–3

Does science trump religion on questions of how the universe began?

- The origins of the universe, including: religious teachings about the origins of the universe, and different interpretations of these; the relationship between scientific views, such as the Big Bang theory, and religious views.

Lessons 4–7

Is the material world of value?

Does nirvana or heaven provide humans with a get-out clause for caring in the 'here and now'?

- The value of the world and the duty of human beings to protect it, including religious teaching about: stewardship, dominion, responsibility, awe and wonder. The use and abuse of the environment, including the use of natural resources, pollution
- The use and abuse of animals, including: animal experimentation and the use of animals for food.

Origin and value of human life

Lessons 8–10

Does science trump religion on the question of how human life began?

- The origins of life, including:
  - religious teachings about the origins of human life, and different interpretations of these
  - the relationship between scientific views, such as evolution, and religious views.

Lesson 11

How do the sanctity of life and free will work together?

- The concepts of sanctity of life and the quality of life.

Lesson 12–14

Have we the right to choose anything for ourselves?

- Abortion, including situations when the mother's life is at risk
- Ethical arguments related to abortion, including those based on the sanctity of life and quality of life
- Euthanasia.

Lesson 15–16

Is any belief in an afterlife nonsensical?

- Beliefs about death and an afterlife, and their impact on beliefs about the value of human life.

Autumn Term (second half) Year 11

Theme D: Religion, peace and conflict

This is chosen as it focuses on some of the most significant issues on the political world stage at the moment. The students are required to focus on violence, weapons of mass destruction and pacifism. Students must be able to explain contrasting beliefs on these issues with reference to Christianity, Buddhism and atheism/humanism.

Religion, violence, terrorism and war

Lesson 1– 2

Is it always right to forgive and seek reconciliation?

- The meaning and significance of:
  - o Peace
  - o Justice
  - o Forgiveness
  - o Reconciliation.

Lesson 3–4

Is human violence inevitable?

Can terrorism ever be acceptable?

- Violence, including violent protest
  - o Terrorism
  - o Reasons for war, including greed, self-defence and retaliation.

Lesson 5–6

Can a Just War ever be holy?

- The just war theory, including the criteria for a just war
  - o Holy war.

Lesson 7–8

Is pacifism just an easy way out?

Why is it so hard to live at peace?

- Pacifism.

Religion and belief in 21st century conflict

Lesson 9–10

Is religion the root cause of war?

- Religion and belief as a cause of war and violence in the contemporary world.

Lesson 11–12

Why bother having weapons as deterrents if they must never be used?

Can WMD ever be justified?

- Nuclear weapons, including nuclear deterrence
- The use of weapons of mass destruction.

Lesson 13–14

If religions are the cause of war, how can they also be the solution?

- Religion and peace-making in the contemporary world including the work of individuals influenced by religious teaching
- Religious responses to the victims of war including the work of one present day religious organisation.

Spring Term (first half) Year 11

Theme F: Religion, human rights and social justice

Human rights provide an interesting focus as they are often unquestionably accepted, without exploring their foundational principles. The concept of social justice is often accepted with limited consideration of motivation. This is very different depending on the answer given to the question of ontological reality. The students are required to focus on the status of women in religion, the uses of wealth and freedom of religious expression.

Students must be able to explain contrasting beliefs on these issues with reference to Christianity, Buddhism and atheism/humanism.

Human rights

Lessons 1–2

Will women ever have equality with men?

Is being religious and gay a contradiction?

- Prejudice and discrimination in religion and belief, including the status and treatment within religion of women and homosexuals.

Lessons 3–4

Should religious believers conform to social norms?

Can religious views and western society's views ever be fully reconciled?

- Issues of equality, freedom of religion and belief including freedom of religious expression.

Lesson 5

Does belief in God take away the notion of human rights?

- Human rights and the responsibilities that come with rights, including the responsibility to respect the rights of others.

Lesson 6

Is social justice an unrealistic dream?

- Social justice.

Lesson 7–8

Can racism ever be acceptable?

- Racial prejudice and discrimination
- Ethical arguments related to racial discrimination (including positive discrimination), including those based on the ideals of equality and justice.

Wealth and poverty

Lesson 9–10

Can you be religious and rich in an age of hunger?

- Wealth, including:
  - o the right attitude to wealth
  - o the uses of wealth
- The responsibilities of wealth, including the duty to tackle poverty and its causes.

Lesson 11–12

Are payday loans immoral?

- Exploitation of the poor including issues relating to:
  - o fair pay
  - o excessive interest on loans
  - o people-trafficking.

Lesson 13

Is it the fault of the poor that they are poor?

● The responsibilities of those living in poverty to help themselves overcome the difficulties they face.

Lesson 14

Is giving to charity more than removing guilt?

● Charity, including issues related to giving money to the poor.

Revision

Throughout the teaching and learning, we would of course expect regular exam question practice, but do ensure you concentrate on the conceptual understanding. This will move the focus from teaching your students how to complete PEEL paragraphs, to ensuring a really solid understanding of the religions and issues studied. Once the students are able to engage meaningfully, their writing will develop so much more easily.

Note

1 See Chapter 8 on virtues assessment.

References

AQA (2016). Assessment Resources. Available online at http://www.aqa.org.uk/subjects/religious-studies/gcse/religious-studies-a-8062/assessment-resources.

Barber, P. (2015) Setting the record straight on the new RE GCSE in Catholic Schools. *The Catholic Education Service* (16/11/15) online. http://www.catholiceducation.org.uk/news/ces-news/item/1003017-setting-the-record-straight-on-the-new-re-gcse-in-catholic-schools.

Bruner, J. (1977). *The Process of Education (Revised Edition)*. London: Harvard University Press.

Cooling, T. (1994). *Concept Cracking: Exploring Christian Beliefs in School*. Nottingham: The Stapleford Centre.

Department for Education (2015). Religious studies GCSE content. Available online at: https://www.gov.uk/government/publications/gcse-religious-studies.

Department for Education (2016). Statement on the religious studies GCSE judicial review. Available online at: http://www.gov.uk/government/news/statement-on-the-religious-studies-gsce-judicial-review.

Hella, E. and Wright, A. (2009). Learning 'about' and 'from' religion: phenomenography, the Variation Theory of Learning and Religious Education in Finland and the UK. *British Journal of Religious Education* 31, no.1, 53–64.

HM Government (1996). *Education Act*. HMSO.

Juss, S. (2016). High Court Ruling on Religious Education: Legal guidance on what it means for local authorities, academies, schools, teachers, Agreed Syllabus Conferences, and SACREs. Available online at: https://humanism.org.uk/wp-content/uploads/2016-04-28-FINAL-High-Court-ruling-on-Religious-Education-legal-guidance.pdf (accessed 25/08/16).

National Association of Teachers of Religious Education (2016). Highest number of entries for full course GCSE in Religious Studies since 2002. Available online at: http://www.natre.org.uk/news/latest-news/highest-number-of-entries-for-full-course-gcse-in-religious-studies-since-2002/.

Pells, R. (2016). Humanists threaten further legal action over 'unlawful' religious studies GCSE syllabus. *The Independent* 02/06/16. Available online at: http://www.independent.co.uk/news/education/education-news/humanists-threaten-further-legal-action-over-unlawful-religious-studies-gcse-syllabus-a7061266.html (accessed 09/08/16).

Piaget, J. (1975). *The Equilibration of Cognitive Structures: The Central Problem of Intellectual Development*. Chicago: University of Chicago Press.

Rocker, S. (2016). Worries over rule to teach Christianity. *The Jewish Chronicle* 02/06/16. Available online at: https://www.thejc.com/news/uk-news/worries-over-rule-to-teach-christianity-1.58002?highlight=GCSE (accessed 15/08/16).

The Religious Education Council (2013). A Curriculum Framework for Religious Education in England. Available online at http://resubjectreview.recouncil.org.uk/media/file/RE_Review_Summary.pdf (accessed 15/08/16).

Wright, A. (2007). *Critical Religious Education, Multiculturalism and the Pursuit of Truth*. Cardiff: University of Wales Press.

Appendix

Ontological Triangle

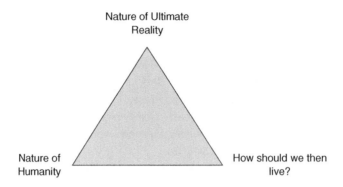

Nature of Ultimate Reality

Nature of Humanity

How should we then live?

Denominational differences in Christianity

The specification requirement is that students have understanding of Protestant, Catholic and Orthodox traditions. The differences which exist in the interpretation of beliefs, the nature of worship and the application of these to ethical responses are really important to understand. It may be useful to use the following grid as a means of locating different Christian denominations (with thanks to the Very Reverend Dr Jeffrey Johns who used this in a King's PGCE session many years ago):

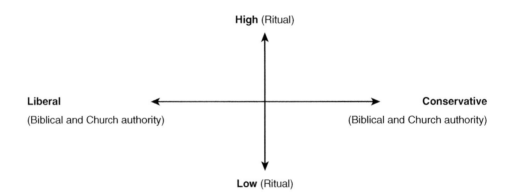

High (Ritual)

Liberal
(Biblical and Church authority)

Conservative
(Biblical and Church authority)

Low (Ritual)

CHAPTER 8

Critical Religious Education and assessment

Assessment in religious education (RE) has always been tricky. To begin with, there is uncertainty over what exactly is being assessed. Is it students' knowledge and understanding? If so, knowledge and understanding of what? Or is it more important to assess the skills they are developing? Perhaps spiritual development is what is of primary importance? Even once we have decided *what* it is we are trying to assess, there remains the further problem of *how* one assesses.

The situation is further complicated as RE has generally sought to fall in line with the curriculum content and assessment expectations of the National Curriculum. These have been the subject of significant reform. In this chapter we will review the current situation and reflect on some of the issues around assessment in RE, before putting forward a framework for assessment developed specifically to fit with a CRE pedagogy.

The current situation with the National Curriculum

There have been many significant changes to the National Curriculum and to its assessment and accountability. The most significant changes which have impacted RE are as follows:

- As part of the government reforms to the National Curriculum, the system of 'levels' used to report students' attainment and progress was removed from September 2014 and not replaced. (Department for Education, 2014)
- New GCSE examinations have been brought in with a new grading system. This replaces A* to G with 9 to 1, beginning with English and Mathematics in 2017 with the other subjects following in 2018. (Department for Education, 2015)
- New A Level examinations have been introduced with the teaching of the RS specifications from September 2016. The AS and A Level qualifications have been decoupled, with AS results no longer counting towards the A Level, and all examinations are now linear. (Department for Education, 2015)
- There are new accountability arrangements – Progress 8 and Attainment 8. These two indicators of school performance are based on students' performance across 8 subjects. Attainment 8 measures each student's average grade from their best 8 GCSE results. These 8 subjects are taken from three

groups: English and Maths (these are double weighted), EBacc subjects and an open group. The school's Attainment 8 figure is the average of its students' Attainment 8s. Progress 8 constitutes each student's progress score, calculated by relating each student's Attainment 8 score to their Key Stage 2 test score in Reading and Mathematics. The school's Progress 8 figure is the average of its students' Progress 8s. (Department for Education, 2016)

The impact of reforms on Religious Education

As Religious Education is not included in the EBacc, its inclusion in Progress 8 and Attainment 8 is dependent on schools choosing to include it as a subject in the 'open group'. RS GCSE counts as a 'high value' academic qualification on this list for the purposes of Attainment 8. However these new performance measures do not recognise short course GCSEs and this has had a negative impact on uptake by some schools (Thomson, 2015).

While schools consider the impact of Progress 8 and Attainment 8, teachers have been tasked with becoming acquainted with the new GCSE and A Level specifications and have also been faced with the significant task of re-thinking assessment at Key Stage 3. Levels were found wanting. They failed to represent performance accurately, distracted from teaching, worked with a 'best-fit' model, were open to interpretation and "did not lend themselves to assessing the underpinning knowledge and understanding of a concept" (Department for Education, 2015, p.13). By removing the levels and not prescribing replacement assessment expectations, the intention was to "allow teachers greater flexibility in the way that they plan and assess students' learning" (Department for Education, 2014, p.2). Whilst this 'flexibility' may appear daunting, it offers a really important and exciting opportunity, allowing us to consider again the intrinsic nature of the subject, and the implications of this for student learning. The report by the Commission on Assessment without Levels stressed that "Assessment of pupils' attainment and progress should be directly linked to the curriculum" (Department for Education, 2015, p.15). RE teachers have an opportunity to put the students' engagement with the subject matter at the very heart of any assessment process.

The current situation with the RE curriculum

In September 2018, the Commission on Religious Education published its final report, following a period of consultation. This project was seeking to respond not only to the changes nationally but also to emerging and concerning evidence that RE provision in many schools was significantly lacking and the subject appeared to be in a precarious position. The Commission sought to tackle issues of entitlement and provision, as well as organisational problems which need addressing to ensure that RE has an appropriate framework, particularly in light of academisation and the impact of this on SACREs and Agreed Syllabuses.

The recommendations are largely welcome and could provide a positive way forward for the subject. They include the re-naming of the subject as Religion and Worldviews. In a very clear way this reveals a growing consensus that a multiplicity of worldviews is the appropriate content for RE, a view which has been central to the CRE pedagogical approach for the last 25 years!

It is interesting to note, however, that there was no reference at all in the Commission report to assessment. It may well be that this was seen as outside of the remit of the report, but it does indicate that the national programmes of study which are a core recommendation of the report, (i.e. the content to be studied) are conceptually at a distance from the process of assessment.

To find the most recent reference to assessment, we need to go back further. It was as a response to the initial National Curriculum reforms, that the RE Review and National Curriculum Framework for Religious Education (NCFRE) was published in 2013. The Review evaluated the state of play for RE, referencing the research project Does RE Work? which was forthright in its evaluation, concluding 'bluntly' that

> RE has tried to do too much, re-inventing itself to include within its brief additional whole-school priorities – 'community cohesion', for example – and seeking to provide social, moral and values education so that the sense of a substantive core or essence of the subject has been eroded
>
> (The Religious Education Council of England and Wales, 2013, p.49).

The review was written with a determination to encourage progress and includes recommendations for developing and sustaining RE in the 21st century. One of these recommendations is to "develop new assessment arrangements for RE" (2013, p.32) The NCFRE did not attempt to replace the levels or prescribe a specific way of assessing the subject, but recognised that this remained an urgent need. What the NCFRE did do was to offer freshly articulated aims for RE which sought to reconstruct the 'substantive core' for the subject. These are listed below:

A. Know about and understand a range of religions and worldviews, so that they can:

- describe, explain and analyse beliefs and practices, recognising the diversity which exists within and between communities and amongst individuals;
- identify, investigate and respond to questions posed, and responses offered by some of the sources of wisdom found in religions and worldviews;
- appreciate and appraise the nature, significance and impact of different ways of life and ways of expressing meaning.

B. Express ideas and insights about the nature, significance and impact of religions and worldviews, so that they can:

- explain reasonably their ideas about how beliefs, practices and forms of expression influence individuals and communities;
- express with increasing discernment their personal reflections and critical responses to questions and teachings about identity, diversity, meaning and value, including ethical issues;
- appreciate and appraise varied dimensions of religion or a worldview.

C. Gain and deploy the skills needed to engage seriously with religions and worldviews, so that they can:

- find out about and investigate key concepts and questions of belonging, meaning, purpose and truth, responding creatively;

- enquire into what enables different individuals and communities to live together respectfully for the wellbeing of all;
- articulate beliefs, values and commitments clearly in order to explain why they may be important in their own and other people's lives. (The RE Council, 2013, p.11)

The NCFRE set appropriately high standards with regard to the scope of RE and the nature of skills which the students should be developing; explanation, interpretation, enquiry and evaluation are all appropriate and necessary. However it did not provide a specific pedagogical framework and this was never its intention. If we understand pedagogy as being "a theory of teaching and learning encompassing aims, curriculum content and methodology" (Grimmitt, 2000 p.16), it is important to recognise the limitations of a *framework*. As a framework it *could* only offer broad 'aims' and exemplification. It is important to be really clear that whilst the NCFRE provides a valuable re-modelling of the subject, it could not fully construct the 'substantive core' needed for the subject. There is a danger of a disconnection between aims, content and methodology such that any pedagogical approach became seen as an after-thought rather than a raison d'etre. It is not possible to put together a coherent embodied vision for RE without acknowledging the pedagogical and philosophical assumptions which inform it. Grimmitt recognised that "all pedagogical models of RE are expressions of certain assumptions about how education and religion can be brought into a relationship within the context of a secular educational system" (2000, p.17). The possibility of programmes of study being introduced in response to the Commission's Final Report, would bring specific content into play. This would reveal more starkly the need for there to be a clear understanding of the specific aims of the subject, as they relate to particular content. With CRE we offer a coherent vision for the subject. CRE has an unfaltering commitment to understanding learning in RE to be about seeking truth. CRE can work with the NCFRE aims, but we would want to move truth-seeking to a centre stage position.

It is of course possible to work with a CRE pedagogy within the NCFRE framework. Applying a CRE pedagogy to schemes of work which were not designed specifically to seek truth, is a bit like focusing the lens of your camera – the object you want to concentrate on will become sharply defined. In a similar way you can use CRE if you are still using levels. (Many schools have kept these on for the moment as they wait to see what alternative models are developed.) For example, CRE requires students to be able to describe (Level 4), explain (Level 5), compare (Level 6) and evaluate (Level 7) religious beliefs and practices (see The Non-Statutory National Framework for RE, Qualifications and Curriculum Authority, 2004, p.37). It is possible to take any religious content and apply a CRE pedagogy to it, and also to work within existing assessment systems. It will just require the focus and purpose of the learning to be shifted to exploring truth claims.

The current situation with RE assessment

For secondary teachers, re-designing KS3 programmes of study in response to the NCFRE and creative re-thinking of assessment are priority concerns. Often curriculum design and assessment have been considered as if they are separate entities. We creatively plan exciting ways of delivering content in the classroom and only then as an after-thought consider how to assess the learning. But content and assessment must go hand in hand.

With the removal of levels, how can we avoid some of their pitfalls? Levels were expressed in the generic language of skills and this meant we over-complicated assessment. It necessitated a process of applying 'disembodied level statements' to any content taught, which could only be done with subjective and time-consuming analysis and interpretation (Expert Advisory Group, 2015, p.13). It is important to recognise that although CRE entails significant skill development, this is not at its heart. Instead this is an outcome of the pedagogy rather than its aim. Instead assessment of student learning in CRE focuses on the subject itself. The Commission on Assessment without Levels encouraged teachers to ensure ". . . assessment directly evaluates pupils' knowledge and understanding of curriculum requirements". In this way "a virtuous circle of teaching and assessment" can be created (Department for Education, 2015 p.16).

The correlation between curriculum content and assessment was explained by Dilwyn Hunt in a keynote lecture on assessment given at the 2015 Culham St. Gabriel's 'Energising RE Conference'. He made reference to the work of the expert panel set up to provide guidance for the National Curriculum and assessment reforms. The panel recommended that teaching should cover fewer topics, in greater depth (Department for Education, 2013). It suggested that there should be a focus on essential knowledge and that the detail of what is to be taught should be specified carefully. Lastly, there should be a direct and clear relationship between that which is taught and learned, and assessment. By prioritising skills in levels assessment, our focus had been forced to move from the curriculum, the *what* of learning, to the process of learning, the *how* of learning. Whilst formative assessment requires an engagement with the metacognitive processes of learning, for any such assessment to be meaningful it must never become dislocated from a student's understanding of the subject itself. It is a student's engagement with knowledge and understanding which is the motivator and characteristic of deep learning.

This emphasis on the assessment of knowledge rather than skills fits naturally with a CRE approach due to its realist roots. If we accept that reality exists independently of our knowledge about it and we seek to come closer to the truth about that reality then the ongoing development of our knowledge is fundamental. This is not to say that skill development is unimportant in CRE. Indeed, one cannot make reasonable judgements about the reality in which we live without developing the skills of analysis and evaluation for example. But the development of these skills is necessarily secondary to the focus on honing our knowledge. In contrast, constructivist frameworks (which either implicitly or explicitly deny that we can discover the truth about an external reality) are more likely to prioritise skill development over the acquisition of knowledge. If we cannot gain true knowledge of the external word (or such a world doesn't even exist) then all we can do is construct ideas (which may or may not be shared depending on the particular constructivist philosophy in play). Thus, the aim of education becomes the development of ourselves and/or social cohesion, hence transferable skills. This profound difference between the aims and outcomes of constructivist and realist pedagogy is highlighted in the ongoing work of both Wright and Goodman as presented at the AULRE conference in 2018. For the purpose of this chapter it suffices to say that a primary focus on knowledge, both for curriculum content and assessment, is necessary in any CRE context.

Given this intrinsic relationship between curriculum and assessment, we must begin our task of developing effective assessment processes with the curriculum. The NCFRE guidance provides principles for curriculum design: being clear about the purpose of RE; balancing areas of enquiry/content and incorporating a model of progression. If these principles are consistently applied, the resulting programme of study can be described as a coherent 'learning journey' within a year, within a key stage and across phases (Expert Advisory Group, 2015, p.5). The NCFRE guidance suggests that a model of progression has the following characteristics:

- The study of specific religions and worldviews should become deeper and more comprehensive
- Vocabulary should become wider, more abstract and used more competently
- Enquiries, concepts, content and source materials should become more challenging and complex and concepts integrated into a coherent narrative in relation to the matters studied
- Pupils should become more challenging and perceptive in the questions they ask
- Pupils' responses should become more complex and more closely identified with the material and sources they are studying (2015, p.5).

When you use CRE pedagogy to develop a programme of study these principles for curriculum design are very useful. You will have a specific understanding of the purpose of RE – to seek truth. You will balance the content; this will be prescribed by your Agreed Syllabus or Diocesan Syllabus but you will prioritise truth claims and introduce significant variation. You will incorporate all the characteristics of a model of progression but these will be grounded in a specific understanding of the nature and purpose of study.

CRE assessment – a way forward

> Learning is always the acquired knowledge of something. And we should always keep in mind what that something is, that is, we should be clear about the object of learning.
>
> (Marton et al, 2004, p.4)

In CRE we are concerned primarily with our students' understanding of the topic being studied. When we plan our lessons, we devise learning objectives which embody what we want them to learn. These learning objectives are also the assessment criteria. We need to assess the extent to which the students have learnt what we have intended them to learn. If they have not learnt what we intended, we must ask why. We must reflect on these intentions (our planning, teaching and resources, their nature, pitch and appropriateness) and the assumptions we may have made and carefully compare these to what the students have actually learnt. We can then make changes if their learning has fallen short, and celebrate if they have been taken further in their learning than we hoped. This process embodies the "virtuous circle of teaching and assessment" we are looking to create (Department for Education, 2015, p.16). It offers us a simple and coherent idea of the process of assessment, strongly and directly correlated to content.

In order to ensure this "virtuous circle" we must consider the nature of CRE pedagogy itself, as "assessment and pedagogy are inextricably connected"

(Department for Education, 2015, p.16). The pedagogy of CRE is concerned with students' exploration of ontological reality, through the consideration of different interpretations embodied in the rich variety of worldviews. This exploration necessitates an acknowledgement of epistemic relativity, and involves students making informed responses, through the process of judgemental rationality. Learning involves a process embodying the principles of critical realism. Thus the principles of critical realism within CRE offer us an inbuilt **framework for assessment**.

Evaluating students' engagement with religious truth can be challenging as they are required to make critical judgements, and it can be difficult for a teacher to assess students' reasoning and critical analysis and to respond to the conclusions they reach. However, CRE's primary concerns are both truth and truthfulness, and the approach stipulates that these are intimately linked. "To be truthful is to act habitually in a loyal, faithful, honest and upright manner" (Wright, 2007, p.15). This resonates with a virtue-based approach and Wright (2012) suggests four intellectual virtues that characterise the type of engagement at the heart of CRE. These relate to the three basic principles of critical realism. These virtues offer us **criteria for assessment**.

1. **ATTENTIVENESS** – This virtue relates to ontological reality. Attentiveness assesses the understanding a student has of the topic, looking for evidence of close attention to it. Attentive students will describe the **beliefs, practices, concepts and issues** explored with accuracy. They will explain how these relate to each other and how they fit into a particular worldview. It is not enough for students to just regurgitate facts; an attentive appreciation of the topic is only possible with the students' active participation, engaging their own worldviews with the new perspectives shared. In this way learning is essentially and necessarily personal. It encompasses each student's thinking, feeling, communicating and acting.

2. **DEPTH** – This virtue relates to epistemic relativity. Depth is dependent on students having the opportunity to engage with sufficient, appropriate and challenging variations within the content. Students will explore a variety of different ways of understanding the nature of reality as this is contested. Their learning will be characterised by a sound comprehension of **significant variations and interpretations**, revealed through clear and detailed explanation. Their engagement with these different interpretations will be thoughtful and carefully considered and will be accompanied by epistemic humility. This is characteristic of an increasing awareness that our knowledge is limited; our beliefs may change, they could be wrong, others could be right, so holding them with humility is always appropriate.

3. **DISCERNMENT** – This virtue relates to judgemental rationality, which is concerned with the pursuit of truth. CRE focuses on critical issues regarding our place in the ultimate order-of-things and requires students to propose carefully balanced and evidenced arguments. Students will need to ensure that their engagement and evaluation are considered, coherent, consistent, justified and wise. In this way, students will seek to be reasonable in their **personal responses** to questions of ultimate truth.

4. **RESPONSIBILITY** – This virtue relates to the implication of judgemental rationality that of **truthful living**. If learning involves the whole person, in thinking, feeling, communicating and acting, then responsibility is about how students will seek to live truthfully. 'Lex Orandi, Lex Credendi': as we act, so we believe,

as we believe, so we act. Through the process of learning, understanding will have been enriched, perceptions may have changed, and students will be encouraged to consider how they are living in light of this. The impact of such learning on students' lives, understood as personal and holistic, is our ultimate concern, but the responsibility for this lies solely with the students.

The first two virtues loosely embody 'knowledge and understanding' and the third virtue, 'evaluation'. To this end it is possible to see how a CRE understanding of assessment could be used with already existing assessment structures and strategies (for example, the legacy *'learning about' and 'learning from'* assessment criteria) in order to imbibe them with new meaning and purpose. However the fourth virtue goes beyond a correlation with a customary understanding of *'learning from'*. It offers something new and requires further attention.

Understanding 'responsibility'

'Responsibility' as an aspect of learning goes beyond the remit of the teacher to assess. This is personal. We can only know what our students are prepared to share with us, and what is evident from the way they are choosing to live their lives. This type of learning is neither linear nor immediate; it may lie dormant, it may be hidden, it may be conflicted or it may appear clearly expressed and self-evident. However it is perceived at any moment in time, it will always be subject to change. On-going engagement with the nature of ontological reality is, after all, a life-long pursuit and not confined to the RE classroom!

There are two issues here. Firstly we need to acknowledge that many within the RE community have rightly and consistently argued that the personal and affective aspects of learning are both difficult and/or inappropriate for a teacher to assess. This has meant the conventional *'learning from'* assessment criteria has often been applied in a woolly or tangential way. It is our assertion however, that no consideration of ontological reality can ever take place without such personal learning happening on some level; it is both inevitable and essential. Hella and Wright (2009, p.10) argue that students "by learning about religion . . . must necessarily learn from religion by considering the relationship between their own worldview and the worldview of the religious or secular tradition they are studying". CRE provides students with the specific opportunity to consider the implications of what they have learnt and to assess for themselves any impact this has had on how they are choosing to live their lives. This is why the virtue of responsibility is self-assessed by the students rather than by the teacher.

Secondly, we need to acknowledge that any such self-assessment is likely to be imprecise and messy! There is an ambiguity around the relationship between beliefs and actions. The impact of one on the other is often unclear, which makes any such assessment both challenging and interesting. Students' reflections need careful articulation and the fact that this may be difficult makes it all the more important. For example, consider Wolff who finds himself "very sympathetic to the moral case for ending animal experiments and for vegetarianism" and yet recognises "the peculiarity is that, for me at least, I do not find that such arguments, however intellectually compelling, of very strong motivational force" (2011, p.32). He understands that it is often difficult and personally challenging to act on beliefs, and that living with some level of hypocrisy is not an unusual position in which to find oneself. This is perhaps an insight which resonates with Muslims in relation to greater jihad, and Christians may see reflected in Paul's writing in Romans (7:18–19). Such ongoing tension and existential concern about the relationship between belief and action is fundamental and unavoidable when seeking to live truthfully. As such we are committed to engaging the students in this way as an essential part of the learning process.

We recognise that students may choose not to share their thinking with us, or to misrepresent their responses, or even to lie. It may be that students' perceptions may alter rather than there being any significant change in their actions. All these possible responses need to be acknowledged, talked about and accepted. It is up to each of your students to complete their self-assessment. It is their decision and their responsibility which makes this opportunity really important. (If you are concerned that this autonomy may lead to final marks which could give a skewed picture of your students' progress, you could choose to record the teacher and student assessment marks separately. This would enable you to use the teacher assessment as the raw marks by which to monitor progress.)

A CRE Virtues Assessment Framework

The concern of any assessment system is always to "advance pupil progress and outcomes" (Department for Education, 2016, p.8). The independent report 'Eliminating unnecessary workload around marking' recommends that teachers "seek to develop a range of assessment techniques to support their pedagogy" (2016, p.11). It identifies that marking should be "meaningful, manageable and motivating" (2016, p.5). These are appropriate characteristics for all aspects of assessment and we used them as guiding principles as we produced the CRE assessment framework.

We believe that the CRE assessment framework exemplifies excellent practice. It has the following features:

- It recognises that assessment must directly relate to knowledge and understanding of the content studied.
- It limits 'deep marking' (Department for Education, 2016, p.6) to an end-of-topic assessment which provides students with the opportunity to show and apply what they have learnt throughout the scheme of work.
- It prioritises formative assessment, understood particularly as meaningful relational communication about learning. This is central to CRE pedagogy.
- It is concerned with the students developing virtues in relation to specific knowledge, rather than developing skills, independent of and disembodied from content.

A suggested process of assessment

At the beginning of the year

- The students will be given a copy of the **virtues assessment framework** to stick in their books at the beginning of the year (see table 1). This will be explained and explored with them.

- The students will also be given a **monitoring sheet** (see table 3) to stick into their books at the beginning of the year. This will involve recording marks awarded for each topic and adding brief comments by the teacher and the student.

Before you start teaching a topic

- Write your scheme of work. This should consist of a series of lesson plans with clearly identified learning objectives, with accompanying resources as needed (see chapters 3–6 as examples).
- Write the summative end of topic assessment. Keep this simple. Look at examples in chapters 3–6. Include group preparation and discussion, before giving an individual task.
- Teachers will produce a **specific mark scheme/feedback sheet** for the end of topic assessment, using the virtues as assessment criteria (see Table 8.2 below for an example). This can be shared with the students when they are reaching the end of the topic and preparing for their assessment.

At the beginning of the topic

- Each scheme of work will have a summative end of topic assessment. This will allow students to show their knowledge and understanding of the topic. The nature of this assessment, its question and format, should be shared with the students at the beginning of the topic, so they have a clear idea both of the purpose of their learning and how they are going to be assessed. They will need to understand that all the lessons are building up to them being able to complete this assessment effectively.
- Explain the nature of the formative assessment you will use with the students throughout the topic. In particular stress that all work will be closely monitored. Classwork tasks will be formatively assessed, and homework tasks will be acknowledged and comments may be given, but only as required.

During the topic

- Teachers will use the learning objectives of each lesson as assessment criteria. Your purpose in monitoring student work carefully is to see whether they have learnt what you intended them to. Remember there is fluidity to this type of learning developed around dialogue. Expect to be surprised by what they have written! They need to know that you have read what they have written – this is essential. Use short comments and symbols – lots of encouraging ticks! But this feedback does not need to be detailed. It needs to be short and pertinent!

At the end of the topic

- When you get to the end of the topic and are beginning the summative assessment, share the mark scheme with the students.
- When the summative assessment has been completed, use the mark scheme to mark and comment on students' work (Table 8.2).

Table 8.1 CRE virtues-based assessment

Virtues assessment framework A *virtue is a good habit or a character trait. It is something admirable and valuable. It is* *a habit, like being friendly. This is something you can get better at* *over time, through practice – whether you're a friendly person isn't fixed.* *The assessment of your learning is about you as a person, not just about what you can* *remember or write down. Virtues assessment looks at you through your work and seeks* *to show how you are growing through your learning. This is about your engagement* *and the quality of your ideas and responses.* Each assessment will be marked against the following criteria: **Attentiveness, depth, discernment and responsibility.** Your teacher will mark the first three of these virtues with a mark from 1–5, with 5 being the highest mark. You will be given a mark out of 15. You will then assess yourself against the criterion of **responsibility**. You will give yourself a mark from 1–5. These marks will be added to give you a final mark out of 20.	
Teacher assessment	**You showed you are developing the virtue of 'Attentiveness' because . . .** You paid careful attention to the topic. You described accurately the **beliefs, practices, concepts and issues** explored. You showed you understood them, by explaining how they relate to each other and how they are part of a specific worldview. You asked questions about how people choose to act on their beliefs (what they look like in practice). You considered carefully how these beliefs and ideas were similar or different to your own. **You showed you are developing the virtue of 'Depth' because . . .** You identified and accurately described the important and contrasting **variations and interpretations** of belief and practice which exist in relation to the topic. You explained these different variations and interpretations, why these differences exist, how they developed and why they are important to different believers. You asked questions about how to make sense of these differences without being afraid. You appreciated that people act on these differences and live in different ways. You also recognised where ideas were similar and what believers hold in common. You recognised the limitations of your own knowledge and responded with humility to the different interpretations as you encountered them.

(continued)

Table 8.1 (continued)

	You showed you are developing the virtue of 'Discernment' because . . . You identified your own beliefs and your own worldview. You understood that different beliefs can sometimes lead people into conflict. You thought carefully about your **response** to the topic; you explained what this was and justified this with careful attention to what you had learnt about the beliefs and interpretations of others. You recognised when aspects of the topic didn't seem to fit together or make sense to you. You thought carefully about how something fitted with or challenged your own beliefs. You were sensitive to beliefs expressed which were different from your own. You understood that different interpretations could be controversial or difficult to make sense of or reconcile. You were careful not to make quick or rash judgements. You evaluated others' responses and asked questions about why one response could be right or better than another. You did not seek to win arguments but you listened and learned from others with the aim of getting to the right answer. You ensured any arguments were **carefully balanced and justified with evidence.**
Student self-assessment	**I showed I am developing the virtue of 'Responsibility' because . . .** I evaluated my own response to the topic carefully and honestly and in this way developed my own beliefs and ideas. I considered carefully what **the implications of my response were for how I should live.** I sought to understand myself better and to understand those who did not share my worldview. I understood the importance of not being fearful, and of keeping an open mind as I encountered new ideas. I considered carefully what could be true and recognised when my perceptions on the topic had changed. I understood that, whatever my faith position, my understanding is limited and that it is right to hold my views humbly, and I have remained open to the possibility that they could be wrong. In light of the topic, I have tried to ensure that **what I believe and what I do mirror each other.**

- The feedback sheet will then be shared with the each student, who will complete the responsibility self-assessment. This will be stuck into their books and the final mark recorded by the teacher.
- A final grade will then be given and recorded on their monitoring sheet (see Table 8.3). Short comments will be added to provide a summary of the longer comments on the specific mark scheme/feedback sheet (see Table 8.2).

Remember there can be no attentiveness, no depth, no discernment, nor responsibility apart from the knowledge-relationship between the students and the subject. Remember too that skill development is inherent within the learning. This model assumes that students' oracy and literacy skills will be improved through the learning without diverting attention from the topic itself.

Tables 8.1, 8.2, and 8.3 are to be used with Key Stage 3 students:

Table 8.1: This table provides an explanation of CRE virtues-based assessment. This can be shared with students and stuck into their books for reference.

Table 8.2: This table is an example of a mark scheme for the Year 7 scheme of work (chapter 3). Mark schemes can be written for each scheme of work and can be used to accurately assess students' attentiveness, depth, reasonableness and responsibility.

Table 8.3: This is a monitoring sheet, which can be used to enable progress to be monitored. Marks and teacher and student comments can be recorded for each scheme of work.

Table 8.2 Mark scheme for the Year 7 scheme of work

ASSESSMENT		
Year 7: Does God exist?		
You will be marked against the following criteria:		
Attentiveness, depth and **discernment**. Your teacher will grade these virtues with a mark from 1–5. You will be given a mark out of 15.		
You will then assess yourself against the criteria of **responsibility**. You will give yourself a mark from 1–5. These marks will be added to give you a final mark out of 20.		
Assessment Criteria	Comments	Mark
Teacher assessment /15		
Attentiveness (to beliefs, practices, concepts & ideas) You have understood that the question 'Does God exist?' is an ultimate question You have understood that this question explores the nature of reality You have understood that there are various ways of thinking about what is real e.g. things do not have to be physical to be real.		

(continued)

Table 8.2 (continued)

Assessment Criteria	Comments	Mark
Teacher assessment /15		
You have understood that people's accounts of reality are limited. You have made reference to the fable of the blind man and the elephant, and to Plato's cave. You explain ways in which people make judgements as to what is real. e.g. theists have holy books. You have identified specific criteria for assessing what is real - evidence, experience and credibility and related these to the question. You discussed key ideas in relation to the question e.g. There is evil and suffering in the world which suggests that there is no God. You used key terms e.g. secular, theist, postmodern.		/5
Depth (of variation and interpretation) You have understood three common worldviews: theism, secularism and postmodernism. You have identified simply whether each worldview accepts belief in God's existence. You have explained how each worldview would go on to respond to the question 'Does God exist?' and the reasons they would give to justify their beliefs You have explored counter-arguments to the reasons given.		/5
Discernment (in response and argument) You have articulated your own worldview and offered your own answer to the question. You have expressed beliefs different from your own with accuracy and respect. You provided balanced arguments, and provided evidence to back these up. You justified your own point of view using reason, evidence and/or examples.		/5
Student self-assessment		
Responsibility (for truthful living) I was honest about my own answer to the question. I tried to keep an open mind but was also confident enough to express my own beliefs. I reflected on the difference that this answer could or should have on how I live my life. I evaluated the difference it actually makes and reflected on why this is and whether I want to change anything.		/5
Final mark		/20

Table 8.3 Monitoring sheet

Example KS3 student monitoring sheet – Year 7				
Schedule	Scheme of work title	Mark/20	Summary of teacher comments and targets	Student response
Yr 7 Autumn	Introduction to CRE			
Yr 7 Autumn				
Yr 7 Spring				
Yr 7 Spring				
Yr 7 Summer				
Yr 7 Summer				

Progress and accountability

While we are grasping the opportunity to creatively re-think assessment in line with our pedagogical commitments, it is also important to recognise that our schools will require us to fit into whole school monitoring and accountability procedures. It is incumbent on us to ensure that we as teachers are both facilitating and monitoring student progress. To this end, we offer a simple and accessible way of doing this.

Progression in the subject depends on the content, on the increasing conceptual difficulty of the schemes of work. Planning a comprehensive programme of study, which comprises schemes of work for the whole of Key Stage 3, is therefore a priority for any teacher wanting to embody CRE pedagogy. Not to do so, would be to produce schemes of work which would be neither systematic nor coherent and would not allow for progression. This was reflected in the feedback from the Year 7 pilot. Much like beginning a bit of DIY, when you refresh the paint in one room, it immediately draws attention to the shabbiness of the furniture or the paintwork in the next room and so you are motivated to carry out further improvements as a result! The teachers who took part in the pilot were eager to create schemes of work which would build on the students' enthusiastic engagement with CRE and allow them to explore and question material in increasingly challenging depth.

Ensuring that the pitch of each scheme of work is appropriate will be essential. Learning must be accessible and therefore differentiation is vital. CRE schemes of work already have the advantage of being student-centred, in that the student's own response to the topic is a central concern. Intrinsic value and relevance is therefore assured and differentiation becomes not so much a matter of employing technical strategies, but of careful and meaningful conversation and engagement.

In light of the current 'libertarian approach' to assessment (Smith, 2015, p.1), it is useful to keep abreast of developments, but not to feel tied down to any one of them. Any assessment system must be able to produce useful data to allow the school to be accountable for students' progress. RE cannot avoid being involved and responsible in this way. Some current developments of Key Stage 3 assessment formulations involve a 'flight path' approach (see Chris Hildrew's and Stephen Tierney's blogs). We have produced a particular version which monitors students'

Table 8.4 Virtues Assessment Flight Path

SAT score	Yr7 aut	Yr7 spr	Yr7 sum	Yr8 aut	Yr8 spr	Yr8 sum	Yr9 aut	Yr9 spr	Yr9 sum	Yr10 aut	Yr10 spr	Yr10 sum	Yr11 aut	Yr11 spr	Yr11 sum	GCSE grade
120	100 / 20	100 / 20	100 / 20	100 / 20	100 / 20	100 / 20	100 / 20	100 / 20	100 / 20	100 / 20	100 / 20	100 / 20	100 / 20	100 / 20	100 / 20	9
115	90 / 18	90 / 18	90 / 18	90 / 18	90 / 18	90 / 18	90 / 18	90 / 18	90 / 18	90 / 18	90 / 18	90 / 18	90 / 18	90 / 18	90 / 18	8
110	80 / 16	80 / 16	80 / 16	80 / 16	80 / 16	80 / 16	80 / 16	80 / 16	80 / 16	80 / 16	80 / 16	80 / 16	80 / 16	80 / 16	80 / 16	7
105	70 / 14	70 / 14	70 / 14	70 / 14	70 / 14	70 / 14	70 / 14	70 / 14	70 / 14	70 / 14	70 / 14	70 / 14	70 / 14	70 / 14	70 / 14	6
100	60 / 12	60 / 12	60 / 12	60 / 12	60 / 12	60 / 12	60 / 12	60 / 12	60 / 12	60 / 12	60 / 12	60 / 12	60 / 12	60 / 12	60 / 12	5
95	50 / 10	50 / 10	50 / 10	50 / 10	50 / 10	50 / 10	50 / 10	50 / 10	50 / 10	50 / 10	50 / 10	50 / 10	50 / 10	50 / 10	50 / 10	4
90	40 / 8	40 / 8	40 / 8	40 / 8	40 / 8	40 / 8	40 / 8	40 / 8	40 / 8	40 / 8	40 / 8	40 / 8	40 / 8	40 / 8	40 / 8	3
85	30 / 6	30 / 6	30 / 6	30 / 6	30 / 6	30 / 6	30 / 6	30 / 6	30 / 6	30 / 6	30 / 6	30 / 6	30 / 6	30 / 6	30 / 6	2
80	20 / 4	20 / 4	20 / 4	20 / 4	20 / 4	20 / 4	20 / 4	20 / 4	20 / 4	20 / 4	20 / 4	20 / 4	20 / 4	20 / 4	20 / 4	1

progress from year 7 through to year 11, using the scaled KS2 SATs data as the starting block and the new GCSE 9–1 grading system as the finishing line.

To create such a mechanism is not overly problematic. The process of progression lies in students' responses to the increasing expectations provided by each subsequent scheme of work. It is a straightforward way of monitoring, which allows teachers to concentrate on planning really effective schemes of work, rather than being separately concerned with monitoring students' progress in terms of their skill development.

The starting block

Since May 2016, SATS are no longer graded, as levels are no longer in use. Instead students are given a 'scaled score'. This information will be available to schools at transfer.

The interpretation of these scores is as follows:

- Below 100: Those that score below 100 will not have reached the nationally set "expected standard".
- Within close proximity of 100: Those that get 100 will have reached the national standard expected of them.
- Above 100: Those that score significantly higher than 100 will have exceeded the standard expected of them.

The progression

Using CRE virtues assessment, it is possible to map progress simply (see Table 8.4). For each scheme of work, each student's work will be given a mark out of 20. The teacher assessment will be out of 15 and the student's self-assessment out of 5. In the columns the top number in each box is the percentage and the bottom number is the mark out of 20. The teacher plans each scheme of work ensuring that the pitch and the expectations of the lesson become increasingly more challenging and complex. The progression is therefore built into the content. Such planning has always happened; it is what teachers do, but now it has greater significance and will need to be done with sufficient thought and care. The schemes of work themselves will become the key mechanism for monitoring students' progress, rather than a subjective and often ambiguous reading and interpretation of level descriptors.

The finishing line

The GCSE assessment constitutes the finishing line. The 9–1 grades have been located in the last column providing a visual representation of students' progression over their time at secondary school, with the expected 100 SATS score correlating to the expected grade 5 (roughly C equivalent) at GCSE. Many schools are now teaching the GCSE specifications over three years. Whether this is the case in your school, there will be a time when you transfer your attention from a CRE assessment framework to the GCSE assessment criteria. This will be necessary for the students' preparation for sitting the exam. However we believe that the quality of engagement at GCSE will still be significantly enriched if CRE pedagogy is used to plan and deliver the specification content and to assess the students' engagement, particularly in relation to responsibility. If students have enjoyed CRE pedagogy in KS3, keeping the basic tenets of critical realism as a means of focusing teaching and learning will continue to empower them and ensure strong performance at GCSE (see Chapter 7).

References

Commission on Religious Education (2018) Final Report Religions and Worldviews: The Way Forward. The RE Council

Department for Education. (2011). The Framework for the National Curriculum: A report by the Expert Panel for the National Curriculum review. Available online at: https://www.gov.uk/government/uploads/system/uploads/attachment_data/file/175439/NCR-Expert_Panel_Report.pdf (accessed 15/08/16).

Department for Education. (2014). Get the facts: GCSE and A level reform. Available online at: https://www.gov.uk/government/publications/get-the-facts-gcse-and-a-level-reform (accessed 23/08/16).

Department for Education. (2014). National curriculum and assessment from September 2014: information for schools. Available online at: https://www.gov.uk/government/uploads/system/uploads/attachment_data/file/358070/NC_assessment_quals_factsheet_Sept_update.pdf (accessed 23/08/16).

Department for Education. (2016). Eliminating unnecessary workload around marking. Available online at: https://www.gov.uk/government/publications/reducing-teacher-workload-marking-policy-review-group-report (accessed 15/08/16).

Department for Education. (2016). Progress 8 measure in 2016, 2017 and 2018. Available online at: https://www.gov.uk/government/uploads/system/uploads/attachment_data/file/536052/Progress_8_school_performance_measure.pdf (accessed 23/08/16).

Expert Advisory Group. (2015). Religious Education in the New Curriculum. Available online at: http://reonlineorg.wpengine.com/wp-content/uploads/2015/03/Religious-Education-in-the-New-Curriculum-2015.pdf (accessed 15/08/16).

Grimmitt, M. (eds). (2000). *Pedagogies of Religious Education*. Great Wakering, UK: McCrimmon.

Hanscomb, S. (2012). Feedback and student virtues. [Unpublished]. Available online at: http://www.psy.gla.ac.uk/~steve/rap/docs/hanscomb.pdf (accessed 31/07/16).

Hella, E. and Wright, A. (2009). Learning 'about' and 'from' religion: phenomenography, the Variation Theory of Learning and Religious Education in Finland and the UK. *British Journal of Religious Education* 31, no.1, 53–64.

Hildrew, C. (2014). Tracking progress over time: flight paths and matrices. Available online at: https://chrishildrew.wordpress.com/2014/04/15/tracking-progress-over-time-flight-paths-and-matrices/ (accessed 23/08/16).

Marton, F., Tsui, A. et al. (2004). *Classroom Discourse and the Space of Learning*. Mahwah, New Jersey: Lawrence Erlbaum Associates.

Qualifications and Curriculum Authority. (2004). The non-statutory national framework for Religious Education. Available online at: http://webarchive.nationalarchives.gov.uk/20090903160937/http:/qca.org.uk/libraryAssets/media/9817_re_national_framework_04.pdf (accessed 15/08/16).

Religious Education Council of England and Wales. (2013). A Curriculum Framework for Religious Education in England. Available online at: http://resubjectreview.recouncil.org.uk/media/file/RE_Review_Summary.pdf (accessed 15/08/16).

Smith, L. (2015). Effects of the new GCSE grading and accountability systems – unpublished paper.

Thomson, D. (2015). What will Progress 8 do for the creative subjects? Available online at: http://educationdatalab.org.uk/2015/03/what-will-progress-8-do-for-the-creative-subjects/ (accessed 8/7/16).

Tierney, S. (2013). Targets, Learning Gaps and Flight Paths. Available online at https://leadinglearner.me/2013/10/02/targets-learning-gaps-and-flight-paths/ (accessed 15/08/16).

Wolff, J. (2011). *Ethics and Public Policy: A Philosophical Inquiry*. Oxon: Routledge.

Wright, A. (2007). *Critical Religious Education, Multiculturalism, and the Pursuit of Truth*. Cardiff: University of Wales Press.

Wright, A. (2012). Towards a Virtue-Based Assessment in Critical Religious Education [email] (Communication to FORASE writing group members, 29/05/2012).

Critical Religious Education and differentiation

There has been growing disquiet around the nature and conceptualisation of differentiation. The concern is about assumptions that are made about students' abilities. These assumptions drive the teachers' provision, through various differentiated means, all of which arise from their understanding of the perceived learning 'needs' of their students. In a recent blog, Zoe Helman, identifies the core of the problem: "Many of us have wondered how exactly we square the fact that children can get cleverer with the need for differentiation. If children really can get cleverer, which they can ….does differentiation really help, does it hold students back, does the answer lie in how we do the differentiating?" Teacher Standard 1 requires teachers to have high expectations of their students – "set goals that stretch and challenge pupils of all backgrounds, abilities and dispositions"; Teacher Standard 5 requires teachers to "know when and how to differentiate appropriately, using approaches which enable pupils to be taught effectively" and "have a clear understanding of the needs of all pupils, including those with special educational needs; those of high ability; those with English as an additional language; those with disabilities; and be able to use and evaluate distinctive teaching approaches to engage and support them." These two aims are often held in tension and classroom differentiation practices often fall short of ensuring that TS1 remains in ascendency throughout! Thus, learning to differentiate effectively is an on-going task for all teachers, whatever their subject and however experienced they are. This chapter begins by clarifying the nature of differentiation. It then considers the specific benefits of using a CRE pedagogy which make differentiation central and organic, rather than additional and mechanic!

Understanding differentiation

The BBC Active website identifies three key aspects of differentiation: readiness to learn, interest and learning needs (BBC, 2010). With CRE, interest and motivation become intrinsic; CRE explicitly requires and values each student's worldview. It may take a while for a reluctant learner to be willing to engage, but the evidence we have from the Year 7 'Introduction to CRE' pilot (see Chapter 3) is that students' interest is easily fostered by CRE and that they tend to become really enthusiastic. Our focus in this chapter is the third aspect of differentiation – learning needs. We are essentially concerned with how to ensure all students have effective access to the curriculum that they are studying.

Differentiation to meet learning needs begins with the teacher considering the individual students in their classroom, getting to know their specific learning needs and planning accordingly. BBC Active proposes that methods of differentiation can fall into seven categories: differentiation by 'task, grouping, resources, pace, outcome, dialogue and support, and assessment' (2010). All these methods and the processes involved in using them will be familiar to you. For CRE, whilst you will see all of these methods exemplified in the schemes of work, there are some which should be given priority. Assessment, dialogue and support are of particular importance. These three processes facilitate the on-going and responsive communication between teachers and students which is essential for effective planning, teaching and learning. Without these processes, which can be understood as forms of differentiation, CRE cannot happen in the classroom.

Factors to consider when planning CRE lessons

When we undertook the Year 7 pilot, the teachers involved provided important feedback. Timing and ensuring that all students have access to the learning were key issues raised. As it was impossible to plan bespoke schemes of work for each department, these issues were inevitable and also arise for the schemes of work presented in this book. The pilot and this book aim to equip teachers to have the understanding and confidence to adapt the schemes of work offered so as to 'fit' their context (including the lesson time available and the students making up their classes). We aim to empower you to create your own teaching and learning opportunities using a CRE pedagogy, not just to provide resources. We want you to use your understanding of CRE to inform your own evaluation of existing schemes of work and to enable their enrichment.

In order to differentiate CRE lessons to meet the 'learning needs' of your students, we ask you to remember that:

1) CRE may be challenging but it is not too difficult

Initially the Year 7 scheme of work was met with a sense of incredulity. How were students going to be able to engage with such complex ideas as truth, relativity and postmodernism? Yet the feedback once the pilot had been taught indicated that such engagement was not only possible, but also empowering and enjoyable. Students loved the difficult stuff! It *is* possible to communicate complex concepts.

There is a quote attributed to Einstein "Everything should be made as simple as possible, but not simpler." Dave Smith, who was Head of RS at Archbishop Tenison's CE Boys School in Lambeth when the pilot was undertaken, reminded us of this. He taught the Year 7 scheme of work and was part of the evaluation team at King's College London. He was concerned that the language and the concepts being explored would need bridging and further explanation in order to make them accessible to his students, and so created a variety of methods for doing this. One method to bridge understanding that he used involved making masks to represent different worldviews. These were decorated with symbols which the students saw as representing these views. He then encouraged the students to wear the masks as appropriate, when giving specific responses to the questions about the possibility of God's existence.

While teaching the pilot, Dave's school had a SIAS (Statutory Inspections of Anglican Schools) Inspection. The impact of CRE was applauded in its report:

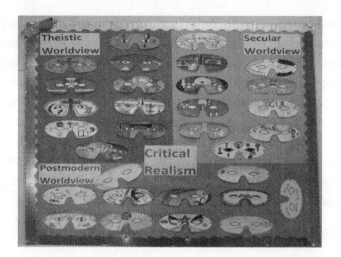

Figure 9.1 The Worldview Masks by Year 7 students Archbishop Tenison's CE School Lambeth

"The school's involvement in piloting a national project with King's College London enables students to develop their higher level skills of enquiry as they benefit from 'cutting edge' thinking. Recognising the successful impact of the pilot project upon raising attainment in RS, the school now plans to develop the project to embed higher level questioning across the curriculum." (National Society, 2012, p.4)

2) CRE is inherently personal

Students' personal involvement in the learning makes CRE a 'high stakes' process. When the students become clearly invested in the learning, particularly with the focus on discernment and responsibility, it has the effect of making aspects of the process almost 'self-differentiating'. This can be seen with the Year 7 scheme of work. It would only have to be adapted minimally to be appropriate for other year groups, up to Year 11 and beyond. This is because the ideas being explored can be unpacked at very different levels of conceptual difficulty, whilst being posed through essentially the same questions. This has the effect of 'handing the reins' over to the students. We can't predict or determine what the students will bring to the learning; we have to facilitate the articulation of their ideas and responses, but we cannot pre-determine these. Something feels different about such learning; there is a shift in the dynamics of the classroom. No longer does the teacher hold all the power and the knowledge, for both teacher and student are in an acknowledged position of epistemic relativity. Such learning cannot happen without both the teacher's and the students' active involvement. This is incredibly empowering and constitutes the kind of shared experience central to CRE.

3) CRE requires you to know your students

Effective assessment is a prerequisite for meaningful personalisation of learning; you cannot do one without the other. You have to really know your students. This 'knowing' is an on-going process – it is neither quick, nor easy, but it is essential and relational. It is achieved through the on-going development of relationships with each individual student. If you are responsible for your students' learning, you must know their strengths and weaknesses, their ways of working, their preferences, and the things that make them fearful. You must come to understand how they feel about their learning, what they are good at, what they are weaker at, what their worries are. You will come to know these things as you build relationships with your students. If you don't know or you are unsure, you just need to ask. Create moments in your classes which allow you to systematically learn about your students, *through* their engagement with the learning. Monitor carefully and build in regular opportunities for feedback. Making the curriculum accessible through effective differentiation involves making no assumptions and doing lots of asking and checking. Differentiation is not a randomly applied mechanistic process.

Marking is also central to the process of differentiation itself. Regular, prompt, responsive marking provides an essential and unique opportunity to foster the relationship you have with each of your students individually.

Phil Beadle (2005) wrote about this in his Guardian column:

> Marking is the secret and special relationship between teacher and student. It is not in the public realm. You can't accidentally humiliate a child by privately praising what they have written. My own devotion to the gospel of marking is the sole reason that the children I teach regard me as being a "good" teacher. If you have a naughty boy or girl, it is also the best way to their heart. And, with the possible exception of being gentle to children whose lives sometimes set them too great a challenge to bear, it is the single most important thing a teacher does. Any fool can come up with a five-step lesson plan (formulated in the five steps before you get to the classroom door), but a teacher who knows exactly who their children are, and what it is they need to learn, is a teacher who is armed with fistfuls of gold and magic.

4) CRE requires you to value and use theories of learning to understand the way your students learn

We know that on-going exploration and evaluation of worldviews is at the heart of CRE, and that this process involves engagement, dialogue and response. This means that you as a teacher must go beyond simply facilitating tasks. To teach meaningfully and effectively, *you* need to become an integral part of the learning, listening so carefully to the dialogue that you are able to analyse and evaluate your students' understanding as they begin to articulate their responses. Different theories of learning are really useful to help you in this task and would warrant further exploration, but are beyond the scope of this book. One particular theory, however, is important to mention here: the 'Variation Theory of Learning'. This theoretical perspective on the nature of learning began with the work of Ference Marton and is aligned closely with CRE.

According to Hella and Wright,

> Variation theory addresses key principles of learning . . . According to the theory, variation is *necessary* for any learning to take place.
>
> (2009, p.59)

Students learn through the process of juxtaposing alternative interpretations to enrich their understanding. Engaging with such variation is essential for deep learning; it is how the learning happens, it is not an optional extra. As you are listening to what your students are saying about how they make sense of different interpretations, about what they understand and what they are confused by, you will be informed by your analysis and able to support them through questions, comments, examples and analogies.

5) CRE has pitching and progression as priorities for effective planning and teaching

You will need to ensure that the pitch of your scheme of work and the learning in individual lessons is appropriate. A CRE KS3 programme of study must have the desired progression built into the curriculum itself. Remember the assessment principles offered by the NCFRE guidance: any study should become deeper and more comprehensive, vocabulary should be wider and more abstract, and whatever you plan to focus on in your lessons, whatever activities and resources you use, it should all be characterised by being challenging, complex and coherent (EAG, 2015). You will know that you're doing well with this, if your students ask deeper and more nuanced questions and if their responses are closely related to the topic you are exploring. The topics in your schemes of work should be incrementally pitched in more complex ways for each year and key stage. As the students complete their study and move from one scheme of work to the next, so the progression in their learning will be evidenced through the assessment (see Chapter 8 on Assessment).

6) CRE will dovetail with formative assessment to ensure effective teaching and learning

When 'Assessment for Learning' was introduced, teachers began to grasp that when it worked well, it was much greater than just a useful strategy to implement, but a re-thinking of the nature of communication and community in the classroom. Both AfL and CRE require a shift in classroom dynamics. This involves both the teacher and the students being organically and reciprocally engaged in the learning process. Marshall and Drummond (2006) comment that teachers whose classroom practice embodies the spirit of AfL are those who "value pupil autonomy and see it as a key goal of their teaching but it also has something to do with how they see the classroom as a site of their own learning" (p.147). CRE can work hand-in-hand with such formative assessment. If AfL demands insightful analysis and evaluation of the processes of learning, within a classroom context where fear of failure is at best banished or at least becomes part of the conversation, then CRE goes one step further. It moves beyond the processes of learning, to the content of learning itself and allows the topic, the subject being studied, to have a transformative effect on both teacher and students.

7) CRE will empower you to apply the schemes of work in this book to your students

As we present these schemes of work, it is clear that there will be specific factors relating to your school's context which we haven't been able to take into account. Your lessons may be of different length and your students will bring with them specific needs. You will read the lesson plans and may think "Well I'm not sure that would work" or "I haven't got enough time for that" or "I'll have to do some PR work with my parents to make sure they understand what's going on!" And that is exactly what we envisage your engagement and your response to be. You are the teacher; the context is yours. James Melligan, then Head of RE at Guildford County School, piloted the Year 7 scheme of work and shared with us how he had amended the lessons and resources to make them accessible for his students. For example, he broke down tasks into shorter activities and provided images and analogies to exemplify concepts when he felt this was needed. For some of the students he included writing frames and sentence starters for aspects of the written work. Where some of the tasks were open-ended, he provided much tighter expectations for the length and nature of the work.

The difference CRE can make

Teaching using a CRE pedagogy brings many exciting opportunities. Differentiation will be a rich and rewarding process. You will enable the learning of each individual student, their religious literacy and their personal and spiritual development. In embracing the virtues of CRE, you will be attentive to both your students and the subject, you will pull them deep into the subject, you will encourage discernment in their responses and you will allow them to share their stories as they are challenged to live responsibly in light of their own commitments. As the teachers of the pilot discovered, this commitment on your part will be worth it. You will see, as they did, significant outcomes from your CRE lessons, including students having much more confidence to ask questions, students having raised expectations as to the nature of RE and increased understanding of its relevance to them individually. Using a CRE pedagogy will ensure that social cohesion becomes an outcome of the learning rather than its aim, that students' attitudes to learning will improve, in particular that they will have a more discerning understanding of what they believe and why, and that the students will become used to practising critical thinking skills. RE will be seen as something 'hard' that 'makes your head hurt'! As Zoe Helman writes: "our 'struggling' students, the vast majority of them, if not all, need more opportunities to learn and remember knowledge. They don't need less, or simpler knowledge. That's an important distinction. They need more high quality, challenging knowledge and they need it even more than the other students." https://unpickingeducation.wordpress.com/2018/10/15/doing-away-with-differentiation/ (accessed 16/10/18).

In order to become an effective teacher of CRE, you will need to learn to trust yourself! You can become a teacher who is empowered to make changes and to be changed yourself. Palmer (1998) argues that "good teaching cannot be reduced to technique; good teaching comes from the identity and the integrity of the teacher" (p.10).

References

BBC. (2010). Methods of Differentiation in the Classroom. Available online at: http://www.bbcactive.com/BBCActiveIdeasandResources/MethodsofDifferentiationintheClassroom.aspx (accessed 09/08/16).

Beadle, P. (2005). Red all over. *The Guardian*. 10/05/2005. Available online at: https://www.theguardian.com/education/2005/may/10/teaching.schools (accessed 09/08/16).

Expert Advisory Group. (2015). Religious Education in the New Curriculum. Available online at: http://reonlineorg.wpengine.com/wp-content/uploads/2015/03/Religious-Education-in-the-New-Curriculum-2015.pdf (accessed 15/08/16).

Hella, E. and Wright, A. (2009). Learning 'about' and 'from' religion: phenomenography, the Variation Theory of Learning and Religious Education in Finland and the UK. *British Journal of Religious Education* 31, no.1, 53–64.

Marshall, B. and Drummond, M. J. (2006). How teachers engage with Assessment for Learning: lessons from the classroom. *Research Papers in Education* 21, no.2, 133–149.

National Society. (2012). Statutory Inspection of Anglican Schools Report on Archbishop Tenison's School Lambeth. Available online at: https://www.churchofengland.org/education/your-local-school/school-details.aspx?id=36&dist=1.54 (accessed 15/08/16).

Palmer, P. J. (1998). *The Courage to Teach*. San Francisco: Jossey-Bass.

Critical Religious Education and the importance of subject knowledge
A guide to useful resources

CRE aims to develop religiously literate students. However, this is, and can only be, possible if religious educators are religiously literate themselves. As discussed in previous chapters, CRE relies on religious educators making professional judgements about the content which is presented to students; the content needs to be authentic and the right variations need to be introduced in order to make the learning as fruitful as possible. Without an authentic understanding of the religions being studied or the correct variation being selected when exploring critical questions (whether of a philosophical or theological nature), the students' ability to give critical answers is severely limited. Thus, any teacher who embarks on the planning and/or teaching of a scheme of work within a CRE framework must take responsibility for ensuring that there is sufficient depth to their subject knowledge in that area.

Recent research into teacher perceptions of the pilot materials for the Year 7 Introductory Scheme of Work (Goodman, 2016) demonstrated that this is an issue which teachers who are already attempting to apply the pedagogy across the curriculum are aware of:

> . . . there was an acknowledgement that, in order to adapt the curriculum to be in line with the approach, teachers really need to invest in it personally and be willing to spend their time and energy on developing their practice;
>
> B1: I think CRE is about going the extra mile, with something . . . it is not just learning about religion, it is not even learning from religion, it is about saying and therefore . . . where does this take us . . .
>
> B2: I think that is where I struggle . . . I did get it but actually it's harder in practice to put in to new contexts or new faiths, particularly if you are less confident in the faith. . . . Doing it with Christianity with the resurrection stuff, easy, doing it with Islam a bit harder, doing it with Sikhism. . . . It also depends on your . . . academic speciality within more theological areas lie . . .
>
> (p.239)

Therefore, in order to begin to address this we have sought to offer sufficient guidance for the teaching of the schemes of work in this publication. However, these are only intended as a springboard from which to begin to plan and design your own curriculums. Consequently, if you wish to wholeheartedly embrace the approach (as we would encourage you to do) it may be necessary to reflect on and, in turn, develop, your own subject knowledge as part of the planning process.

We acknowledge that this is easier said than done. Teachers face all sorts of time pressures and having lots of spare time for subject knowledge development wouldn't be very typical! In addition, RE is renowned for a being a subject which is handed to non-specialists in order to fill up their timetables. Even specialist RE teachers will likely only be true 'specialists' in certain curriculum areas, having often studied *either* Philosophy *or* Theology/Religious Studies at University (if that!). The potential scope of the CRE curriculum is vast and the idea of anyone being an expert in it all is fanciful. Thus for some practitioners there may be large areas of subject knowledge which need development and this may seem daunting. However, we wish to encourage you that this task is very worthwhile.

Critical Religious Education is not a process which is confined to the school years. We are all on a journey of discovery. We interact with various phenomena on a daily basis which may challenge or deepen our current convictions and this is both unavoidable and potentially enriching. If we accept a critical realist philosophy, we all have a responsibility to adjust appropriately as we come into contact with new information about the world. Furthermore, if we really wish to be 'truth seekers' (and to encourage our students to be likewise), we should not only adapt when confronted with new knowledge, but we should actively seek it out. The critical questions which CRE puts at the centre of religious education are exciting and important and as religious educators we have a unique opportunity to explore these in a community of enquiry on a daily basis. Thus, if there are areas of our own subject knowledge that need to be strengthened in order to do the approach justice, this can be seen as an opportunity; not only for developing our teaching practice, but also for developing ourselves and our own understanding of the reality in which we live.

We recommend as starters:

Useful resources

Buddhism

Cush, D. (1993). *Buddhism: A Student's Approach to World Religions*. London: Hodder & Stoughton.
Hanh, T. N. (1999). *The Heart of the Buddha's Teaching*. London: Broadway Books.
Rahula, W. (1974). *What the Buddha Taught*. Oxford: Grove Press.
Smith, J. (1999). *Radiant Mind*. New York: Riverhead Trade.

Christianity

Jones, D. A. (2012). *Christianity: An Introduction to the Catholic Faith*. Norwich: Catholic Truth.
Lane, T. (2013). *Exploring Christian Doctrine*. London: SPCK.
Lewis, C. S. (1996). *Mere Christianity*. New York: Touchstone.
Migliore, D. L. (2014). *Faith Seeking Understanding*. Cambridge: Eerdmans.
Ware, T. (1993). *The Orthodox Church*. London: Penguin.

Islam

Armstrong, K. (2002). *Islam: A Short History*. London: Phoenix.
Bdaiwi, A. and Hussain, Z. (2017). *Shi'a Islam: Beliefs and Practices*. London: Al Khoei Foundation.

Sawar, G. (2006). *Islam: Belief and Practices*. London: Muslim Educational Trust.
Watton, V. (1993). *Islam: A Student's Approach to World Religions*. London: Hodder.

Judaism

Braybook, M. (1995). *How to Understand Judaism*. London: SCM.
Kushner, H. (1994). *To Life: A Celebration of Jewish Being and Thinking*. New York: Warner Bros.
Magonet, J. (1998). *The Explorer's Guide to Judaism*. London: Hodder & Stoughton.
Sacks, J. (2004). *A Letter in the Scroll*. New York: Free Press.

Hinduism

Flood, G. (1996). *An Introduction to Hinduism*. Cambridge: Cambridge University Press.
Fowler, J. (1996). *Hinduism Beliefs and Practices*. Eastbourne: Sussex Academic Press.
Klostermaier, K. (2007). *A Survey of Hinduism: Third Edition*. Albany, New York: Suny.

Sikhism

Cole, W. O. (2004). *Understanding Sikhism*. Edinburgh: Dunedin Academic Press.
Guninder Kaur Singh, N. (1993). *Sikhism World Religions*. New York: Facts On File Inc.

CRE

Wright, A. (2007). *Critical Religious Education, Multiculturalism and the Pursuit of Truth*. Cardiff: University of Wales Press.
Wright, A. (2016). *Religious Education and Critical Realism*. Abingdon: Routledge.

Critical Realism

Bhaskar, R. (2016). *Enlightened Common Sense: The Philosophy of Critical Realism*. Abingdon: Routledge.

Variation Theory

Marton, F. (2015). *Necessary Conditions of Learning*. Abingdon: Routledge.
Marton, F. and Tsui, A. (2004). *Classroom Discourse and the Space of Learning*. London: Lawrence Erlbaum Associates.

Reference

Goodman, A. (2016). Critical Religious Education (CRE) in Practice: Evaluating the reception of an introductory scheme of work. *British Journal of Religious Education* 40, no.2: 232–241.

Index

abortion 106, 107, 153, 154
academic debate, skills of 8–9, 34
academisation 162
Adams, R. 71
afterlife 46, 51, 145, 154
age appropriateness 42, 44
agency 95
agnosticism 21–2, 103, 104
Agreed Syllabuses 162
Akhirah 46, 51
A Levels 21, 70, 76, 102, 161, 162
'Al Khaaliq' (Yusuf Islam) 51
animals, treatment of 78, 135, 153, 154
anti-realism 2
arguments, evaluation of 73–5, 81, 95, 134
assessment 161–78; baseline assessment
    27–8; Commission on Religious Education
    (Report, 2018) 163; and differentiation
    181–2, 183; formative assessment 165,
    169, 170, 183; GCSE 129–30, 133–8;
    knowledge versus skills 165; libertarian
    approaches to 175; marking guidance
    27, 37, 170, 182; models of progression
    166, 175–8, 183; peer assessment 33,
    35, 37, 54, 57, 121; removal of levels 161,
    162, 163, 164–5, 175; self-assessment
    37, 54, 57, 99, 124, 168, 169; summative
    assessments 170; virtues assessment
    framework 147, 150, 168–77; virtuous circle
    of teaching and assessment 165, 166
Assessment for Learning (AfL) 183
atheism: and Buddhism 104, 117; and ethics
    103; at GCSE 152; introducing worldviews
    22; and philosophy 76, 94, 96
Attainment 8 161–2
attentiveness 14, 167
AULRE conference (2018) 165
authenticity 40, 43, 138–9
authentic understanding of others' beliefs 10, 11
authoritativeness 43–4, 52, 103, 104, 111, 113
autonomy 16, 111, 169
Ayer A. J. 101

balloon dilemma exercise 122
baseline assessment 27–8
Beadle, Phil 182
behaviour, implications for 78, 105, 150, 168
beliefs - practices - ethical issues ordering 40
Bible: creation accounts 72–5, 91, 93–4;
    ethics 107, 113, 116, 123; GCSE 131–2,
    134, 135, 144; Genesis 72–5, 91, 93–4;
    interpretation of religious texts 44; and

philosophy 74; and the Qur'an 46; and truth
    claims 22
Big Bang theory 83–4, 89–90, 95, 153
Billingsley, B. 73, 76, 77
Blind Men and the Elephant, The 30, 31
boo-hurrah theory 101
boxing exercise (RE boxing) 8, 34, 37, 65
Brighouse, H. 15
British values 7, 13–15
Bruner, Jerome 140
Buddhism: and atheism 104, 117; ethics 117;
    and fasting 55; GCSE 143, 147–50, 151–3;
    useful resources 186; world religions 39
Bunnin, N. 101

card sort activities 29, 87, 96, 116, 122
Catholic Christianity 8, 84, 116, 127–8, 129,
    131, 143, 160
cause and effect 95
certainty 77
challenge, differing levels of 58, 179–84
charitable giving 157
chocolate temptation activity 55
Christianity: Catholic Christianity 8, 84, 116,
    127–8, 129, 131, 143, 160; denominational
    theological differences 145, 160; as focus 78;
    GCSE 128, 131–2, 140, 143–7, 151–3; and
    Islam 45; in non-Christian faith schools 128;
    Orthodox Christianity 51, 131, 143, 144, 160;
    Protestant Christianity 8, 116, 131, 143, 144,
    160; useful resources 186; as world religion 39
classroom culture 8–9
cognitive conflict 142
coherence 20, 40, 134, 138–9
Commission on Assessment without Levels
    162, 165
Commission on Religious Education (Report,
    2018) 162–3
community of enquiry approach 71, 186
complex concepts, ability of students to
    grasp 180
conclusions, drawing 73–5, 81, 84, 86, 95
conflict, classroom 7–8
conscience 104, 115
conservative beliefs 94, 113, 116
constructivist frameworks 2, 165
contingency of knowledge 2
contradictory beliefs 9, 11
controversial issues 7–18; classroom culture
    8–9; leaving unresolved 5, 11; and liberalism
    15; and philosophy 84; and social cohesion
    12–13, 184; tendency to avoid 7–8